MORE PRAISE FOR *YOU C...*

"To read this book is to visit tenni...

..., ...inio, TV tennis analyst and
1977 French Open mixed doubles champion

"Started reading and couldn't stop. . . . La Rochefoucauld and John Bartlett would have approved. These are maxims for the modern tennis fan."
—Christopher Clarey, tennis writer,
International Herald Tribune and *New York Times*

"Out of the mouths of tennis players comes Paul Fein's wonderful, witty, profound, catty collection of quotations from a who's who of tennis past and present."
—Donna Doherty, former editor of *Tennis* magazine

"*You Can Quote Me on That* is as fascinating for its historical dimensions as its human revelations. It's informative and entertaining."
—Louis Cayer, head national coach, Tennis Canada

"It's a must for both tennis cognoscenti and all those who enjoy a light and entertaining read."
—Greg Hunter, former editor, *Inside Sport* (Australia)

PRAISE FOR PAUL FEIN'S PREVIOUS BOOK, *TENNIS CONFIDENTIAL*

"Paul Fein hits an ace with *Tennis Confidential*."
—Pete Sampras, fourteen-time Grand Slam champion

"An excellent addition to sports collections."
—*Library Journal*

"A must-read for tennis fans!"
—Jon Saraceno, sports columnist, *USA Today*

"*Tennis Confidential* is the kind of thought-provoking book you'll return to again and again. Highly entertaining and always engaging, it makes a terrific addition to any collection of tennis literature."
—Alan G. Schwartz, chairman of the board
and president of the USTA

YOU CAN QUOTE ME ON THAT

Also by Paul Fein

Tennis Confidential: Today's Greatest Players, Matches, and Controversies

YOU CAN QUOTE ME ON THAT

GREATEST TENNIS QUIPS, INSIGHTS, AND ZINGERS

PAUL FEIN

Potomac Books, Inc.

Washington, D.C.

Library of Congress Cataloging-in-Publication Data
　　Paul Fein.
　　　You can quote me on that : greatest tennis quips, insights, and zingers / Paul Fein.
　　　　p. cm.
　　　Includes index.
　　　ISBN 1-57488-925-7 (alk. paper)
　　　　1. Tennis—Quotations, maxims, etc.　2. Tennis players—Quotations.
　　I. Fein, Paul, 1944–　II. Title.
　　PN6084.T44Y682005
　　796.342—dc22　　　　　　　　　　　　　　　　　　　2004013322

Printed in the United States of America on acid-free paper that meets the American National Standards Institute Z39-48 Standard.

Potomac Books, Inc.
22841 Quicksilver Drive
Dulles, Virginia 20166

First Edition

10 9 8 7 6 5 4 3 2 1

To my twin sisters, Jane and Betty,
for their loving support and valuable advice

CONTENTS

PHOTOGRAPHS

FOREWORD

You Can Quote Me on That brought back a flood of wonderful memories, and I discovered plenty of juicy quotes I never heard before.

Ever since I first picked up a tennis racket as an eleven year old in Long Beach, California, I've crusaded to improve the sport I love. I battled country club elitism and snobbery, the reactionary establishment, "shamateurism," racism, homophobia, and sexism.

Winning thirty-nine Grand Slam titles, including twenty at Wimbledon, and thumping Bobby Riggs in the famous "Battle of the Sexes" match gave me the public platform I needed. Early on, I learned the power of words. They can make people laugh and cry, think and argue, and ultimately inspire us to do good and great things.

Tennis history has always been a huge fascination for me. I loved stories about the tradition-breaking flamboyance of Suzanne Lenglen, the classic elegance of Helen Wills Moody, and the serve-and-volley boldness of Alice Marble.

As an enthusiastic teenager, I not only dreamed of playing like these champions, I wanted to be like them. Lenglen liberated tennis women in the 1920s with her attitude as much as her then-risqué attire. "I just throw dignity to the wind and think of nothing but the game," she proclaimed.

Those words stuck in my mind, as did the eloquence of Helen Wills Moody, the first American to dominate women's tennis. Seventy years ago she said, "Concerning the limits and limitations of the women's game— why should we believe there are any?" My thoughts exactly!

That passion for tennis is reflected every day around the world, whether it be at a gritty public court in Compton, California, where Venus and Serena got started, or Centre Court at Wimbledon—my favorite place in the world. Tennis players tell it like it is. They praise and lambaste opponents, confide their hopes and fears, talk tennis issues, and express themselves in every conceivable way.

Andre Agassi is one of my favorite players because he's a champion off the court, too. He's raised millions of dollars for charities, and his college preparatory academy in Las Vegas has given hope to hundreds of disadvantaged children. After Andre rebounded from a devastating career slump to win Roland Garros in 1999, he said, "I've got to say, what turns me on more than anything is just making a difference in people's lives. That's one thing I've taken with me and I'll keep. Probably even more so than the accomplishments itself at the French Open is the fact that somewhere along the line it gave hope to people."

Paul Fein, an award-winning journalist, is also a sectional tournament player, former satellite tournament director and regional TV commentator, and teaching pro, who knows first-hand about the pressures, joys, and disappointments of competition.

Paul's *You Can Quote Me on That* contains hundreds of funny, informative, and provocative quotes by and about present and past stars on thirty-five different topics. No one and nothing is spared.

I found the entire book engrossing. I'm sure you will, too. And you can quote me on that!

—*Tennis superstar Billie Jean King*

ACKNOWLEDGMENTS

The greatest pleasure in collecting the most entertaining and enlightening tennis quotes uttered and written was doing the fascinating research. That entailed reading new sources—chiefly newspapers, magazines, books, press conference and TV transcripts, and information found on the Internet—and rereading old sources.

Several people have supplied me with much of that valuable information over the years. I would most like to thank Matthew Suher, of Stanmore, England, for his generous assistance and Bernie Bloome, another old and loyal friend from my hometown of Springfield, Massachusetts. Joe Salfas of Carnegie, Australia; Fara Kearnes of Denver, Colorado; and Joy Parker of Lake Lotawana, Missouri, have also helped me.

Quite a few of the quotes in this compendium come from my own interviews. I am grateful to the players, coaches, officials, and authorities for giving me their time and expertise as well as the communication staffs of the ATP, WTA, ITF, and USTA, and client managers from management companies for arranging the interviews.

Harry Kirsch, a tennis authority from Auburndale, Massachusetts, corrected errors and made substantive suggestions. I am most of all indebted to Suzi Petkovski, my longtime friend and colleague from Kew, Australia. She superbly critiqued the content and style of the book.

INTRODUCTION

Quotes are great fun. They amuse, shock, inform, enrage, enlighten, and inspire. The most compelling quotes provoke thought and debate and can even incite us to take action.

My favorite is, "Be not ashamed to say what you are not ashamed to think." Tennis players heed Montague's advice more than athletes in other sports. Tennis pros speak out freely because as free agents they don't worry about antagonizing teammates, coaches, or owners. They vent emotions and voice opinions on the court and in press conferences afterward, when the heat of battle has barely cooled.

In individual sports, such as tennis, we follow our heroes more closely and root for them more passionately. When Andy, Serena, Andre, Jennifer, Martina, Anna, Marat, and others bare their souls, they make an emotional connection with their legions of fans that adds immensely to the entertainment they create in competition.

You Can Quote Me on That captures the power and range of tennis quotes past and present in thirty-five chapters that contain almost 1,700 quotes—far surpassing any previous tennis quote collection.

For a good chuckle, go directly to "Did They Really Say That?" You'll find Agassi quip, "Sex doesn't interfere with your tennis. It's staying out all night trying to find it that affects your tennis." And Ilie Nastase, when asked why he didn't report the loss of his credit card, replied, "Whoever stole it is spending less than my wife."

In "True Confessions," Steffi Graf confides, "I never wished to live this life. I just wanted to play tennis, not become a public person. That is why I can be quite bitchy toward people." You'll be shocked by admissions, such as stoical superstar Bjorn Borg's, "I was never that cold inside. It was always an act—an act I came to perfect—but an act just the same."

Zingers abound in our fiercely competitive international sport. Check out "Nothing Personal." There Kournikova rants, "I'm not Venus Williams.

I'm not Serena Williams. I'm feminine. I'm not masculine like they are." And master-blaster John McEnroe skewers archrival Jimmy Connors, "He's a bit anal, he thinks the whole world is against him and that everyone is screwing him on some level. He's always been like that and he always will be." Rest assured, Johnny Mac takes plenty of deliciously wicked hits, too.

Those seeking advice and inspiration will find it in "Stuff of Champions." I'm especially moved by whiz-kid-turned-burnout-case-turned-champion Jennifer Capriati, "There is always a light at the end of the tunnel. . . . You are in control of everything. Just believe in yourself. You make or break yourself."

Chapters on styles and strategies, doubles, race and gender issues, rackets, and Open Tennis offer provocative viewpoints that may make you reconsider your own. For example, legendary Australian coach Harry Hopman controversially contended, "There are no hard and fast rules for learning to play tennis or for developing your game, and there is no one style which could be laid down as the 'correct' way to play."

Who was tennis's first nonstop serve-and-volley champion—Jack Kramer, Joe Hunt, Maurice McLoughlin, or even "the Wizard," Norman Brookes, early in the twentieth century? Hint: it was an American star in the late 1880s and early 1890s. *You Can Quote Me on That* can settle that and other arguments, too.

Some quotes are less known but eloquent or powerful. I bet you don't know who said this about Wimbledon, "This is hallowed ground, the field of dreams for tennis players. It's great. It's legendary." Or who uttered this about the men's ranking system, "You can be dead and still be No. 1." Or who predicted, "Women's tennis won't draw flies." Bet you'll be surprised to find out who said that.

You Can Quote Me on That taps into universal themes, such as love, God, country, and the meaning of life, or at least life on the tour. The context for most quotes is given, and their sources and years are cited when they could be discovered.

This book is for the casual fan, the tennis fanatic, the quote lover, the raconteur, the journalist, the historian, and the merely curious. It contains (almost) everything you ever wanted to know about who said what about who and what in the fascinating, ever-changing world of tennis.

I hope you thoroughly enjoy *You Can Quote Me on That*. I've told you some of my favorite quotes. Feel free to e-mail me at lincjeff1@cs.com and tell me yours.

"Be not ashamed to say what you are not ashamed to think."
—Montague

THEY CALL IT A GAME

"People don't seem to understand that it's a damn war out there. Maybe my methods aren't socially acceptable to some, but it's what I have to do to survive. I don't go out there to love my enemy. I go out there to squash him."

—Jimmy Connors (1973)

"To be a top tennis player you have to have a tough streak. I was ruthless and determined . . . because I really wanted to win. It's good for women to have a tough streak, just like it's important for a guy to be sensitive."

—Chris Evert

"I was always a believer in stamping on my opponent if I got him down, at Wimbledon or anywhere else. I never wanted to give him the chance to get up."

—Fred Perry, 1930s British champion

"This is something you'd die for. The intensity of playing against Pete is something above and beyond anything I feel against anybody else, and beyond the rivalry there's that hunt for No. 1."

—Andre Agassi, fired up about his rivalry with Pete Sampras (1995)

"I began to understand that you could walk out on the court like a lady, all dressed up in immaculate white, be polite to everybody, and still play like a tiger and beat the living daylights out of the ball."

—Althea Gibson, who saw the importance of manners during her odyssey from Harlem to Wimbledon, which she won in 1957 and '58

1

"Jimmy was taught to be a tiger on the court. When he was young, if I had a shot I could hit down his throat, I did. And I'd say, 'See, Jimmy, even your mother will do that to you.'"

—Gloria Connors, mother/coach of all-time great Jimmy Connors

"There is nothing I wouldn't do on court in order to win."

—Boris Becker

"I have always considered tennis as combat in an arena between two gladiators who have their rackets and their courage as weapons."

—Yannick Noah, 1983 French Open champion

"Unlike other sports, in tennis if you are getting killed, you are expected to stay out there and continue to get killed."

—Actor and comedian Bill Cosby, who once hired a teaching pro to travel with him

"There is a stronger version of structural competition in which one contestant must *make* the other(s) fail in order to succeed himself. War is one example. Tennis is another."

—Alfie Kohn. From his 1986 book, *No Contest: The Case Against Competition*

"Tennis is an assassin's game. I'm not just talking about the players. In all that I do in tennis, I'm surrounded by strong men, and virility is institutionally rivalistic."

—Ted Tinling, tennis historian, WTA Tour impresario, renowned dress designer, and raconteur, in *Sports Illustrated* (1984)

"I know what people think—they hear me on television and I sound like a nice guy. . . . The truth is that nice guys win nothing on court—you have to be hard and ruthless."

—Tim Henman (1999)

"I'm a competitor. Unfortunately, it's a war out here. If there's a weakness, someone's going to have to be attacked."

—Serena Williams, who noticed her sister Venus suffering with a sore shoulder but did not let up during her straight-sets Wimbledon final victory (2002)

"I'm not backing down from anybody. You don't play this game to win. You play to kill people out there."

—Lleyton Hewitt (2000)

NOTHING PERSONAL

"I'm not Venus Williams. I'm not Serena Williams. I'm feminine. I don't want to look like they do. I'm not masculine like they are."

> —Anna Kournikova (2001)

"She thinks she's the f—ing Venus Williams, and she's not going to move out of the way. That's it. I'm sorry she feels that way."

> —Irina Spirlea, blaming her on-court collision with Venus Williams in the U.S. Open on her opponent's imperious attitude (1997)

"She's a big, ugly, tall, white turkey."

> —Richard Williams, father/coach of Venus, terming the bumping episode "a racial thing." He later apologized to Spirlea. (1997)

"Borotra was the artist and charlatan of the French; undoubtedly, the greatest showman and faker in tennis history."

> —Bill Tilden, revealing his hatred toward French rival Jean Borotra. From his 1948 memoir, *My Story*

"I'm getting tired of saying hello to Stan Smith and not getting any reply. I'm cocky and confident and maybe I'm too bullheaded sometimes, but I think I have some fan and player support. I know what the others say, but I'm not that obnoxious. I am not a punk. I'm 5'10", 155 pounds. I've got broad shoulders, and I can pack a punch. Most of these guys are windbags anyway. If they ever try anything with me, I'll be to the net fast."

> —Jimmy Connors, twenty-one, after beating veteran Stan Smith at the Masters and seeing Smith stalk from the court instead of leaving with his opponent, as is tradition (1973)

3

"He's always complaining and doing bad things. But not just against the players. He talks against the crowd too much."

—Bjorn Borg, on Jimmy Connors (1976)

"We're good friends. He has his friends, and I have mine."

—Bjorn Borg, asked if he was good friends with Jimmy Connors (1978)

"He [Jimmy Connors] has one weakness. He can never say his opponent played well. That's why it feels good to beat him, and that's why other players would rather beat him than any other player."

—Bjorn Borg. From HickokSports.com

"His day is done, and now we're doing it. And we're doing it pretty well and not with fingers in the air and our hands on our crotches."

—Jim Courier, firing back after Jimmy Connors criticized the leading players for being boring (1994)

"Pancho's no saint. But whoever saw a saint with a tennis racket?"

—Pancho Segura, on his close friend and fiery competitor Pancho Gonzalez

"Fred's extremely bright and hard-working and didn't miss much as a businessman. But he's an opportunist, a selfish and egotistical person, and he never gave a damn about professional tennis."

—Jack Kramer, on 1930s British champion Fred Perry. From his 1979 autobiography, *The Game: My 40 Years in Tennis*

"There is no place for Stich in German tennis."

—Boris Becker, transferring his antipathy to former rival Michael Stich, who beat him in the 1991 Wimbledon final, to German tennis politics (1997)

"For Boris, every other German player was just a supplement to him. They came after him [in priority], people who were not at his level and were never able to take any fame away from him. Most of the German players, including me, never really got the respect we deserved."

—Michael Stich. From the 1997 book, *Becker Advantage*

"We're out there busting our guts, and he doesn't show a lot of respect at the end of the day. He tries to play down the reason he lost, giving no respect to the other player. And that is what really upsets me about him and the reason I try to piss him off as much as I can."

—Patrick Rafter, on the day he claimed the No. 1 ranking, blasting Pete Sampras. Rafter later apologized for the remarks. (1999)

"He's a bit anal, he thinks the whole world is against him and that everyone is screwing him on some level. He's always been like that and he always will be."

—John McEnroe, on long-time nemesis Jimmy Connors (1999)

"John McEnroe was my idol. He was the player I really liked to watch but, as a person, I don't think too much about him. He says I only have one shot. That makes me a genius or that makes the other guys very bad. . . . [He] gives everybody shit. Who cares about John McEnroe now. . . . He's an idiot."

—Goran Ivanisevic, after beating Tim Henman in the Wimbledon semis, en route to the championship (2001)

"I don't know him, I don't like him and I wouldn't want to like him."

—Nike chairman Phil Knight, on rival Reebok chairman Paul Fireman (1989)

"He's an old man, he walks like a duck, he can't see, he can't hear, and besides, he's an idiot."

—Rosie Casals, Billie Jean King's doubles partner and a TV analyst when King played Bobby Riggs in the "Battle of the Sexes" match (1973)

"Tennis judges are usually frustrated tennis guys who didn't make it, or old people who want to be around the sport."

—John McEnroe

"He has never been my favorite guy. The minute one of his stars would turn pro, Hopman would turn on him. No matter how close he'd been to a player, as soon as he was out of Hopman's control, the guy was an outcast. 'It was as if we'd never existed,' Rosewall once said."

> —Jack Kramer, a former champion and pro promoter, on Australian Davis Cup captain Harry Hopman. From Kramer's 1979 autobiography, *The Game: My 40 Years in Tennis*

"Cash is not one of my favorite people. He's one of the most aggressive, obnoxious players. I don't talk to him very often, and I'm not the only one."

> —Boris Becker, after he whipped Cash 6–4, 6–3, 6–4 in the 1988 Wimbledon quarterfinals

"Pat Cash is an arrogant little bugger who will probably finish up in the gutter."

> —Dawn Fraser, Australian Olympic swimming champion and then a member of the New South Wales parliament (1989)

"For Jimmy, tennis meant money, and Davis Cup wasn't money."

> —John McEnroe, on why American superstar Jimmy Connors rarely played Davis Cup. From his 2002 autobiography, *You Cannot Be Serious*

"I've got more talent in my pinkie than Lendl has in his whole body."

> —John McEnroe

"The guy hasn't been good for tennis. He's been so selfish. And he's certainly not the kind of guy who brings out the best in others. He's hurt the popularity of the game so much. . . . Do you like a robot being No. 1?"

> —John McEnroe, blasting Ivan Lendl, in *Esquire* magazine (1987)

"Most people still hate Lendl with a passion. It's not hard to see why. He was arrogant and, amazingly for a Czech guy who took American citizenship, unquestionably a racist."

> —Former Wimbledon champion Pat Cash. From his 2002 autobiography, *Uncovered*

"Ivan doesn't lose very often. But when he does, he's a bad loser."

> —Yannick Noah, on Ivan Lendl. From the 1983 exposé, *Short Circuit*

"What a monster! I want nothing to do with him. All that money and he never has time to smile. He gives the game a bad image."

> —Yannick Noah, on the dour Ivan Lendl (1983)

"I think Connors believes he has to hate everyone he plays [in order] to play better, and McEnroe hates just about everyone who can beat him. He used to hate Connors and me. Now he has to hate the top 50."

> —Ivan Lendl, in *USA Today* (1987)

"I'm sad anyone can cherish Agassi. The kids see him as a rebel with his earring, hair and no-shave look."

> —Ivan Lendl (1990)

"These people are animals. Rome is the asshole of the universe."

> —Vitas Gerulaitis, exasperated by a frenzied crowd at the Foro Italico in his loss to local hero Adriano Panatta (1977)

"Bob Kain couldn't create an image out of a bar of soap. I've had my image ever since I was a junior. You can ask the players that."

> —Flamboyant Vitas Gerulaitis, on his IMG manager Bob Kain. From the 1983 book, *Short Circuit*

"Agents are merely parasites who promise so much, only to leave you totally let down . . . ninety-nine percent of them are the epitome of sleaze."

> —Pat Cash. From his 2002 autobiography, *Uncovered*

"After living in Czechoslovakia so long, I can't understand how anybody who wants a free life can go the liberal line. As much as I like and respect Martina, I just cannot see her point of view. Liberal is just a different name and a different stage for Communism."

> —Ivan Lendl, in *Tennis* magazine, on how he and fellow Czech Martina Navratilova turned out so differently (1995)

"The kids see [Agassi] as a rebel with his earring, hair and no-shave look."—Ivan Lendl (*Fred Mullane/Camerawork USA, Inc.*)

"How can he say that? Would he say that if he were a gay man? No. Because the Republicans, if they had their choice, would not recognize me as a species at all. They would either try to indoctrinate me into heterosexuality or lock me up somewhere. Now the

Republicans are telling you more and more how to lead your life. They are just like the Communists were. They're always claiming we should get the government off our backs, but on certain social issues, *they* are the culprits on our backs."

> —Martina Navratilova, replying to Lendl's antiliberal remarks (1999)

"He thinks he's Bob Hope, but he's about as funny as bloody Marcus Welby."

> —Australian veteran Phil Dent, not amused by Jimmy Connors's crude attempts at humor in the early and mid-1970s

"Yeah. But he's my *favorite* asshole."

> —Arthur Ashe, in answer to the question, "Is Jimmy Connors really just an asshole?" From Peter Bodo's 1995 book, *The Courts of Babylon: Tales of Greed and Glory in the Harsh New World of Professional Tennis*

"I don't think I could ever be that phony."

> —John McEnroe, on the nice-guy image Jimmy Connors cultivated late in his career

"I consider Flip—and I say this with all due respect to him, and nothing condescending—he's one of the greatest underachievers in the history of the sport."

> —Scott Draper, on fellow Australian Mark Philippoussis (2002)

"One of the most uncommitted people to rise to prominence in sport."

> —How Pat Cash branded Mark Philippoussis, his compatriot and former protégé, in an article in the *Sunday Times* (London) that appeared on the day Philippoussis played the 2003 Wimbledon final

"He has that comfortable middle-class look about him. The English middle class basically don't have the stomach for a fight."

> —1987 Wimbledon champion Pat Cash, on why he thinks Tim Henman lacks the right stuff to win a major tournament, in the *New York Times Magazine* (2002)

"He's a very good [tennis] player. I think he's a much better player than he is a vice president."

> —Humor columnist Art Buchwald, on then vice president George Herbert Walker Bush

"Her tennis isn't going to straighten out until she straightens out her life."

   —Chris Evert Lloyd, on Martina Navratilova (1981)

"At some point, I would be amazed if someone didn't whack him in the locker room. If I was on the other end of his antics, I would have snapped by now."

   —Brad Gilbert, Andre Agassi's coach, warning fist-pumping Lleyton Hewitt to tone down his act (2001)

"An asinine, pompous, overstuffed bunch of little men trying to run a big sport. Anything I've said or done to them goes redoubled."

   —Bill Tilden, on the leaders of the USLTA, with whom he frequently locked horns, in *SPORT* magazine (1951)

"I can't rationalize talking to press people because they're not rational people."

   —John McEnroe

"They're an intense breed who rarely travel without a thesaurus and their analyst's telephone number."

   —Michael Calvin, of the *Telegraph* (UK), on American tennis writers (1993)

"Gilbert, you don't deserve to be on the same court with me! You are the worst. The f—ing worst!"

   —John McEnroe, enraged while losing to heavy underdog Brad Gilbert in the Masters tournament at Madison Square Garden (1986)

"I've never seen anybody as negative on a tennis court . . . and he never seemed satisfied until he got you feeling pretty gloomy, too. . . . Perhaps there was something about Gilbert that made me look into myself and think, 'Oh my God, can I possibly be that unbearable?'"

   —John McEnroe, on Brad Gilbert. From his 2002 autobiography, *You Cannot Be Serious*

"I appreciate him more now, he amuses me. There's depth to the man I didn't recognize before, and a generosity in advising younger players. But when he's out there on court he's still Pancho the bastard."

—Rod Laver, on longtime rival Pancho Gonzalez. From his 1971 autobiography, *The Education of a Tennis Player*

"Nastase does not have a brain; he has a bird fluttering around in his head."

—Ion Tiriac, Ilie Nastase's longtime sidekick and Davis Cup teammate (1976)

"Comparing Pat Cash to Mats Wilander is likening a crack in the wall to the Grand Canyon."

—John Newcombe, on the eve of the 1983 Australia-Sweden Davis Cup final, with the cheap shot that created a lifelong feud with Pat Cash. In his 2002 autobiography, Newcombe wrote, "I take total responsibility for the hurt it caused Pat because I'd been too busy to okay the [ghost] writer's copy."

"I regard her as the coldest, most self-centered, most ruthless champion ever known to tennis. Her complete disregard for all other players and her fixed determination to play tennis only when she herself wished to and felt it was to her advantage let her make little or no contribution to the advancement of the game or the development of younger players."

—Bill Tilden, blasting 1920s and '30s superstar Helen Wills Moody. From his 1948 memoir, *My Story*

"She was very hard for me to play against. She was not ladylike. She was rude, she was unsportsmanlike, and it upset me."

—Hazel Hotchkiss Wightman, on fellow American May Sutton Bundy, the first foreign woman to win Wimbledon, in 1905

"Virginia doesn't think anybody should beat her—including God."

—Wendy Turnbull, sick of Virginia Wade's claims that she shouldn't lose to a player of Turnbull's caliber, during a joint postmatch interview (1977)

"I thought ProServ did a great job marketing Tracy, especially given her personality and her public-speaking ability."

—Pam Shriver, on Tracy Austin. From her 1986 book, *Passing Shots: Pam Shriver on Tour*

"I guess she should be cocky. She beat me three years ago."

—Superstar Chris Evert, with a zinger for Hana Mandlikova, who claimed Evert was past her prime

"They were supportive of me the day I was stabbed, but by the next Monday in Rome they were already standing up to take my ranking away. Gaby [Sabatini] was the only person who thought of me as a human being and not as a ranking position they wanted to grab."

> —Monica Seles, feeling betrayed by her fellow players, who, aside from Sabatini, voted against freezing her No. 1 ranking while she was off the tour recuperating from her on-court stabbing (1995)

"Anna has never had an idol, she is her own idol."

> —Nick Bollettieri, who coached Anna Kournikova before she turned pro

"I like her, but who does she think she is when she parades around like a queen at the French Open, so absorbed that she does not even notice hands holding out for autograph books."

> —Frenchwoman Nathalie Tauziat, 1998 Wimbledon finalist, talking about Anna Kournikova. From her controversial book, *The Underside of Women's Tennis*

"I'm not the next Kournikova—I want to win matches!"

> —Russian beauty Maria Sharapova, sixteen, on being branded the new Anna Kournikova (2003)

"I hate saying this, but I haven't found a girlfriend I want to be with more than a week at a time."

> —Enrique Iglesias, the handsome singer who had been dating tennis sex symbol Anna Kournikova since last summer, when asked in August 2003 by America's *Parade* magazine about their relationship

"You are the pits of the world!"

> —John McEnroe's infamous rant to Wimbledon chair umpire Edward James (1981)

"I want to let my racket do the talking. I thought the way they [John McEnroe and Jimmy Connors] acted on the court was embarrassing. I didn't want a reputation like that. I have always wanted to present myself as a class act, not lose my temper, not rub it in to anyone if I beat them. Just go out there and win."

> —Pete Sampras (1995)

"Nobody should be ranked No. 1 who looks like he just swung from a tree."

> —Andre Agassi's cheap shot at Pete Sampras, for which he later apologized (1993)

"I would never feel like I could have a relationship with a person I'm in competition against that would allow them to understand me completely. You're always guarded."

> —Andre Agassi, explaining why he can't be friends with Pete Sampras

"I think both of our worst nightmares would be to wake up the next morning and be the other."

> —Andre Agassi, on being polar opposites with archrival Pete Sampras (2002)

"Ten Grand Slams."

> —Pete Sampras's reply when asked what is the difference between him and Patrick Rafter, ranked No. 2 (1997)

"Musumba Bwayla is a stupid man and a hopeless player. He has a huge nose and is cross-eyed. Girls hate him. He beat me because my jockstrap was too tight and because when he serves he farts, and that made me lose my concentration, for which I am famous throughout Zambia."

> —Lighton Ndefwayl's original excuse after his defeat by fellow Zambian Musumba Bwayla (1993)

"If I had limited knowledge, how did I get him to where he is? He has earned $35 million or $45 million. He's got the best Davis Cup record in the country. He's been to three Grand Slam finals and won Wimbledon, and he spent ten years with me as his coach. If I was so limited, what the hell did he stay with me for?"

> —A bristling Nick Bollettieri, in response to Andre Agassi's calling him "insignificant" and his knowledge of tennis "limited" (1994)

"I'm a Republican, but I'll never vote for him again."

> —Cliff Richey, part of the triumphant U.S. Davis Cup team hosted at a White House reception by President Richard M. Nixon in 1969, after Nixon presented each player with a golf ball. From the 2003 book, *Bud Collins Total Tennis: The Ultimate Tennis Encyclopedia*

Journalist: "You used to win matches like that."
Jim Courier: "And you used to ask good questions, too."

> —Former world No. 1 Courier, after losing a tiebreaker-in-the-third-set cliffhanger to Marcelo Rios (1997)

"During all the years in which we both were playing, we never once exchanged an unpleasant word!"

> —1930s star Helen Jacobs, denying she and longtime rival Helen Wills Moody hated each other as newspaper accounts insisted, in a magazine piece Jacobs wrote titled "There Was Never a Feud"

"Every time I played Steffi Graf—and I beat her a couple times—there was always something wrong with her."

> —TV analyst Pam Shriver, dubious about Graf's injury claims (2004)

"Billie Jean has changed tremendously from the person I first met at Wimbledon in 1962. We got on very well then despite our intense rivalry. She had high moral standards and was a good person. She'd talk about her faith in God and reading the bible and having a family—that's a long way from the Billie Jean who told the whole world about her abortion, when she became an active women's libber. Once I admired Billie Jean a lot, but I don't anymore. There is only one person she thinks about these days and that's Billie Jean."

> —Margaret Court. From her 1975 book, *Court on Court: A Life in Tennis*

"He has a habit of creating controversy where none exists."

> —Martina Navratilova, on provocateur Richard Williams, father/coach of Venus and Serena (2001)

"What's love got to do with it? I don't have time to come along slowly; we both want to be No. 1."

> —Serena Williams, on her sibling rivalry with Venus (1997)

"People criticize me for being arrogant [but maybe it's] because I'm a little smarter than the others."

> —Venus Williams, whose educational goal is to graduate from fashion school (2002)

"They have made excuses and not given credit to their opponents. They're afraid to show any kind of humility. Humility doesn't mean you're weak."

> —Martina Navratilova, critical of Venus and Serena Williams (2001)

"These players for the most part don't get along. That's what makes it so interesting."

> —Lindsay Davenport, on the sassy "Spice Girls" of tennis: Martina Hingis, Anna Kournikova, Venus Williams, and Serena Williams (2001)

"Professional sports are like that in general. Most of the great players are assholes or bitches."

> —Former No. 1 Lindsay Davenport (2002)

TALK IS CHEAP!

"Women's tennis won't draw flies."

> —Arthur Ashe (1970)

"It is its want of variety that will prevent lawn tennis in its present form from taking rank among our great games. . . . For in all probability the monotony of the game as compared with the others would choke him off before he had time to excel in it."

> —Spencer Gore, first Wimbledon champion, with the worst call in tennis history (1890)

"Boris needs an amazing amount of concentration and willpower. . . . I don't think he'll be playing tennis for long."

> —Gunther Bosch, after quitting as Becker's coach in 1987. Becker retired in 1999.

"Other girls say they're going to replace us at the top, but we just laugh."

> —Chris Evert, then reigning with Martina Navratilova, in *Life* magazine (1986)

"I'm still the best women's tennis player in the world. Steffi will never be No. 1 again."

> —Monica Seles, after Steffi Graf whipped her 6–2, 6–1 for the Wimbledon title (1992)

"The Steffi Graf era is over."

> —German Davis Cup coach Boris Breskvar, after unseeded Lori McNeil upset Graf in the first round at Wimbledon. Graf went on to win seven more Grand Slam titles. (1994)

"Look honey, we all like Alice. She's a real nice person, but she doesn't have it."

> —Legendary actor Clark Gable, at the 1937 Pacific Southwest tournament in Los Angeles, watching struggling champion Alice Marble. Marble, winner of the U.S. Championships in 1936, overheard Gable's remarks and went on to win the U.S. Championships again in 1938, '39, and '40 as well as Wimbledon in 1939.

"You have put sin and vulgarity into tennis."

> —A Wimbledon committeeman, on why Ted Tinling, who designed Gussie Moran's scandalizing lace panties, was banned from Wimbledon (1949)

"I may have exaggerated a bit when I said that 80 percent of the top 100 women are fat pigs. What I meant to say was 75 percent of the top 100 women are fat pigs."

> —1996 Wimbledon champion Richard Krajicek, who later apologized for his oinkish remarks (1992)

"Women's tennis is two sets of rubbish that last only half an hour."

> —Pat Cash (1987)

"If anybody ever manages to get the female fraternity equal prize money with men, that person should be awarded a gold medal and then locked away for robbery!"

> —Pat Cash. From his 2002 autobiography, *Uncovered*

"I have never believed a woman can successfully play the net."

> —Bill Tilden (1924)

"No broad can beat me."

> —Aging hustler and male chauvinist Bobby Riggs, before Billie Jean King whipped him in their celebrated "Battle of the Sexes" at Houston Astrodome before a record crowd of 30,472 and 60 million TV viewers (1973)

"She expects to scrape me up off the Astrodome floor. I will scrape her up. She is a woman and is subject to women's emotional frailties. She will crack up during the match."

> —Bobby Riggs, trash talking before the match (1973)

"Women are brought up from the time they're six years old to read books, eat candy, and go to dancing class. They can't compete against men, can't stand the strain."

> —American Davis Cupper Gene Scott, a TV analyst for the "Battle of the Sexes" match, predicting a Riggs romp (1973)

"He played like a woman."

> —Billie Jean King, on Riggs's wimpy performance in their "Battle of the Sexes" (1973)

"There are hundreds of players like her in America."

> —Tracy Austin, dismissing thirteen-year-old debutante Steffi Graf after routing her 6–4, 6–0 in Filderstadt, Germany (1982)

"If I ever lost to a fourteen- or fifteen-year-old, I'd die right on the court."

> —Pam Shriver, before losing to fourteen-year-old Gabriela Sabatini at the Family Circle Cup (1985)

"Remember, he's still a young boy. . . . McEnroe will be good practice for me."

> —Jimmy Connors, before losing to John McEnroe for the first time at the Grand Prix Masters (1979)

"With the right kind of guidance, he could turn his brashness into something really great that people would admire and respect. But what's he going to get from [his mother] Gloria? Win, win, win, to hell with the rest of the world? Jesus, emotionally that kid is a vegetable. He can't stand confrontation, and he can't make a decision. I'd be surprised if he didn't have an unhappy life. All that potential that's never going to be shaped. Jimmy—Jimmy is a tragedy."

> —Bill Riordan, Jimmy Connors's manager. From Peter Bodo's 1979 book, *Inside Tennis: A Season on the Pro Tour*

"The USTA should be shot for making us play in these conditions. They should drop an A-bomb on this place."

> —Wimbledon finalist and new U.S. citizen Kevin Curren, blasting the U.S. Open after a first-round debacle against Guy Forget (1985)

"I am not playing Wimbledon because I am allergic to grass."

> —Ivan Lendl, who skipped Wimbledon in 1982 and was photographed during the fortnight playing golf

"The grass court is passing. I must admit this truth, greatly as I deplore it. It will not be long, possibly twenty-five years, before grass courts will be a rarity, and all championships will be played on clay or some dirt surface."

> —Bill Tilden. From his 1925 classic, *Match Play and the Spin of the Ball*

"They get rid of the grass here next year. That's when they better watch out for me."

> —Bjorn Borg, after he was upset by Vijay Amritraj at the 1974 U.S. Open. Borg would never win the U.S. Open, either on clay (Har-Tru) or on hard courts.

"Many people say to me that it was easier for a player to win the Grand Slam in my day. I always reply, 'Well, if that is so, why couldn't someone else do it?'"

> —Don Budge, winner of the first Grand Slam of tennis in 1938

"If we paid the women more, we wouldn't have so much to spend on petunias."

> —Chris Gorringe, All-England Lawn Tennis Club secretary, smugly dismissing women players' demands for equal prize money at Wimbledon (1999)

"How old are you now Pancho?"
"I'm twenty-eight."
"I'll give you one more year."

> —Ted Schroeder, to Pancho Gonzalez in 1956. Gonzalez would rule the pro tour for the next five years and continue to beat the world's top players into his forties. From the 1973 book, *The Return of a Champion: Pancho Gonzalez' Golden Year 1964*

"Two or three more years, that's all. . . . With so much money, I think they lose their competitive urge."

> —Pancho Segura, Jimmy Connors's former coach, on how much longer Connors, then twenty-five, would play. Connors retired at age forty, then founded and starred on a senior tour. (1978)

"I always say that if I can't play with the big boys, then I don't want to play."

> —Jimmy Connors, in 1985, scoffing at the notion of playing on after his pro tour days. In 1993 he started his own thirty-five-and-over Champions Tour

"If he's the best young player we got, we're in big trouble. He's flimsy."

> —Pancho Segura, erring on the young John McEnroe

"I don't see anybody in McEnroe's or Connors's class in the U.S. In about three years, the bottom is going to fall out at the top of American men's professional tennis."

> —Arthur Ashe, who lived to see the "Greatest Generation"—Sampras, Agassi, Courier, and Chang—in American men's tennis (1985)

"If Agassi ever wins Wimbledon, I'll eat my T-shirt. Not only has he no chance to win, but if he doesn't pull himself together soon, he could be out of tennis in two or three years."

> —*Miami Herald* sports editor Edwin Pope, just before Andre Agassi won his first major title at Wimbledon (1992)

"Who's Rostagno? Nothing personal but I could have had a harder draw. There's at least twenty guys tougher than him, and I'm not planning to lose."

> —John McEnroe, before Derrick Rostagno bounced him out in straight sets in a Wimbledon first-round match (1990)

"My gut tells me Pat Rafter is a one-Slam guy. I think the U.S. Open last year was it."

> —John McEnroe, whom Rafter proved wrong three months later by winning a second straight U.S. Open (1998)

"Marriage probably is going to ruin his tennis. He hasn't been able to really play [well] since he got married."

> —John McEnroe, during the summer of 2002, before Pete Sampras ended his storied career by winning the U.S. Open

"Sampras is a step and a half slow coming into the net. He's just not the same player. . . . I'll be surprised if he wins the next match."

—Greg Rusedski's infamous words after Pete Sampras beat him in a third-round match at the 2002 U.S. Open. Sampras went on to capture his fifth U.S. and fourteenth Grand Slam title, a record, in his final tournament.

"To say that tennis today is clean, you have to be living in a dream world."

—French Davis Cupper Nicolas Escude, minus the benefit of proof, telling *Le Parisien* that he believes the ATP covers up the extent of the drug problem, particularly among American players (2003)

"I think it's arranged. I have no information, nothing at all, but, looking at the matches, I think it may be arranged."

—Amelie Mauresmo, who lost to Serena Williams in the 2002 Wimbledon semifinals, charging that matches between Serena and Venus are rigged, despite an absence of evidence

"If it's fixed, how come I've only won once?"

—Serena Williams, debunking nonsensical speculation that her father Richard orchestrates the results of her matches with sister Venus (2001)

"He has so much talent that he can't fail to be a champion."

—All-time great Fred Perry, after American Scott Davis nearly upset Ivan Lendl at Wimbledon in 1984

"I wouldn't mention his name in the same breath. . . . With his talent, he should never have allowed himself to drop out of the top four or five."

—Jimmy Connors, bristling when asked if Andre Agassi deserves to be linked with Pete Sampras and retired greats like himself, John McEnroe, and Bjorn Borg (1999)

"As they say in sports, the older you get, the better you used to be."

—John McEnroe (2002)

"I think he should start thinking about quitting tennis when he is beaten by Corretja, especially on grass. That loss should tell him something, and it's a disrespect to himself to keep playing."

—Yevgeny Kafelnikov, on slumping Pete Sampras, who won the U.S. Open five months later (2002)

"Don't worry about me. I'm the best tax expert in Germany."

> —Peter Graf, a few years before he went to prison in 1995 for tax evasion on his daughter Steffi's earnings

"I would like to thank the sponsor, even though I think it is a disgrace to smoke cigarettes."

> —Pat Cash, after winning the Salem Open in Hong Kong (1990)

"I'm going to take him out."

> —Serena Williams's brash prediction about playing No. 203–ranked Karsten Braasch in a "Battle of the Sexes" match during the 1998 Australian Open. The bespectacled German, who had played a round of golf earlier in the day, slammed Serena 6–1, rubbing it in by smoking cigarettes on changeovers. Braasch also whacked Venus 6–2 to silence, temporarily, the Williamses' claim that they could compete on the men's tour.

"It's like Martin Luther King Jr. said, 'A lie cannot live.' I was never controversial."

> —Serena Williams (2003)

"Agassi couldn't beat my mum now. He's finished."

> —British Davis Cup captain David Lloyd, in early 1999 before Andre Agassi resurrected his floundering career at age twenty-nine and went on to win five more Grand Slam titles

STUFF OF CHAMPIONS

"Champions are people who want to leave their sport better off than when they started."

—Arthur Ashe (1988)

"A truly great player should be able to win on all surfaces."

—Former Wimbledon and U.S. champion Stan Smith (1983)

"Cedric Major showed wisdom and analysis when he summed up the great match player as the one who has the ability to scramble in the pinch."

—Bill Tilden, from a 1924 article he wrote in *American Lawn Tennis* magazine

"I want to reach absolute perfection. And I think I can reach it."

—Steffi Graf, owner of the unique "Golden Slam" in 1988, and the only player to win each Grand Slam title at least four times and, to many experts, the greatest ever (1991)

"Sacrifice. Giving up enjoyment of life for the sake of practice."

—Pancho Gonzalez on what makes a champion. From the 1992 book, *Tough Draw*

"Nobody but the world's top-ranked player knows what it takes to get to the top. You have to sacrifice everything."

—Bjorn Borg, eleven-time Grand Slam champion (1981)

"Often after I lost a tournament, I'd be out practicing harder than ever to make up my mind I wasn't going to lose the next one."

> —Margaret Court, who captured a record sixty-two Grand Slam titles in singles, doubles, and mixed doubles between 1960 and 1975. From the 1997 book, *The Tennis Lover's Book of Wisdom*

"My only drug is work. I have worked really hard for the last year . . . sometimes it made me cry. I pushed myself so hard."

> —Justine Henin-Hardenne, winner of the 2003 French and U.S. Opens, denying insinuations by former French Open semifinalist Filip Dewulf and Leo Clijsters, father of world-ranked No. 2 Kim Clijsters, that she uses performance-enhancing drugs (2003)

"If only people knew how hard I worked to make it [look] that easy."

> —Pete Sampras, winner of a record fourteen Grand Slam singles titles

"What I like is his consistency, his concentration. He's not bothered what people are thinking about him, the way he looks, the way he walks. All that he's bothered about is playing good tennis and being competitive and I feel that's remarkable."

> —Indian cricket superstar Sachin Tendulkar, in praise of Pete Sampras (2003)

"I hated it at Bollettieri's academy. The only way I could get out was to succeed. That became my goal—to do well so I could escape."

> —Andre Agassi, on his teenage years at the Bollettieri Tennis Academy (1998)

"You may play the match everybody says is the best they ever see, but by next year it is forgotten. A tennis player must paint the Mona Lisa two, three times a year."

> —Guillermo Vilas, four-time Grand Slam champion and published poet, on the drive required to succeed in tennis

"You should never complain about an injury. We believe that if you play, then you aren't injured, and that's that."

> —Roy Emerson, holder of a record twenty-eight Grand Slam singles and doubles titles, on the famous Australian sporting code

"Lance Armstrong, the cyclist, says he owes everything to cancer because the cancer—the adversity—made him the champion he is today. . . . Wheelchair tennis taught me how to adapt, it taught me to compete with myself, not to compare. Wheelchair tennis is not about forehands and backhands, trophies and money—it's about taking a risk, looking at what you can do and getting outside your comfort zone. . . . To paraphrase Michael Jordan, it is not that you fall down that is important, but whether you get back up that is significant."

> —Randy Snow, ten-time U.S. Open champion, 1991 ITF Wheelchair Tennis world champion, and 1991 double Paralympic gold medalist. From the 2001 ITF book, *More Than Tennis: The First 25 Years of Wheelchair Tennis*

"I used to lay in my bed dreaming of being a champion and living the life of an athlete. I did it like many athletes before and after. Let's not forget where we came from, a hospital bed wondering what next, and there are people there today wondering the same. Give back."

> —Randy Snow, ten-time U.S. Open champion, 1991 ITF Wheelchair Tennis world champion, and 1991 double Paralympic gold medalist. From the 2001 ITF book, *More Than Tennis: The First 25 Years of Wheelchair Tennis*

"You continually need to sell the sport. That's one of the sad things about the current athlete, there's too much taken for granted."

> —Former doubles champion Pam Shriver, saying women players today need to do more than just hit tennis balls and collect prize money (2001)

"The best players are always the ones who remember their losses, because they remember the pain and they hate it."

> —Billie Jean King, on seeing a distraught Rod Laver after an upset loss to Roger Taylor at Wimbledon (1970)

"Champions are not born. They are made. They emerge from a long, hard school of defeat, discouragement, and mediocrity, but they are endowed with a force that transcends discouragement and cries 'I will succeed.'"

> —Bill Tilden. From his 1920 book, *The Art of Lawn Tennis*

"I know I would hate life if I were deprived of trying, hunting, working for some objective within which there lies the beauty of perfection."

> —Helen Wills Moody, who during the zenith of her brilliant career, from 1927 to 1933, not only won *every match* she played—158 straight—but also *every set* to achieve the perfection she coveted. From her 1937 autobiography, *Fifteen-Thirty*

"I thought that if ever I became a champion I'd want to behave just like her."

> —A young Don Budge, after meeting Helen Wills Moody at the Berkeley Tennis Club about 1932. From the 1988 book, *The Goddess and the American Girl*

"Outwardly, I appeared calm, but inside I was boiling. To be the best, you have to care mightily."

> —Don Budge

"You're always striving to play that perfect match."

> —Chris Evert, eighteen-time Grand Slam singles champion

"What? Don't tell me that! That's the biggest crock of dump! Being the U.S. Open champion is what I've lived for. If these guys are relieved at losing, something is wrong with the game—and wrong with them."

> —A raging Jimmy Connors, when told—during his memorable run at age thirty-nine to the U.S. Open semis—that Pete Sampras, after failing to successfully defend his title, expressed relief that the "bag of bricks" had just been lifted from his shoulders (1991)

"It's not a good year unless I win two majors. They're what count."

> —Pete Sampras (1996)

"He's all blood and guts."

> —Singer Seal, on why Jim Courier is his favorite tennis player

"He tries to the maximum on every single point of every game of every single set. He just has an amazingly high level of intensity during a match. I get the feeling he probably brushes his teeth ferociously."

—Brad Gilbert, on Jim Courier's ferocious determination, in his 1993 book, *Winning Ugly*

"The most amazing effort I think I've ever seen, man or woman."

—Praise from Martina Navratilova for U.S. Open champion Justine Henin-Hardenne, whose final victory over Kim Clijsters came less than twenty-four hours after a momentous semifinal triumph over Jennifer Capriati, which resulted in painful cramps and required an IV injection of fluids (2003)

"A champion in modern lawn tennis needs three attributes: a burning determination to succeed, a sound attacking game, and perfect physical condition."

—Tony Mottram, English Davis Cup player from 1947 to 1955, and Joy Mottram, English Wightman Cup player from 1947 to 1952. From their 1957 book, *Modern Lawn Tennis*

"Tennis is a sport for all-sized people, so there will always be some good little kids, but I'll know tennis has really made it to the very top when we develop a champion from the inner city who's six-foot-five and moves like Rosewall with a serve like Vines."

—Jack Kramer. From his 1979 memoir, *The Game: My 40 Years in Tennis*

"There hasn't been a British Wimbledon men's champion since me in 1936, and a lot of people keep wondering when we will produce another one. Well, it's not a matter of *producing* anybody, to begin with. It's a case of somebody, somewhere, who wants to succeed badly enough and is determined and bloody-minded enough to make sure he does."

—Fred Perry. From the 1984 book, *Fred Perry: An Autobiography*

"If Evonne [Goolagong Cawley] and I had been in a squad [like players today] at a very early age, we would never have made it. You've got to go back to individual coaching, not groups. They [kids] begin to look like robots because nobody is bringing out their individualism."

—Australian tennis legend Margaret Court, slamming the state of Australian junior tennis (1998)

"No matter what accomplishments you make, somebody helps you."

> —Althea Gibson, first black tennis champion

"In the perfection of his stroking, he is a machine . . . but, more than that, he is a charming, cultured gentleman."

> —Bill Tilden, on French star Rene Lacoste. From the 1971 book, *Tennis: Its History, People and Events*

"Learning to play tennis was easy after my father got through teaching me ethics, integrity, and fairness. He told me to be a standup guy, with no alibis; shake hands firmly and look people in the eye. That's corny and old-fashioned, but there's plenty of time to get to the forehands and volleys."

> —Jack Kramer. From his 1979 memoir, *The Game: My 40 Years in Tennis*

"If the other guy gets a bad call, it's going to bother me. I want to beat him because I play better, not because someone made a mistake. If I didn't miss the next shot, my game would be affected. I'll think I'm taking advantage of him."

> —Manuel Orantes, 1975 U.S. Open champion, who sometimes purposely missed a shot after his opponent was victimized by an incorrect line call

"My mother always told me to never give up but to play by the rules. I think my mother would be proud of me."

> —Magnus Norman, who conceded his 2001 Australian Open fourth-round match against Sebastien Grosjean when he refused to replay match point after being aced on a serve that the net machine registered as a let

"I don't know of any player who doesn't wish he had some of Lleyton's mongrel."

> —Todd Woodbridge, on world-ranked No. 1 Lleyton Hewitt (2002)

"This year I particularly think that those firefighters from all over Australia who gave up their Christmas and put their lives in danger to help out their mates—I think of every one of them as Australian of the Year."

> —Patrick Rafter, paying tribute to the efforts of the firefighters who battled the New South Wales Christmas bushfires, after he was honored as Australian of the Year (2002)

"I don't come to tournaments to make friends, to go to parties, to hold conversations. I come to be the best, and I'm not mean and cruel and dirty."

—Venus Williams (1997)

"You can have a certain arrogance, and I think that's fine, but what you should never lose is the respect for the others."

—All-time great Steffi Graf, on the trash-talking teen queens (1999)

"I never had time for friends or anything else. I didn't even know anybody in school. I was too busy. I used to leave class every day at noon to practice tennis."

—Jimmy Connors, saying that as a child all he ever wanted to do was play tennis

"The hunger, the drive, a lot of that will stem from negative things, like insecurity, or wanting to get attention. When I started playing tennis, I was painfully shy. But I liked the attention. I'd go, God, people are accepting me because I'm winning."

—Chris Evert, on one source of the burning desire that made her a champion, in *Esquire* magazine (1988)

"If you want tantrums or comedy, don't come and see me."

—Ivan Lendl, the no-nonsense champion (1987)

"I've been reading about how I don't have much talent. There are many different talents besides hitting a tennis ball. Having guts on the court is a talent; having desire is a talent; having courage to go for a shot when you are [down] love-40 is a talent."

—World-ranked No. 1 Jim Courier, after routing Andre Agassi—who had said, "I don't think he has a lot of natural talent to fall back on"—for his third win over Agassi in the past four French Opens (1992)

"Skill and confidence are not the only determining factors—the champion's edge exists solely in the mind. He uses any success as a spur to greater ambition; he has the ability to peak when the stakes are the greatest; and he has what is known as the killer instinct."

—Mark McCormack, CEO and Chairman of the Board of International Management Group, equating the qualities of great athletes to those of successful businessmen, in *RACQUET* magazine (1985)

"Now that I'm losing some, I can see how tough I was—the killer instinct, the single-mindedness, playing like a machine. Boy, that's what made me a champion."

>—Chris Evert, near the end of her illustrious career, in *TIME* magazine (1989)

"I think self-awareness is probably the most important thing towards being a champion."

>—Billie Jean King, in *The Sportswoman* magazine (1973)

"To the contender, written criticism is as wind in the trees."

>—All-time great Helen Wills Moody, in 1933, addressing criticism of sportswriters that she had become haughty and cold. From the 1988 book, *The Goddess and the American Girl*

"Nothing is worse than when people say you're washed up."

>—Martina Navratilova, thirty, after beating Steffi Graf, eighteen, in the 1987 U.S. Open final. Navratilova also defeated Graf in the Wimbledon final, but Graf (75–2) captured the season-ending No. 1 ranking.

"I'm living proof that, just when you think it is like the worst ever, there is always a light at the end of the tunnel, and you are in control of everything. Just believe in yourself. You make or break yourself."

>—Jennifer Capriati, after a Lazarus-like comeback to win the Australian Open (2001)

"I've always had a strong character, a strong personality, and I'm not going to let someone ruin my life or control my life. I'm not a victim."

>—Jennifer Capriati, former whiz kid turned burnout victim turned tennis champion (2001)

TRIUMPH AND DISASTER

"If You can meet with Triumph and Disaster, and treat those two imposters just the same. . . ."

—words above the players' entrance to Wimbledon's Centre Court, from Rudyard Kipling's famous poem "*If*"

"The moment of victory is much too short to live for that and nothing else."

—Martina Navratilova, in the *Guardian* (UK) (1989)

"Sports for me is when a guy walks off the court, and you really can't tell whether he won or lost, when he carries himself with pride either way."

—Jim Courier

"Unlike many school authorities, I believe there is more character-building to be found in tennis than in so-called team games. . . . If the sharing of triumph and disaster—and the necessary teamwork to achieve one and overcome the other—are required, I can recommend the understanding and teamwork of the successful doubles combination."

—Legendary Australian Davis Cup captain Harry Hopman. From his 1972 instruction book, *Better Tennis*

"The ultimate connection between tennis and life is 'in the doing,' not the winning. Vince Lombardi's statement—'Winning is not everything, it's the only thing'—is taken too literally. Success is a journey, not a destination. The going is usually more important than the outcome. Not everyone can be No. 1. What happens to the person who ends up No. 2 or No. 20?"

　　—Arthur Ashe. From his 1981 book, *Off the Court*

"In tennis, you can only lose; the other guy can't eat you."

　　—Brazilian star Gustavo "Guga" Kuerten (1998)

"You are not next to God if you win. And if you lose, you are not next to the devil."

　　—Boris Becker

"Greatness in sports is the ability to win in a stadium filled with people who are pulling for you to lose."

　　—Quotation from ex-football coach George Allen that 1970s transsexual pro player Renée Richards carried with her at all times

"When you look at the big picture, tennis, and any sport for that matter, is insignificant to life in general. It's important for every sports person to learn that."

　　—Former No. 1 Patrick Rafter (2001)

"If I'd lost, I suppose I would have started thinking about quitting tennis altogether. Really, I'd have felt that down. . . . I needed that title and I needed it badly. Nick needed it and my father needed it. I also think my fans needed it because they had to have a reason to keep believing. Then there were my critics. They needed a dose of reality, that not only can I actually play this game, but that I can be a winner."

　　—Andre Agassi, after he won Wimbledon for his long-awaited first Grand Slam title after losing his first three major finals with disappointing performances (1992)

"When you are a young man, you are looking for your own identity, and winning is a way of expressing yourself. When I lost, I wanted to die. And because I thought in victory I became somebody, in defeat, it followed, I was nobody."

　　—Boris Becker

"It's very dangerous to have your self-worth riding on your results as an athlete."

—Jim Courier, former No. 1 and four-time Grand Slam singles champion

"I can't understand it. I thought, 'I hope I never come to this.' I'll know something's wrong if I do. Games aren't something to cry over."

—Evonne Goolagong Cawley, on coming upon Chris Evert crying in the locker room, after Evert had lost a close match in 1972 to Billie Jean King in Dallas. From the 1979 book, *Famous Women Tennis Players*

"Tennis is just a game, but if I were getting terrible grades, that's disappointing."

—World No. 5 and part-time college student Venus Williams (1998)

"It was almost like a death."

—Oracene Williams, describing her distraught daughter Venus's heart-breaking 6–1, 4–6, 6–4 semifinal loss to Martina Hingis at the 1999 U.S. Open

"What kind of message does this send to the world? Mr. Parche has admitted that he stalked me, then he stabbed me once . . . [and] now the court has said he doesn't have to go to jail for his premeditated crime. He gets to go back to his life, but I can't because I am still recovering from this attack, which could have killed me."

—A "shocked and horrified" Monica Seles, after a German court handed out a two-year suspended sentence to Gunther Parche who stabbed her in the back during a match in Hamburg (1993)

"Competition is grand, but people also like watching a victim twitch. In fact, some prefer it."

—Tennis historian Ted Tinling, on the ruthless reigns of such champions as Suzanne Lenglen and Helen Wills Moody, in the *Wall Street Journal* (1989)

"Tennis is a diversion, not a career."

—Helen Wills Moody, winner of eight Wimbledon and seven U.S. crowns during the 1920s and '30s while also a noteworthy artist and novelist. From her autobiography, *Fifteen-Thirty*

"Pressure? I'll tell you what pressure is. It's a man struggling to support a family—not playing a game."

> —Boris Becker

"I didn't start a war. Nobody died. I only lost a tennis match, nothing more."

> —Boris Becker, struggling to keep his head while all others were losing theirs, after a shock second-round loss to journeyman Peter Doohan at Wimbledon (1987)

"The fascination of playing is paramount, the victory a minor consideration."

> —Bill Tilden

"Too great a degree of importance is placed on victory, either for the money, the prestige, the club, or the country."

> —Jean Borotra, flamboyant French champion in the 1920s and early '30s. From the 1997 book, *The Tennis Lover's Book of Wisdom*

"If I had known that this is what it's like to have it all, I would have settled for less."

> —Martina Navratilova, quoting Lily Tomlin, after winning the 1986 U.S. Open. From the 1987 book, *Tennis Trivia*

"My girl, if you're going to win this thing, you'd better do it soon. There's going to be a war that will make all of us forget about tennis."

> —American ambassador Joseph Kennedy, at the 1938 Wimbledon Ball, talking to U.S. star Alice Marble, who lost in the semis to Helen Jacobs, but won the title in 1939, two months before the outbreak of World War II

"It was the worst loss of my life, a devastating defeat: Sometimes it still keeps me up at nights. It's even tough for me now to do the commentary at the French—I'll often have one or two days when I literally feel sick to my stomach just at being there and thinking about that match. Thinking of what I threw away, and how different my life would've been if I'd won."

> —John McEnroe, on losing a two-sets-to-love lead in his heartbreaking 1984 French Open final defeat, to hated rival Ivan Lendl. From his 2002 autobiography, *You Cannot Be Serious*

"I had losses on the court that were so devastating I'd go back to my room and sob inconsolably. When you're a teenager, you cry; when you're twenty-five, you break a racket; and when you're thirty, you pour yourself a drink and say 'what the hell.' But you learn to cope and you come back strong."

> —Pam Shriver, on the agony of defeat. From the 2001 book, *Venus Envy*

"After a defeat, they [the press] made me feel as if I'm [sic] on trial."

> —Arthur Ashe. From his 1975 book, *Portrait in Motion*

"Defeat lasts a long time; victories only a moment. I'll never get over it."

> —Billie Jean King, on her upset loss to Ann Jones in the 1969 Wimbledon final. In a documentary in the series *Man Alive* on BBC 2

"I had that great summer run, then I lost that match. It was a heartbreaker. I've never felt more lonely on a court or more disappointed in the game."

> —Andre Agassi, on his 1995 U.S. Open final loss to Pete Sampras, the start of a two-year downward spiral in his career

"It made me realize just how bad it feels to lose a Grand Slam final. How the only player that people care about is the one who gets his name engraved on the trophy."

> —Pete Sampras, on how his disappointing loss to Stefan Edberg in the 1992 U.S. Open final changed his attitude and fueled his desire to become a great champion

"When I lose, I'm devastated. It can take me weeks to get over a big loss. I sometimes feel so debilitated I can hardly get up in the morning. It hurts me more now than it did ten years ago. I believe it's a good thing, because it tells me I still care."

> —Pete Sampras (1999)

"I have seriously thought about retiring, but that was on a good day. On a bad day, I've thought about killing myself."

> —Ivan Lendl

"It's tougher for the single guys—I think anyway, maybe because I'm single. My chief focal point is tennis. I have a lot of other interests, but no one single counterbalance, like a family. Defeat is always hardest for me the next day, because it stays with me and swells. The married guys seem to have more of a safety valve. How many times have I seen a guy come off the court, really way down after a hard loss, and he walks out of the locker room, and his pretty little daughter runs up to him, and it's all forgotten."

> —Arthur Ashe, on dealing with defeat alone. From his 1975 book, *Portrait in Motion*

"The one match that took my confidence was the loss to Mary Joe at the [1993] French [Open]. First, you can't believe it happened to you. Then you stop believing in you. It's been a long time since I've been able to sleep a really deep sleep. A loss like that doesn't leave you."

> —Gabriela Sabatini, still haunted by her 1–6, 7–6, 10–8 quarterfinal loss to Mary Joe Fernandez after leading 6–1, 5–1 and not converting five match points (1994)

"In America you're conditioned to regard everything as a contest. You have to make the Ten Best Dressed List, win this, win that. It drives me nuts sometimes. Who cares, for Christ's sake?"

> —Arthur Ashe. From www.tennisontheline.org

"Nobody beats Vitas Gerulaitis seventeen times in a row!"

> —Vitas Gerulaitis's famous reply when reporters asked him how he had upset Jimmy Connors 7–5, 6–2 at the Colgate Grand Prix Masters after losing to Connors sixteen straight times (1980)

THE FAME GAME

"People will pay to see anybody they hate."

> —Promoter C. C. "Cash and Carry" Pyle, after he signed the incomparable Suzanne Lenglen to a pro contract in 1926

"She was a rock star long before there was rock. There was such anticipation before her matches. Everybody wondered about Suzanne, what she would wear, what she would look like. I would love to be like that."

> —Monica Seles, who, as a teenager, idolized charismatic Suzanne Lenglen, tennis's first female superstar, in *Sports Illustrated*

"Glory is often worth the price one pays for it."

> —Charles Lenglen, the hard-driving father/coach of Suzanne Lenglen. From the 1997 book, *The Tennis Lover's Book of Wisdom*

"We're living in the year 1990 and in sport it's still all about money. It's sad but true. It's sad because man is in this circus forever. Money and fame don't make you happy. The values we have are false."

> —Three-time Wimbledon champion Boris Becker, at twenty-two

"People can bring you so high up and put you on a pedestal, and so quickly they can push you off. And you can't be caught up in that."

> —Lindsay Davenport, U.S. Open champion and world-ranked No. 2 (1998)

"If I'd done everything they said, I'd be dead by now."

> —Former tennis superstar Bjorn Borg, forty-four, denying that he ever attempted suicide or took cocaine (1999)

"When you haven't got it, you really want it; when you have it, you really don't want it."

> —Patrick Rafter, Australian hero and dual U.S. Open champion, on the paradox of fame

"I can stand crowds only when I am working in front of them, but then I love them."

> —"Big Bill" Tilden, 1920s superstar

"It's a totally unreal world we live in. It's very dangerous to know you can have anything you want."

> —Yannick Noah, on the temptations heaped on pro players (1989)

"We're setting athletes apart in a society in which everyone knows there are lots of people who smoke joints. When you take up sport, your goal is not to become a model for the young but to be the best. I'm not saying smoking a joint is good, but it's not serious. In no way does it affect sporting values because an athlete smoked a joint one evening."

> —Yannick Noah, admitting to smoking dope during the 1983 French Open, which he won, in a 1996 interview with *L'Equipe*

"I never wished to live this life. I just wanted to play tennis, not to become a public person. That is why I can be quite bitchy toward people."

> —All-time great Steffi Graf

"At the top, no one leaves you alone. Everyone tells you lovely little lies. I learned that most of the people in the world are fake, and I learned there is more to life than tennis."

> —Disillusioned Andrea Temesvari, a statuesque Hungarian who ranked No. 7 at age seventeen before she declined, in part from serious ankle and shoulder injuries (1991)

"When I was twelve, every little girl in Russia was trying to wear her hair like mine and playing tennis."

> —Anna Kournikova

"For years and years, I was trying to find out who my true friends were. Obviously, I lost the ones I had before I was famous. I cut all my ties to childhood long before I won Wimbledon. Then I became famous and for years I was trying to work out whether the person was interested in me for the fame. Now I couldn't care less because one fits to the other. Even Barbara, I don't know 100 percent, she loves me for me. I know as much as a man can know but there's no proof that she would love me if I was poor and not famous, working at a nine-to-five job in some small town in Germany."

—Boris Becker, on the price of fame, in the *Telegraph* (UK, 2001)

"People don't remember who finishes second."

—Pete Sampras

"I think ordinary people are much more happy than the jet-set and celebrity people. My parents, whom I respect as my greatest friends, taught me early that happiness is often a modest thing. It has nothing to do with money or fame."

—Stefan Edberg (1990)

"Nothing is ever like you think it's going to be. If I've learned anything over the past few years, that's it."

—Monica Seles, on her star-crossed life. From her 1996 autobiography, *Monica: From Fear to Victory*

"I used to go into pubs and people would want to pick a fight with me. I would hear a group of girls say: 'Oh look, there's Pat Cash.' And then one of them would come up to me and say, 'You think you're so good' and throw a drink in my face. That kind of reaction from people was a bit of a shock initially, and you don't ever really get used to it."

—Pat Cash (1996)

"If I didn't play well, or lost a match, the public was often violent. Spectators would grab me by the arm and say, 'I came out for a good day and you ruined it for me.' They did everything but hit me. This happens to every public character."

—1930s champion Alice Marble

"Becoming a champion, one learns many things, but nobody teaches you how to deal with the sudden glory."

—1983 French Open champion Yannick Noah, who fled suffocating fame in France for relative anonymity in New York

"Wimbledon is like my second birth place. It's so long ago now. But I remember very clearly, at the moment of match point in the final of 1985, I remember thinking 'Something has changed.' I didn't know what it was, but *I had the clear feeling that something dramatically had changed.* I had become the public Boris Becker. Talk about being put in the spotlight. And I couldn't find out what you were supposed to do or say or act like. Even my closest advisers, parents, and friends were more in a state of shock than I was. I was about to live a life not many human beings have ever known. People get to know you in places you didn't even know existed. In the smallest islands, without any electricity, I found people knew who I was. I'm one of the most famous people on the earth, yes."

—Boris Becker, recalling his life-changing Wimbledon triumph at age seventeen, in the *Telegraph* (UK, 2001)

"I'm leaving, I can't be a normal person here. I've thought about it a thousand times. I can't go to a restaurant or do anything young people do. I don't have a private life. Here, if you can knock down idols, you do it."

—Marcelo Rios, the former world-ranked No. 1 named the Chilean sportsman of the century, after being cleared of assaulting two policemen in Chile (2003)

"I feel like a horse in a circus. Sometimes, I'm getting crazy because people come and see me, and they point their finger at me: 'Look! Look! Look, how she plays.' I understand it's different, and people will react, but sometimes I can't stand it."

—Russia's ambidextrous Yevgeniya Kulikovskaya during the French Open (2003)

"Before I was the hunter. Now I'm the hunted."

—World No. 1 Martina Hingis, after she staved off Serena Williams before losing to Venus Williams at the Lipton Championships (1998)

"Politics aside, her logic was questionable. How uplifting is a song illuminated by such abrasive lyrics? But Capriati made a wish, and it was granted. Star power has its privileges on the women's tour, but it is often misspent on petty demands instead of tennis reform."

—The *New York Times*, on Jennifer Capriati requesting "Bombs Over Baghdad" by rapper Outkast during the warm-up for one of her matches in Miami (2003)

"When I looked at the eyes of my fans, I thought I was looking at monsters. When I saw this kind of blind, emotional devotion, I could understand what happened to us at Nuremberg."

—Boris Becker, telling *Radio Times* (UK) that he was unnerved by German fan adulation during his halcyon days (2001)

"I don't want to be promoted. I am already too much promoted. I want to be unknown."

—Gustavo "Guga" Kuerten, after winning a second French Open in 2000 and hitting national hero status (2000)

"I believe in freedom of the press—but what about freedom from the press?"

—Martina Navratilova, after being harassed by the British press

"Even though I'm on a salary, I still don't have a comprehension of what the real world functions like."

—Andre Agassi, owner of three Grand Slam titles and a $100 million Nike contract (1998)

"If you compare me to Andre or Boris, they're what I would call big stars. They want to be big stars so they act like they think big stars should act. I'd rather not be known by anybody."

—Stefan Edberg (1990)

"People know me. I'm not going to produce any cartwheels out there. I'm not going to belong on Comedy Central. I'll always be a tennis player, not a celebrity."

—Pete Sampras (1997)

"They want me because I give the finger and get mad. I'm not the best player in the world. Borg, Connors, Vilas—they all win more than me. But they don't want them on *Laugh-In* [TV show]. They want me."

—Ilie Nastase. From the 1978 book, *Nasty: Ilie Nastase vs. Tennis*

"They want me because I give the finger and get mad." —Ilie Nastase (*Fred Mullane/ Camerawork USA, Inc.*)

"It became twenty-four hours a day. When I slept, I suspected a secret camera under the sheet. The more I worked to live up to my nationalistic obligations, the more harassed I became. It's tough to handle at age twenty-three, but much harder at seventeen or eighteen."

> —Boris Becker, admitting to paranoia after becoming a teenage German icon (1991)

"I'm glad I made it out alive, to tell you the truth. There were difficult times. I played fourteen years in a row. The first ones were very hectic, and all of a sudden I became a star, and I didn't know how to handle everything. I was always praying that I somehow would have a long career, and I managed to do that without any major scars in my soul. I'm not drug-addicted, I'm not alcoholic, I'm not three times divorced. I'm quite normal. I manage to have a quite normal life. For me that was always my biggest achievement."

> —Boris Becker, with the first of his retirement announcements at the 1997 Wimbledon. An extramarital sex scandal, divorce, tax evasion trials, and an admission of sleeping-pill addiction later ended that normalcy and sullied his reputation.

"All my career I dreamed of being No. 1. But when I finally achieved it [in 1988] and the initial excitement wore off, I felt nothing. I had no sense of elation or pride. I was world champion but so what? It got to the stage where I got more satisfaction out of cutting the grass than playing tennis."

> —A disillusioned Mats Wilander

"I have a fear of being No. 1. I am a quiet, private person who likes to be with his family, and I don't think I'd like to be No. 1 for five years."

> —Boris Becker, after winning his first Australian Open title to take over the No. 1 ranking. As it turned out, Becker stayed No. 1 for only three weeks (1991)

"It's funny how you guys seem to harp on, focus on negative points. God, isn't it great to be No. 1? Nobody asks me that. It's the old case of build a guy up and try to knock him off the hill."

> —Jim Courier, tired of being asked about the pressure of being No. 1, after he was upset by No. 36–ranked Andrei Chesnokov at Indian Wells (1992)

"It's a real shame that two Americans reached the finals of the French Open for the first time since 1954 and not one good thing could be said about either."

> —Jim Courier, responding sharply to *Sports Illustrated*'s unflattering French Open article with a letter to the editor (1991)

"All of the great international games are deprived of some of the good they otherwise do by the type of writer who looks for mischief—ferrets out and exaggerates personal incidents; writes about tennis as if it were a civil (and not very civil) war; and ends up producing all the news *not* fit to print."

> —Robert Gordon Menzies, Australia's long-serving prime minister, in a timeless essay, titled "The Great Game of Tennis," written in 1955

"My life has become a prison. My new haircut helped. It gave me breathing space for about a week. But then the first pictures came out and that blew it."

> —Monica Seles, on the burden of being No. 1 (1992)

"I would gladly give back a quarter of my prize money every year if I were able just to be left alone."

> —John McEnroe, with a Garboesque plea

"People don't listen to losers. Now, when I say something, people listen."

> —Arthur Ashe, tennis star and human rights activist, on the one true benefit of fame, after winning the 1968 U.S. Open to become the first black man to win a Grand Slam title.

"I was thrown into a lake full of crocodiles."

> —Pete Sampras, on how unprepared he was for fame and fortune after winning the 1990 U.S. Open as a nineteen year old (1997)

"If she won just one major, she'd become the most famous athlete of all time."

> —Charlie Pasarell, Indian Wells tournament director and former U.S. No. 1 player, on wildly popular glamour girl Anna Kournikova, in *Sports Illustrated*

"It's over for her in tennis as far as being a serious tennis player. She's a tennis model now."

> —*Tennis Week* publisher Gene Scott, on Anna Kournikova (2002)

"Winning just doesn't matter as much as it used to. There are other ways these athletes can capture the public's attention: by being gorgeous or by being a 'bad boy.' And getting the public's attention is all these companies really care about."

> —Jim Andrews, editorial director of the *IEG Sponsorship Report*, on tennis sex symbol Anna Kournikova, who earns about $15 million a year in endorsements, and eighteen-year-old basketball phenom LeBron James, who has scored more than $100 million in deals with Nike, Coke, and Upper Deck Trading Cards (2003)

"Really, this whole world, being a tennis player, being famous, it's crazy. It really is."

> —Venus Williams, on May 24, 2003. Ironically, less than four months later Yetunde Price, one of her elder half-sisters, was shot dead in Los Angeles.

"I didn't change much over the years. I was true to myself. I didn't sell out for anybody. That's one thing I'm proud of."

> —Pete Sampras, looking back at his legendary career during a poignant ceremony at the 2003 U.S. Open

"Sometimes I'll get recognized out somewhere, and then the next question they ask me is what I do."

> —Andre Agassi (1995)

"It's difficult [to play him] because Agassi is like Jesus wherever he goes."

> —Yevgeny Kafelnikov (1994)

ALL IN THE MIND

"Do not think that tennis is merely a physical exercise. It is a mental cocktail of very high 'kick.'"

—Bill Tilden

"When I am within a point or two of losing a game, I *do* feel very determined and remember that I must keep a strict command over myself."

—Charlotte "Lottie" Dod, who became the youngest Grand Slam champion in 1887 by winning the first of her five Wimbledon singles titles at fifteen years, ten months. From the 1997 book, *The Tennis Lover's Book of Wisdom*

"Pancho Segura [his new coach] wants me to think about situations. But I am not the type of player who responds well to a lot of thinking."

—Andre Agassi, after being upset by Thomas Enqvist in the U.S. Open first round (1993)

"He plays like a Zen master. It's very in the moment."

—Superstar Barbra Streisand, once romantically linked to Andre Agassi (1992)

"In action, Sampras lets go, and gives over to that inner momentum . . . in the Orient, not knowing is highest wisdom."

—Zen master Sister Elaine McInnes, in her 2003 book, *Zen Contemplation*

"Never relax for a second no matter what the score—the body will usually respond if you have willpower, pluck, and determination to spur yourself to fresh efforts."

—Tony Wilding, the 1910–13 Wimbledon and 1906 and '09 Australian champion from New Zealand, on the importance of concentration

"If I were asked to name one aspect of tennis that is the biggest weakness of players of all levels, I would probably say concentration. However good your shots, however fast your movement and reflexes, all is lost if the mind is not controlling every move."

—Ken Rosewall, eight-time Grand Slam singles winner. From the 1975 book, *Play Tennis with Rosewall: The Little Master and His Method*

"I used to step on the court and walk around and step on those land mines of words like 'expectation' and 'potential.' Those things used to destroy every ounce of desire I had."

—Andre Agassi, after beating Todd Martin to reach the U.S. Open final, on why he felt he was an underachiever (1994)

"My nerves were getting the best of me. It happens to everybody. Anybody who says they don't choke, they're lying."

—Pete Sampras, who squandered six match points before beating Gustavo Kuerten in the Miami final (2000)

"More than anything, winning the Grand Slam is a battle within yourself. It really gets down to how you handle the pressure, more than how you handle anybody else."

—Margaret Court, winner of the Grand Slam in 1970

"When calm alertness is maintained on the tennis court, you are ready to perform nearer the limit of your ability."

—Dr. W. Timothy Gallwey, author of the best-selling book, *The Inner Game of Tennis*

"A lot of Iron Curtain countries are ahead of us in this. You ask any Western coach about concentration, and they say it's thinking about doing something right. But concentration at its best is the absence of thought, allowing the subconscious mind to respond to the moment. Using the inner game effectively is not a series of gimmicks, it's an art."

—Dr. W. Timothy Gallwey, in *Tennis* magazine (1980)

"The neurotic more often 'is aware not of his fear but of the resulting inhibitions. When such a person plays tennis, for example, he may feel when he is close to victory that something holds him back and makes it impossible for him to win.' What holds him back is the fear that the person he beats will resent him for this and dislike him."

> —Alfie Kohn, quoting Karen Horney (author of *Neurotic Personality*). From his 1986 book, *No Contest: The Case Against Competition*

"In every close match ever played, you always fought two things—your opponent and the fear inside you, and the worse of the two was the fear."

> —Gordon Forbes, world-class player from South Africa. From his classic 1978 book, *A Handful of Summers*

"My father taught me one important lesson: to not be afraid to lose."

> —All-time great Chris Evert, on how she learned to play without the fear of failure

"Martina goes from arrogance to panic with nothing in between."

> —Astute tennis observer and couturier Ted Tinling, on the young Martina Navratilova's mental game

"Ivan Lendl is the only East European who ever believed he could be the No. 1 player in the world."

> —Wojtek Fibak, former Polish star and mentor of Lendl. From the 1983 book, *Ivan Lendl's Power Tennis*

"The most difficult thing is to believe in yourself. And now I'm believing. I know I'm going to lose matches, but now I have a different feeling. I feel very proud."

> —Albert Costa, who surprised everyone, including himself, by winning the 2002 French Open

"It's like love. When you look too hard, you don't find it. When you let it come naturally, it happens."

> —Marat Safin, expounding about confidence (2002)

"Essentially, *match temperament* boils down to having confidence in your strokes. . . . Erratic temperament stems from what are really erratic rather than brilliant strokes."

> —Paul Metzler. From his 1968 instruction book, *Advanced Tennis*

"Basically, the reason you choke is that you don't have the strokes."

> —Noted coach, researcher, and author Vic Braden

"The older you get, the more nervous you become [in close matches] because it means more to you."

> —Mary Joe Fernandez, finalist at the 1993 French and 1990 and '92 Australian Opens and now a TV tennis analyst (2003)

"I see one coming and visualize where I'm going to hit it, and the shot's perfect—and I feel beautiful all over."

> —Billie Jean King. From the 1999 book, *Smart Tennis: How to Play and Win the Mental Game*

"What really kills me is this sports psychology crap. The USTA has these monthly seminars and all they do is this sports science. You're fifteen, sixteen, and they've got you on the couch. At fifteen, what the hell do you want to know more about yourself for? . . . What all this sports psychology is about is appeasing a lot of egos, and it just kills me."

> —Brad Gilbert, former world No. 4 and then coach of Andre Agassi, in *Tennis* magazine (1995)

"Agassi's forehand is not the biggest weapon in tennis today; Mats Wilander's brain is."

> —Former top tenner Jay Berger (1988)

"You could set off dynamite in the next court and I wouldn't notice."

> —Maureen Connolly, nine-time Grand Slam champion during 1951–54. From the 1999 book, *Smart Tennis: How to Play and Win the Mental Game*

"It's really impossible for athletes to grow up. On the one hand, you're a child, still playing a game. But on the other hand, you're a superhuman hero that everyone dreams of being. No wonder we have such a hard time understanding who we are."

—Billie Jean King

"Boys of twenty, playing some game under the eyes of the entire world, under strain, would be phenomenal if they knew how to deal with the mental problems of ignoring or evaluating criticism. If some become swollen headed, as a result of extravagant praise, and others sullen or moody under extravagant blame, it is not to be wondered at."

—Australian prime minister Robert Gordon Menzies, in a 1955 essay titled "The Great Game of Tennis"

"In the future, if there is too much pressure, too much publicity, maybe I won't want to be No. 1."

—Swedish star Mats Wilander, who became No. 1 in 1988 (1983)

"It's too much pressure. I'm tired of all the talk about it. Everyone is obsessed with it. . . . If I was the type of person who had tennis, tennis, tennis all the time and I went to bed and ended up dreaming about tennis, I would go nuts."

—Marat Safin, freaking out at the thought of making a run at No. 1

"Don't ever show anything negative to your opponent."

—John Newcombe, winner of seven Grand Slam singles titles, on sage advice he learned from Australian Davis Cup captain Harry Hopman. From an ESPN "Sports Classics" interview with Dick Schapp

"The minute you feel yourself getting upset, you have to remind yourself that the only person you're hurting by getting angry is yourself. Anger only produces sloppier play and saps your energy. In the end, it's your opponent who will benefit."

—Dennis Ralston, the No. 1–ranked American player in 1964–66 and coach of four triumphant U.S. Davis Cup teams. From his 1977 instruction book, *Six Weeks to a Better Level of Tennis*

"Pressure—I love it. I don't know why. Why do you rise to an occasion? It spurs you on. I feel the adrenaline flowing."

—Billie Jean King. From the 1975 book, *The World of Tennis*

"People used to ask me, 'How did you become so mentally tough?' I'd tell them, 'Because you get mentally strong just doing the physical work before you even step on the court. You walk out there knowing you're in better shape than your opponent.'"

> —Martina Navratilova, in *Tennis* magazine (2004)

"You just lie on a couch, they take your money, and you walk out more bananas than when you walk in."

> —Head case Goran Ivanisevic, on why he would never see a sports psychologist (1995)

"The trouble with me is, every match I play against five opponents— umpire, crowd, ball boys, court, and myself. It's no wonder sometimes my mind goes to the beach."

> —Goran Ivanisevic, who finally put it all together to win Wimbledon in 2001

"If I didn't play tennis, I probably would have to see a psychiatrist."

> —Arthur Ashe. From www.tennisontheline.org

"If you can't control your mind and emotions, you can't be great at anything. Temperament and mental condition make the difference between a good player and a great one."

> —Jack Kramer. From his 1949 book, *Winning Tennis*

"The greatest lapses in concentration come when we allow our minds to project what is about to happen or dwell on what has already happened."

> —Dr. W. Timothy Gallwey, author of the best-selling book, *The Inner Game of Tennis*

"What chance do I stand against you at my age? Over five sets you'll murder me!"

> —What Pancho "Sneaky" Segura, an expert in psychological warfare, used to whisper to opponents before a match. From Mike Davies's 1962 autobiography, *Tennis Rebel*

"There is not time to think on the tennis court; the less you think, the better off you are."

> —Jack Kramer, apostle of efficient "percentage tennis"

"When badly overmatched, never descend to weak dejection or loss of interest; play as strongly as you can and keep your self-respect. You may earn your opponent's and the gallery's as well, but that is not as important."

    —Paul Metzler. From his 1968 instruction book, *Advanced Tennis*

"Me, I'm not a complete nutcase. I'm just different. Sometimes when I'm losing, I have to push myself, I have to break a racket or hit the ball out of the court. It helps me."

    —Tempestuous Russian Marat Safin (2002)

"The difference is almost all mental. The top players just hate to lose. I think that's the difference. A champion hates to lose even more than she loves to win."

    —Chris Evert

"The strongest part of my game is my head. The rhythm and the timing are much more important to me than power. I never had power. I needed something else. Instead I had to be smart. I had to think until my head broke."

    —Martina Hingis, the champion exponent of killing them softly. From the 1998 book, *The Best of the Best in Tennis*

"This game is 50 percent mental, 45 percent physical and 5 percent tennis."

    —Juan Carlos Ferrero, 2003 French Open champion (2003)

"We all choke. That's all right. We're not machines. What you have to learn is to accept the fact and not panic. It's the panic that loses you the matches, not the nerves."

    —Rod Laver. From the 1988 book, *Open Tennis: The First Twenty Years*

"Lawn Tennis may be only a game, but when it is seriously and properly played, it is a valuable mental training, and you may be quite certain that the same characteristics which enable a man to win at tennis will, if properly applied, help him to win in the more important game of life."

    —Ernest G. Meers, a standout American player, in 1904. From the 1947 instruction book, *Lawn Tennis Courtcraft*

CHILD'S PLAY

"Many a parent is prejudiced against her daughter having so much freedom, but my mother was lenient—and I consider most sensible—in that respect, and turned a deaf ear to anyone who advised her not to allow my sister and myself to travel about."

> —Charlotte "Chattie" Cooper, who won singles and mixed doubles gold medals for Great Britain in the 1900 Olympic Games

"She's as sexy as a sixteen-year-old can be."

> —Chris Evert, on Anna Kournikova, nicknamed "The Russian Lolita" (1997)

"I started when I was four, but I didn't play seriously until I was eight."

> —Kathy Rinaldi, fourteen-year-old French Open quarterfinalist (1981)

"When Tracy was eight, she would beat the best ladies at the local tennis club and then go over to the baby-sitting area and play in the sandbox."

> —Jeanne Austin, mother of whiz kid Tracy, who appeared on the cover of *World Tennis* at age four and won the U.S. Open at sixteen

"She has potential and should be developed wisely. Keep her tennis 'career' in perspective. Keep it fun! Be careful not to push her progress too quickly."

> —A 1985 tennis camp evaluation in the Capriati family scrapbook. It proved ironic because father/coach Stefano Capriati did not heed it, and the destructive pressure of "too much, too soon" caused Jennifer to drop out of both the pro tour and school and get into trouble for shoplifting and drug use.

"In parent groups I tell them that as parents they mustn't use guilt to manipulate the child. They'll quickly assure me, 'Oh, I would never do that.' And what shoots out of the parent's mouth a minute later but, 'After all I've done for you, you lost that match to a nobody.' Parents can develop savage, brutal mouths without realizing it."

—Sports psychologist Dr. Bruce Ogilvie. From the 1983 book, *Little Winners: Inside the World of the Child Sports Star*

"Pressure? Do you realize how many times I had my picture on the cover of *Sports Illustrated* at the age of twelve?"

—Teenage phenom Tracy Austin

"Sure there are children who are musical prodigies and young gymnasts, but none of them is under as much pressure or stand to gain as much as young girls playing tennis. . . . They are supposed to be professional athletes, 'killers' on the courts. At the same time, because of the show-business aspect of professional sports, they are supposed to be sweet and charming—almost a cliché of femininity—off the court. It is another level of pressure and confusion for these kids."

—Karen Stabiner, author of the book, *Courting Fame: The Perilous Road to Women's Tennis Stardom*, in the *Los Angeles Herald Examiner* (1986)

"I was always doing things younger, and it hasn't hurt me so far."

—A naïve Tracy Austin, after dethroning Chris Evert at the 1979 U.S. Open, where she became its youngest champion at sixteen years, nine months. Only five years later, she retired after a series of painful back and neck injuries.

"I promised myself years ago that I'd play the U.S. Open when I was thirteen. And in my mind I did because I was still thirteen in the qualifying [event]."

—Kathy Horvath, who clipped nine months off Tracy Austin's record to become the youngest player in the history of the U.S. Championships

"I don't think any agent should be able to talk to a youngster until he has either graduated from high school or reached graduation age. Nor to the parents. It's really the buying of these children's youth. It's unconscionable. All these agents are like drug pushers in the playgrounds."

—Hall of Fame journalist Bud Collins, railing against the exploitation of tennis prodigies in a *60 Minutes* program segment titled "Million Dollar Babies" (1994)

"I was brought up never to give up. I don't think I ever will."

—Andrea Jaeger, American whiz kid who reached the Wimbledon and French Open finals and climbed to No. 2, before chronic shoulder pain forced her to retire at age twenty

"God, I hope no one has to go through what I did. But from thirteen on, he really wasn't my father, just my coach."

—Andrea Jaeger, on her hard-driving father, Roland, in *Vanity Fair* magazine (1995)

"When it really goes wrong, it can be like *Lord of the Flies* with kids trapped on an island turning into savages."

—Ann Thomas, a sports psychologist who has worked with many Florida junior players, asserting that tennis academies may improve a girl's tennis game but they can exacerbate other problems. From *Ladies of the Court: Grace and Disgrace on the Women's Tennis Tour* (1993)

"I think it's great we have all these people like Kobe Bryant and Tiger Woods. But how many kids who are trying to be that and don't make it, at the end of the day feel like a failure? How do you know a child at age two wants to play tennis?"

—Andrea Jaeger, a whiz kid who played competitive tennis at ten, was No. 2 in the world at sixteen, and left the pro circuit at twenty after a chronic shoulder injury, agreeing with the American Academy of Pediatrics warning that youngsters should be discouraged from specializing in a single sport before adolescence to avoid physical and psychological damage (2000)

"I've always looked at it as if, if I just make it, I'll be rich and I won't need to do anything else. Now I don't really know; I have to wait and see if I will be rich and won't have to worry. If not? I'll marry a rich man. If I play tennis, I've *got* to meet some guy with money."

—American junior star Debbie Spence, who wound up with a career-high No. 31 ranking and less than $150,000 prize money in her five-year pro career. From the 1986 book, *Courting Fame: The Perilous Road to Women's Tennis Stardom*

"It's no use to keep asking me, because I don't know anything anyway."

> —Bjorn Borg, far better at tennis than at school at age thirteen, replying to a teacher who was pushing him to answer a question. From the 1975 book, *Carnival at Forest Hills: The Anatomy of a Tennis Tournament*

"I like it, but I miss my puppy back in Florida."

> —Fourteen-year-old Jennifer Capriati, asked if she liked Wimbledon (1990)

"Why should I envy my friends? It is they who envy me. They get to have a soda at the shopping mall. I get to see the world."

> —Jennifer Capriati (1991)

"Golly, I have a great life for seventeen, don't I? Everyone would choose my life, wouldn't they?"

> —Steffi Graf (1987)

"I never myself had the feeling that I've stolen her childhood. I mean, what is it that she should be doing, playing with puppies? Look at her: she's a happy girl."

> —Melanie Molitor, contemptuous of critics who claimed her own vicarious ambition cost her daughter, Martina Hingis, her childhood (1997)

"She might be No. 1 in two years, but will she last five years?"

> —A critical and concerned Martina Navratilova, on her namesake Martina Hingis, who turned pro at fourteen, became No. 1 at sixteen, and retired at twenty-two with serious foot injuries (1994)

"If she was my daughter, she would be back in school. You can get eaten alive out there."

> —Martina Navratilova, on whiz kid Martina Hingis (1994)

"I don't say she's too old to play, do I?"

> —Martina Hingis, rejecting Martina Navratilova's claim that she was too young to turn pro at fourteen (1994)

"In the future we will see younger players coming up becoming No. 1 in the world at an early age, but they will not last as long. They will retire when they're twenty-three or twenty-four. Martina Hingis will be the first one to do it, so she will be remembered for that. Maybe in ten years, nobody will be surprised when you have a Grand Slam champion at fifteen or fourteen."

> —Jana Novotna, with a near-perfect prediction (1997)

"When I had children, I knew that if I had boys I would want them to play tennis and to be as good as they could be at it. But if I had a girl, she would never be a world champion. I wouldn't want her to go through all that. I think all that pressure in the hot sun is too tough for a woman. I'm not passing judgment on any of the girls on the tour. I have a lot of respect for every one of them. I'm just talking from my heart."

> —Gloria Connors, who with her mother, taught the game to her all-time great son, Jimmy Connors (1981)

"The only thing that could stop Jennifer is getting knocked up by a ball boy. Something like that. But she's a sure thing."

> —Tennis historian Ted Tinling, on thirteen-year-old sensation Jennifer Capriati, after she reached the final in her pro debut (1990)

"I learned that it will be fun if it's all like this."

> —Jennifer Capriati, after reaching the final in her first pro tournament at age thirteen (1990)

"Kids don't burn out, parents do."

> —Mindless reassurance from Stefano Capriati, on the danger posed by burn-out to his daughter/prodigy Jennifer

"When the fruit is ripe, you eat it."

> —Stefano Capriati, justifying pushing his daughter Jennifer, whom he trained from the cradle to be a pro tennis player

"I didn't expect this to be as tough as it is. Maybe for someone else it would be easier, but not with the route that I've taken."

> —Former whiz kid Jennifer Capriati, floundering in the eighties in the rankings at age twenty-three (1999)

"You know, it's funny. I was such an early starter, early prodigy, whatever, but really I feel like a late bloomer."

> —Jennifer Capriati, who played the final of her first pro tournament at thirteen but required another eleven years to capture a major title, the Australian Open (2001)

"They said my mom tried to make me look like a little girl. But I *was* a little girl. I didn't mature quickly, physically or emotionally."

> —Tracy Austin, as an adult, recalling how she first appeared at Wimbledon at fourteen, weighing ninety-five pounds and dressed in pinafores

"You can't have little girls face the responsibilities and pressures and tensions of women. It's stupid. It's not going to work. Children act like children at thirteen. They're not supposed to serve out the third set at Wimbledon."

> —Mary Carillo, highly regarded TV analyst, 1977 French Open mixed doubles champion and mother of two children, in *Australian Tennis Magazine* (1996)

"For every one player who can point to someone like Arantxa Sanchez Vicario and say, 'Look at this success story,' there are a couple of hundred girls that we'll never hear about who never made it. They turned into head cases and burnouts."

> —Mary Carillo, in *Australian Tennis Magazine* (1996)

"I wonder if she knows what's going on yet. That's great. She's winning. Wait until she learns how to choke."

> —Veteran Billie Jean King on fourteen-year-old Tracy Austin, after Austin upset Sue Barker in the U.S. Open (1977)

"It was very, very hard. There's no question I gave up my childhood to become a tennis player. Personally, I think it was worth it. That doesn't mean there weren't times I hated it. The first year, every Sunday night when my parents dropped me off, I would go off by myself and cry. But I got through it."

> —Jim Courier, on his teenage years at the Bollettieri Tennis Academy, in the 1991 book, *Hard Courts*

"When I had Andre for six and one-half years, my main job was to keep him out of jail."

> —Nick Bollettieri, coach of Andre Agassi when he was a teenage phenom (2001)

"I don't know. I've never lost before."

> —Venus Williams, in her first pro tournament at age fourteen after going unbeaten as a junior, asked how her second-round loss to world No. 2 Arantxa Sanchez Vicario compared to previous defeats

"I've known I could be No. 1 since the age of six. I heard my parents telling me so many times that I would become the world's best one day and that I would write my name in every Grand Slam's records, that I ended up believing in it. At that time I even thought I would be able to beat John McEnroe."

> —Venus Williams, after becoming the tenth player to top the world rankings since they began in 1975 (2002)

OH, BEHAVE!

"You'll be sorry you hit me, you f—ing Communist asshole."

—John McEnroe, after being hit in the side by a ball struck by his Czech opponent, Tomas Smid (1983)

"You cannot be serious!"

—John McEnroe's most memorable outburst at Wimbledon (1981)

"My son is better behaved than you. I'll bring him to play you."

—Jimmy Connors, in a changeover blast at archrival John McEnroe, who was hectoring officials during their Wimbledon semifinal (1980)

"I don't know that I changed all that much. They just found somebody worse."

—Aging bad boy Jimmy Connors, referring to John McEnroe (1984)

"McEnroe is a good friend now, but he should have been suspended on several occasions. Spectators had a love-hate relationship with him. He's a great champion, but sometimes he went over the limit."

—Bjorn Borg, McEnroe's former archrival (1999)

"He's not so brash. But he's not docile. It's just that he's a New Yorker."

—Legendary Australian Davis Cup captain Harry Hopman, on the young John McEnroe

"I didn't want to risk the embarrassment, as an American, of seeing an American disgrace our country."

—Actor Charlton Heston, on why he refused to sit in the Royal Box at Wimbledon while John McEnroe was playing

"When you're twenty-six, who are you gonna listen to, Jagger and Nicholson or some old farts in the United States Tennis Association?"

> —John McEnroe, recalling in *Sports Illustrated*, his being rebuked by the USTA in 1985 for loutish Davis Cup behavior in Sweden only to have Mick Jagger and Jack Nicholson advise him never to change (1996)

"He's probably the most controversial player in modern tennis. He took whining to the next level. I think we ought to hold off that induction until John apologizes."

> —Dr. Eric Heiden, Olympic speed skating champion, introducing John McEnroe at his induction into the International Tennis Hall of Fame (1999)

"Those whom God wishes to destroy, he first makes mad."

> —The Euripides maxim that Dr. Robert Walter Johnson, coach and mentor of young Arthur Ashe, Althea Gibson, and many promising African Americans used often to promote calm and dignified behavior on the court

"At their best [or worst], they could do more to hurt you without even hitting a tennis ball than most players could do with a racket. They're like Bart Simpson's evil twins."

> —Brad Gilbert, on the gamesmanship of Jimmy Connors and John McEnroe, in his 1993 book, *Winning Ugly*

"People want to know why I can't always control myself—or why Connors and McEnroe can't. The problem is that we all have something of a split personality, and I always fear that if I give in to one side—that nice, polite me—then I'll stop caring about victory, and my sweet indifference will defeat me."

> —Billie Jean King. From her 1982 autobiography, *Billie Jean*

"I like the way he loses his temper. It shows how desperately he wants to win all the time."

> —Cricket superstar Sachin Tendulkar, of India, with a positive spin on John McEnroe (2003)

"Kiss me before you do that to me. . . . You son of a bitch. . . . Get out of the chair. . . . You're a bum. . . . Get your ass out of the chair. . . . Don't give me that crap. . . . You're an abortion."

> —The ugly invective thirty-nine-year-old Jimmy Connors spewed at chair umpire David Littlefield for overruling a line call during his dramatic comeback victory over Aaron Krickstein at the 1991 U.S. Open. He was never warned or penalized for the outburst.

"In football, they're breaking the rules on every play, and nobody gets nearly so worked up about that as they do when some poor linesman blows one call in the third set."

—Jack Kramer, a gentleman champion in the 1940s and early '50s.

"I was shocked by what I saw. Martina acted like the teenager she is out there. She plays like a champion but has to learn to behave like one."

—Chris Evert, TV tennis analyst, on Martina Hingis's spoiled-brat antics in her French Open final loss to Steffi Graf (1999)

"One or two years ago, I didn't know who I was on court and I used to swear a lot. But now I've learned how to cope and can therefore win ten matches in a row. I want to be remembered as a good player rather than an idiot on court."

—Roger Federer (2003)

"Tennis doesn't need brashness or bad manners. The sport's bigger than any individual."

—Roy Emerson, all-time men's leader in total Grand Slam titles with twenty-eight

"I want to let my racket do the talking. I thought the way they [John McEnroe and Jimmy Connors] acted on the court was embarrassing. I didn't want a reputation like that. I have always wanted to present myself as a class act, not lose my temper, not rub it in to anyone if I beat them. Just go out there and win."

—Pete Sampras, after doing a pizza commercial with McEnroe "to show the lighter side of me," nonetheless distanced himself from McEnroe (1995)

"I've never heard them ever talk crap about today's players. And that's what I aspire to be like. To me, that's untouchable. Guys who know they're great without having to say they're great."

—Pete Sampras, on moral exemplars and tennis legends Ken Rosewall and Rod Laver

"Imagine how it feels to be twenty years of age, sitting in front of more than one hundred media people from around the world, and they are asking you about your father's alleged infidelities."

—John Newcombe, blasting the way insensitive reporters, especially from "the English gutter press," handled Steffi Graf's father's off-court indiscretions, in *RACQUET* magazine (1994)

"First and foremost in a tennis match, the players must abide by the decision of the linesmen and the umpire. It makes an unpleasant feeling if, at any time, their calls are ignored or questioned."

—Helen Wills Moody, from her 1929 book, *Tennis*

"All close balls are good. If you remember that, you'll never cheat an opponent. In tournament tennis, you don't question a call by the umpire or a linesman. You continue to play."

—Perry T. Jones, the czar of southern California tennis during the 1930s and '40s

"In the old days, say the '50s and '60s, cheating was rare enough to be a rather noteworthy event, a glaring and conspicuous violation of social decorum, a scandal more or less. Not so today. Cheating has become no more than a trifling peccadillo. In some circles— especially among Yuppies and the X-Generation crowd—cheating has become almost routine."

—Jake Barnes. From his 2000 book, *Social Tennis: The Decline and Fall of Manners and Civility*

"If you're not sure if a ball is in or out, give your opponent a reasonable benefit of the doubt."

—Rod Laver. From the 1997 book, *The Tennis Lover's Book of Wisdom*

"They [today's male stars] are getting too big for their britches. All they do is take out of the game and put nothing back in. It's a shame."

—1938 Grand Slammer Don Budge (1979)

"I guess you could basically say I got too big for my britches. . . . The way I handled things—throwing rackets and losing my temper—was a disgrace to myself."

—Andre Agassi (1989)

"It used to give me cardiac arrest sitting there and watching him, because I didn't know if he'd walk out and tank or if he'd walk out and just be *unbelievable*. At the time I was traveling [with him, from 1990 through 1992], it was either one or the other. There was no middle ground."

—Wendi Stewart, Andre Agassi's former girlfriend. From the 1997 book, *Agassi and Ecstasy: The Turbulent Life of Andre Agassi*

"How old do you have to be before people forgive you for your past?"

—Andre Agassi, a changed man at thirty-one (2001)

"There are a lot of guys in the press who have huge egos that get off putting players down, and that puts me off. I hate when people ask me caustic questions. . . . There are circumstances where I have to be a jerk because people are being jerks."

—Jim Courier, four-time Grand Slam titlist, in *Tennis* magazine (1993)

"It's a question I ask myself a lot. Is it me or is it the sport? If I was playing golf and won twelve majors and acted the way I act, and with the sense of history I have, I think I'd be a Jack Nicklaus or an Arnold Palmer. It just tells you that tennis, unfortunately, is struggling and people want to find something to talk about or write about, and the easiest thing to do is say I'm boring. That was a big thing early on in my career, and it's kind of died down a little, but that will always baffle me."

—Pete Sampras (1999)

"If Richard Williams had danced in front of me after I had lost to one of his daughters, I probably would have hit him. What he did was absolutely horrible and has no place in sports."

—Martina Navratilova, on Richard Williams's obnoxious on-court antics following Venus's victory in the 2000 Wimbledon final (2001)

"Manners are manners. Jimmy Connors and Ilie Nastase have no respect. I don't want my kid seeing Nastase play. The demeanor you show on the court is important to tennis. . . . Maybe we [yesterday's stars] were too stereotyped. But we were told to behave or they'd take our racket away."

—Rod Laver (1980)

"I am a little crazy, but I try to be a good guy."

—Ilie Nastase

"I feel like dog trainer who teach dog manners and graces and just when you think dog knows how should act with nice qualities, dog make big puddle and all is wasted."

—Ion Tiriac, on being Ilie Nastase's coach (1972)

"With children, temper tantrums are normal. When older people act up, it's usually because they're getting something out of it. Nastase likes attention and because tennis has been considered a gentleman's game, he keeps his opponents so shook up they can't concentrate."

—Noted psychologist, columnist, and radio personality Dr. Joyce Brothers, psychoanalyzing Ilie Nastase, in *Tennis* magazine (1976)

"The only reason he gets away with it is because the officials and tennis directors don't have the strength or will to stop him."

—Sandy Mayer, on bad boy Ilie Nastase

"Petulance and outright vulgarity have become a lamentable part of tennis, at an incalculable cost to the well-being of the game."

—Jack Kramer, in *World Tennis* magazine (1978)

"The English have always liked good losers rather than winners. . . . One can imagine the impact Perry had on Britain of the '30s, for he was the first Englishman to see tennis as a battle rather than a game."

—Tennis historian Ted Tinling

"I never misbehaved because I was afraid if I did anything like that my father could come up and kick my ass."

—Arthur Ashe. From his 1993 book, *Days of Grace*

"He's always been that way, and no one ever told him to stop. So he didn't. He's probably scared to, equating the competitive urge with anger. Look, he's not that hard to understand. He's just like any other twenty-three-year-old millionaire college dropout."

—Arthur Ashe, psychoanalyzing John McEnroe (1982)

"There is peer pressure in the [pro golf] locker room that is missing in tennis. Arnold Palmer will tell another player, 'Hey, we don't do that here.' Beginning with my generation, the peer pressure stopped. Maybe it was because we felt tennis had been too much of a gentleman's game. But none of us had the guts or will to go up to Connors and Nastase and say, 'Hey, you don't do that here.'"

—Arthur Ashe, in the *New York Times* (1983)

"If you keep that up, I'll just have to knock you out."

> —Australian Bob "Nails" Carmichael, disgusted with John McEnroe's antics during a doubles match. Carmichael and Kim Warwick won the match against McEnroe and Peter Fleming (1978)

"He spent the entire match complaining and whining about line calls and his own play. I figured that was my turf! I also figured that at that point I had a lot more basis for my attitude than he had for his. I told him he should win something before he started complaining."

> —John McEnroe, on his first match against Boris Becker, then seventeen, in Milan. From McEnroe's 2002 autobiography, *You Cannot Be Serious*

"If you start behaving like a beast during the match, I will turn into a bigger beast and I will destroy you."

> —Boris Becker's warning (threat?) to miscreant John McEnroe—although it came at least a decade too late (1990)

"I am not a monster. I'm not all bad. Maybe 10 percent. I think I'm 90 percent good."

> —John McEnroe (1984)

"If guys do it, it's macho, and if women do it, it's not very nice."

> —Wendy Turnbull, former world No. 3, on the double standard for bad on-court behavior

"All one hears over here is what great sportsmen the British are. I've got news for you; the English are no better sports than the spectators in other countries, and, in my opinion, worse than some. And I've seen them all. The British talk about sportsmanship until they believe it. But they don't practice what they preach."

> —Gardnar Mulloy, American star of the 1940s and '50s. From his 1959 autobiography, *Advantage Striker*

"The first law of tennis is that every player must be a good sportsman and inherently a gentleman."

> —Bill Tilden

"I liked it better when I could just pull them off their chairs and stick a racket down their throats. Players don't have one right anymore."

—Unreformed and unrepentant Jimmy Connors, thirty-nine, at the Volvo/Los Angeles tournament (1992)

"There is a temptation to win by any means, and when that happens, it is the finish of sport."

—Jean Borotra. From the 1997 book, *The Tennis Lover's Book of Wisdom*

"Lawn Tennis has always been an exemplar of the highest type of sportsmanship. The spirit of fair play permeates the game and is one of its most cherished traditions. It is not confined to the players and the court. It manifests itself on every side in the bearing and acts of all connected with the sport."

—Don Budge. From his 1939 book, *Budge on Tennis*

"Chris Evert never threw a tantrum, groused at opponents, or blamed officials. A bad call produced a steely stare at most. Chris behaved like an adult, taking full responsibility for her performance and deportment."

—Camille Paglia. From her 1994 book, *Vamps and Tramps*

"Pete [Sampras] is No. 1 in the world and such a great role model for kids. He's a gentleman on the court. It's funny, because when McEnroe and Connors were acting up, everyone said, 'Where are the gentlemen, like the Australians Rod Laver and Ken Rosewall?' Along comes Pete, who is exactly that way, and now everyone is saying, 'Where are the showmen?' Everybody wants what they don't have."

—Tracy Austin, 1979 and '81 U.S. Open champion and later a TV analyst (1997)

"The biggest compliment I could ever receive. It means more now that I'm a father, because you want so much for your child. For parents to come up to me all the time and say, 'You've been a good representative for my kids,' and to feel like you've made a difference with people. I think that's worth the few extra *Sports Illustrated* covers I might've gotten had I acted a different way."

—Pete Sampras, in *USA Today* (2003)

"Pete [Sampras] is No. 1 in the world and such a great role model for kids."
—Tracy Austin (*Fred Mullane/Camerawork USA, Inc.*)

"I used to carry on like an idiot. [Now] I think it's funny when somebody freaks out."

> —Wimbledon champion Roger Federer, who took anger management classes as a teenager (2003)

"I've never met a great champion who couldn't be an absolute bitch."

> —Ted Tinling

OPEN TENNIS

"The nightmare is over. I have escaped from bondage and slavery. No one can order me about any longer to play tournaments for the benefit of club owners. Now I will be able to make some money, have some fun, and see the world."

> —Suzanne Lenglen, tennis's first female superstar, telling the Associated Press why she decided to give up amateur status and accept a $50,000 guarantee from American promoter C. C. "Cash and Carry" Pyle to become the first touring pro (1926)

"Under these absurd and antiquated amateur rulings, only a wealthy person can compete, and the fact of the matter is that only wealthy people *do* compete. Is that fair? Does it advance the sport? Does it make tennis more popular—or does it tend to suppress and hinder an enormous amount of tennis talent lying dormant in the bodies of young men and women whose names are not in the social register?"

> —Suzanne Lenglen, in an article that appeared in her pro tour's program. From the 1988 book, *We Have Come a Long Way*

"Why, my dear fellow, I can't afford to."

> —Superstar amateur Bill Tilden, asked in the mid-1920s why he didn't turn professional, in a 1951 *SPORT* magazine article.

"It was a standing joke that the foreign amateurs couldn't afford to turn pro because they'd have to take a cut in pay."

> —Billie Jean King

"At my first pro tournament [in 1960], they showed us into a room for dressing without furniture, carpet—nothing. I was with Tony Trabert. He pulled a six-inch nail out of his bag and nailed it to the wall. Then he said, 'Rookie, you're a professional now; you've got to bring your dressing room with you.'"

—Mike Davies, on what it was like in the "good" old days (1980)

"If tennis is to realize its full potential, it must find a solution to the professional/amateur problem which has plagued it for so many years. Only through such a solution can there be free competition among not just a few of the great players of the world—but among all of them. The sporting public wants to see the best. It doesn't give a hoot whether that best is amateur or professional."

—Bill Tilden. From his 1948 memoir, *My Story*

"When I was amateur tennis champion of the United States in 1946 and 1947, I wasn't an amateur."

—Jack Kramer's frank admission in *This Week* (1955)

"We all deserve Oscars for impersonating amateurs."

—Arthur Ashe

"Amateur tennis has become a living lie."

—Herman David's memorable declaration at the All England Club's annual meeting in December 1967. David, the AEC's chairman and a driving force for Open Tennis, proposed that Wimbledon be open to both amateur and professional players the following year. Britain's Lawn Tennis Association endorsed the club's stand and approved an "open" Wimbledon in 1968.

"We don't know what we're getting into. Nobody's prepared for Open tennis, or even knows what it means. But I believe the time is now, even if I get tarred and feathered for it."

—Robert Kelleher, intrepid president of the USLTA, after its sections voted overwhelmingly (15–1) in favor of Open Tennis, in the *Boston Globe* (1968)

"We knew Open Tennis was going to be a success, but we didn't know it was going to be a bonanza."

—Derek Hardwick, of the Lawn Tennis Association, after Ken Rosewall beat Rod Laver in the final of the world's first "open" tournament, the British Hardcourt Championships, in Bournemouth (1968)

"We gave up the fun for the money."

—Arthur Ashe, on the arrival of Open Tennis

"Lamar Hunt, in my opinion, has done more for pro tennis and pro tennis players than anybody else who has ever come into the game."

—Bobby Riggs, a 1930s and '40s champion and later a pro promoter himself, on the wealthy Texas entrepreneur whose World Championship Tennis (WCT) circuit transformed and professionalized big-time tennis from 1967 to 1990. From Riggs's 1973 autobiography, *Court Hustler*

"If you want to know what's happened in tennis in the last twenty years, well, I signed my first professional contract for $75,000, and to earn that I had to play about 360 days in the year. The other day Jimmy Connors played one exhibition match and earned $75,000 in two and a half hours."

—Roy Emerson, all-time men's recordholder with twenty-eight career Grand Slam titles (1984)

"I have a paper route."

—How colorful Whitney Reed, top-ranked American "amateur" in 1961, once sarcastically responded when asked how he managed to support himself while devoting much of his time to tennis

"I am an amateur by profession."

—The stock answer of Gordon Forbes, a fun-loving South African player, when asked what he did for a living

"Amateur tennis will be unable to compete with the increasing attractions of the true professionals until it takes a long, hard look at itself. As for me, I was becoming tired and bored with the hypocrisy and evasion I had to practice almost daily. It is scarcely surprising that I was ready to make an honest living for a change."

—Mike Davies, a driving force behind the fledgling International Professional Tennis Players' Association in 1965 and later executive director of the World Championship Tennis pro tour, angry at the "shamateurism" that infected world-class tennis. From his 1962 book, *Tennis Rebel*

"Television is an incredible vehicle. Nothing in the history of communications can compare with it. It is quite possible for a player to play one match on national television before more people than he would ever play live to in his whole career."

> —Mike Davies, executive director of the World Championship Tennis tour, after the spectacularly successful 1972 WCT Finals showdown between Ken Rosewall and Rod Laver that helped turn Americans on to tennis and convince TV moguls that the once-elitist sport was perfect for the viewing masses

"The first two times I won Wimbledon, I got a forty-five-pound gift voucher. It was ridiculous. The same officials who made the rules broke the rules and paid players under the table."

> —Billie Jean King, winner of a record twenty Wimbledon titles (1999)

"I was a tennis slave. . . . The contract makes the player the property of the [national tennis] association. If I go through a rugged tournament such as Wimbledon and say afterwards I am tired and would like a rest, the association says, no, you have commitments to play here and there."

> —Lew Hoad, on his bitter amateur experience, in a magazine article after he turned pro (1957)

"The thing I remember most is the absolute authority of Bill Clothier, the USLTA representative for the international circuit. He could tell you when to go to the bathroom if he wanted. He'd come around the second week of Wimbledon, hand you your fifty pounds, and say, 'See you at Merion [grass court tournament] in three weeks.' You showed up at Merion in three weeks."

> —Arthur Ashe, on the not-so-good old amateur days. In *World Tennis* magazine (1978)

"I can make more money as an amateur. It is a good life, easy life, and I get as much as $400 a week."

> —Italy's Nicola Pietrangeli, a world top-tenner in the late 1950s and '60s, explaining why he spurned offers to turn professional. From the 1971 book, *Tennis: Its History, People and Events*

"The ideal that amateur tennis should be preserved as the focus of the game was in dispute with the facts of the modern world. It was no more rational to ask a young man of twenty-three or twenty-five to use his special talents playing tennis for free as it is to ask him to play baseball for free or to sell insurance or to drive a bus for the sheer pleasure of it."

> —Don Budge. From his 1969 book, *Don Budge: A Tennis Memoir*

"I feel clean for the first time. I don't have to take dirty money anymore."

> —U.S. Davis Cup player Barry MacKay, who turned pro in 1961 and no longer had to take under-the-table payments that characterized "shamateurism"

"The problem wasn't which tournament to play next. The problem was how to get from your match in New York to your match in Los Angeles with three dollars in your pocket."

> —Billie Jean King, on the predicament facing women players in the early days of Open Tennis. From the 1986 book, *Courting Fame: The Perilous Road to Women's Tennis Stardom*

"After talking to the players in the last twenty-four hours, I've decided that this is more politics than the politics I've been in."

> —Hamilton Jordan, former White House chief of staff under President Jimmy Carter, after becoming executive director of the Association of Tennis Professionals, the players' union (1987)

"The craziest thing about 'shamateurism' is that it was no secret, and yet it was tolerated. Everybody knew the kids were taking money under the table, and everybody agreed that the system hurt the game."

> —Jack Kramer, former champion and pioneer pro promoter. From his 1979 memoir, *The Game: My Forty Years in Tennis*

"We're [International Management Group] by far the most powerful influence on sport in the world. We could turn any individual sport—golf, tennis, skiing—on its ear tomorrow."

> —Mark McCormack, head of IMG and acknowledged as the founder of athlete management and sports promotion (1975)

"Professionalism in tennis . . . only resulted in making billionaires out of rude children, producing an onslaught of moody defectors, and a lot of guys with hair that looks as if bats slept in it. . . . Meanwhile, my head swims with the thought that I have watched tennis progress from Don Budge and Alice Marble to Farrah Fawcett becoming John McEnroe's mother-in-law."

    —Dan Jenkins, in *Playboy* magazine (1985)

"Great and godlike as all these players are, the sport will have to be destroyed—and then completely rebuilt again—before it will ever be sane. Ever since the game's been professional, there's been nothing but chaos. Now, they all smack their lips and count their money. It won't last, though. It can't."

    —Ted Tinling, tennis historian (1990)

"I won three Wimbledons in the 1960s and didn't make any money. I've played only three matches this year and have won over $300,000."

    —Billie Jean King, Hall of Famer and women's pro tennis pioneer

"He coulda been the Marlon Brando of tennis, but the best years of his tennis were spent in exile as a barnstorming pro, while pasty-faced amateurs with half his talent won the Grand Slams."

    —Tribute to Pancho Gonzalez in *Sports Illustrated*, "20 Favorite Athletes of the 20th Century" (1999)

"I hope the amateur officials from that era who were guilty and who are still alive feel terrible about what they continued for so long, because they have been proven wrong and they deserve rebuke. There is no reason why sports and money can't go well together, and Open Tennis has proved the point I started making forty years ago."

    —Jack Kramer, amateur and pro champion and pioneer pro promoter (1979)

"Going Open lent respectability to the sport. Now when asked what a person did for a living he or she could say, 'I'm a professional tennis player.' Suddenly, it was as valid as being a lawyer or doctor."

    —Super-agent Donald Dell, in *World Tennis* magazine (1981)

THE FEMININE MYSTIQUE

"Concerning the limits and limitations of the women's game—why should we believe that there are any?"

> —Helen Wills Moody, the first American to dominate women's tennis

"Lawn tennis is a game not alone of skill but of endurance as well, and I fail to see why such a radical change should be made to satisfy a few players who do not take the time or do not have the inclination to get themselves in proper condition for playing."

> —Elizabeth Moore, who lost the first five-set women's final at the U.S. Nationals in 1892 and played the last five-set final there in 1901, protesting, with other leading female players, the male-dominated United States Lawn Tennis Association's decision to shorten the finals of all women's matches to best-of-three sets (1901)

"Is the essential feature of a woman her weakness, just as the essential feature of a man is his strength, not merely physical but mental and moral strength? I do not think so. Woman is a second edition of man, if you will; therefore, like most second editions, an improvement on the first."

> —Dorothea Lambert Chambers, the indomitable Englishwoman who won seven Wimbledon titles from 1903 to 1914, including two after the birth of her first child and two more after the birth of her second. From Virginia Wade's 1984 book, *Ladies of the Court*

"To slide, lunge, dive, does not conform to good style in tennis, but there is the dignity of sincerity in the scramble."

> —Helen Wills Moody, 1920s and '30s superstar who rarely scrambled for balls

"I just throw dignity to the wind and think of nothing but the game."

> —Suzanne Lenglen, the incomparable 1920s champion, on her all-out
> style of play

"Monsieur Tilden and I played, but whether he won six games, or
I did, I really don't know."

> —Suzanne Lenglen, first female superstar of tennis, talking to the press
> after they watched Bill Tilden overwhelm her 6–0 in an impromptu match
> in France in the game's first "Battle of the Sexes" (1921)

"I find that the girls generally do not hit the ball as hard as they
should. I believe in always hitting the ball with all my might, but
there seems to be a disposition to 'just get the ball over' in many
girls whom I have played. I do not call that tennis."

> —Molla Bjurstedt Mallory, powerful eight-time U.S. champion from 1915
> to 1926 (1920)

"All women tennis players should go on their knees in thankfulness
to Suzanne for delivering them from the tyranny of corsets."

> —American doubles star Elizabeth Ryan, who captured nineteen
> Wimbledon doubles and mixed doubles titles—including six with Suzanne
> Lenglen—between 1914 and 1934. From the 1979 book, *Famous Women
> Tennis Players*

"My mother was always saying, 'Be a lady.' What does that mean?
I loved to get out there and run around, and if you really love
something that way, nothing's gonna stop you."

> —Billie Jean King. From the 1974 book, *A Long Way, Baby—Behind the
> Scenes in Women's Pro Tennis*

"It doesn't do girls any good to be stuck around together all the
time. They become de-sexed, a terrible thing. It's easy to get caught
up, not caring how you look, and lose the good points of one's sex."

> —British star Virginia Wade, on femininity on the women's tour (1972)

"People ask me, 'Why do you have to look good on the court? Why
not just play?' But to me, whenever I'm on the court, it's like theatre and I have to express myself. Why should I have to look ugly
just because I'm an athlete?"

> —Anna Kournikova, then sixteen, in *Sports Illustrated*

"That's the one thing women's tennis has, is femininity. If women looked like men or played like men, it would be boring. I know some women who lift weights—they say Margaret Court did. But even if it would make me stronger, I'd never do it. It's *important* to look feminine for your self-confidence. I want to be known as a woman, not just as a tennis player."

—Chris Evert. From the 1974 book, *A Long Way, Baby—Behind the Scenes in Women's Pro Tennis*

"No point is worth getting your dress dirty over."

—Chris Evert, early in her career—a comment she later regretted

"A big deal was made of my femininity when I was younger, and I carried this image as the most feminine of the women players to the hilt. I took advantage of it. I made sure everything was perfect, from my earrings to the color of the pom-poms on my socks."

—Chris Evert. From Peter Bodo's 1979 book, *Inside Tennis: A Season on the Pro Tour*

"I'm often asked what I think I'll be remembered for. I hope it's that I helped the notion that it's okay for a woman to be athletic, to be tough, to be competitive. It's always been okay for men to be those things, but it's not until the last twenty years or so that it's been okay for a woman to be those things."

—Chris Evert, at her induction into the International Tennis Hall of Fame (1995)

"If anyone had told me that I played like a man, that would have been the highest compliment I could have received."

—Former champion and TV analyst Chris Evert, on comments that Serena Williams, Amelie Mauresmo, and other women play like men (2002)

"Richards is still physically a man, and that gives her a tremendous and unfair advantage. [She] has to be stopped."

—Doubles star Rosie Casals, on transsexual Dr. Renee Richards, formerly Richard Raskind until he underwent sexual reassignment, at age forty-one, in 1975. Although a small group of pro players objected to, and resisted, playing against Richards, a 1977 New York State Supreme Court ruling permitted her to compete as a woman (1976)

"I had no idea tennis girls could look so pretty."

> —Queen Elizabeth II of England, after witnessing her first Wimbledon (1977)

"But no matter what the type of outfit worn in tennis, it is always of one color—white. . . . To play in any other color is a great mistake in the eyes of one who knows tennis. I know that I am greatly disturbed when I see a colored dress or blouse on the court. In tennis it is not done."

> —Helen Wills Moody. From her 1929 book, *Tennis*

"Confidence can mean the difference between winning and losing. . . . If a woman feels she looks better than her opponent, that is an edge."

> —Renowned couturier Ted Tinling, on why dress is such an important part of the game. In *Tennis* magazine (1980)

"I prefer to be appreciated for my beauty and other qualities rather than only being seen as a tennis champion."

> —Gabriela Sabatini, the divine Argentine (1990)

"I would never go on court without makeup. Now they make fun of a girl if she does that."

> —Lea Pericoli, standout Italian player in the 1960s and now a correspondent (1993)

"There's so much emphasis on appearance. We all look in the mirror and think we're too heavy. When I first started talking about being an anorexic-bulimic, I actually had younger girls coming up to me and saying, 'Gee, what a great way to lose weight.' I looked at them and said, 'Are you crazy? Do you know how dangerous this is?'"

> —Carling Bassett-Seguso. From the 1992 book, *Tough Draw*

"The sweating female is no longer considered a social deviant."

> —Feminist author and publisher Gloria Steinem (1999)

"I love women. I think every man should have two of them."

> —Bobby Riggs

"A woman's place is in the bedroom and in the kitchen, in that order."

> —Male chauvinist and tennis hustler Bobby Riggs, before losing to Billie Jean King in their "Battle of the Sexes" at the Houston Astrodome (1973)

"People come up to me every single day of my life since that match. I have people say, 'I saw that match. You changed my life. I started to believe in myself. I went to my boss and asked for a raise. I started getting better grades in school. I started thinking of myself very differently.'"

—Tennis legend Billie Jean King, on how her victory in the celebrated 1973 "Battle of the Sexes" changed attitudes

"Of course, the crowds always cheer for Temesvari because of her looks. She spends more time putting makeup on than the rest of the girls combined. Her wraparound skirts barely cover her tennis pants, which barely cover what should be covered."

—Pam Shriver, on Hungarian beauty Andrea Temesvari. From her 1986 book, *Passing Shots: Pam Shriver on Tour*

"I wonder who we shall see today, Jane or Mary?"

—Because it was not unusual for one of French superstar Suzanne Lenglen's breasts to pop out during matches, wealthy winter habitués of the Riviera who watched her every day named her breasts Jane and Mary, and inquired about them at breakfast. In a 1984 *Sports Illustrated* article

"It is appalling the way so much of women's tennis is treated like soft porn. The media should concentrate more on women tennis players' abilities rather than their underwear and figures."

—British sports minister Tony Banks, condemning as "sexist" the British tabloid press, which focused heavily on the bodies and clothing of sixteen-year-olds Martina Hingis and Anna Kournikova and also ran unflattering photos of Monica Seles, with close-ups of her thighs (1997)

"I think it's really sad that they have to sell her like that. Sexuality sells, but she's going to be a good player without that."

—Meilen Tu, after beating sixteen-year-old Ashley Harkleroad, who wore an attention-grabbing, snug, low-cut outfit in their U.S. Open match (2001)

"It's all blonde. It's stupid. I think it's a Marilyn Monroe complex of males forty and up."

—Rising African-American player Alexandra Stevenson, resenting the heavy media and endorsement attention given to Ashley Harkleroad, an Anna Kournikova look-alike (2002)

"All the women play harder against her to make her realize that, on court, being the prettiest is useless. If she gets results as impressive as her beauty, she will be the most adored player in history. But if she fails, the system will crush her."

> —Frenchwoman Nathalie Tauziat, 1998 Wimbledon finalist, on Anna Kournikova. From her controversial book, *The Underside of Women's Tennis*

"If someone is outplaying me and her outfit isn't nice, I refuse to lose to her."

> —Tennis star and budding designer Serena Williams, in *W* magazine (2001)

"JoAnne Russell has a unique explanation for why there is no drug problem in women's tennis. 'Women players are too tight with their money to get high at their own expense.'"

> —Pam Shriver. From her 1986 book, *Passing Shots: Pam Shriver on Tour*

"I'm sure steroids haven't been used. We women are too vain, petrified of what it might do to our bodies. Girls today are just big-boned. I'm no puff cake, but compared to them I am. They'd terrify me in a dark alley."

> —Tennis legend Martina Navratilova (2002)

"Venus has escaped a lot of that stuff because she's not loose out there. I think a lot of things that go on are very demeaning for the woman. When it comes to that, I'm a rampant feminist. Every time a photographer takes a picture, it's always the behind. Or the bust. I hate seeing that. I don't want my girls to be part of that."

> —Oracene Price, mother/coach of Venus and Serena and a former history teacher, telling the *Daily Telegraph* (UK) about today's sex-obsessed world (1997)

"Every Arab woman who does something big stays in the history of the Arab world. Everyone is desperate to see our situation evolve. If I do well, it opens the door for Arab women everywhere."

> —Selima Sfar, a twenty-four-year-old Tunisian who is the first Arab woman to make it on the pro tennis circuit (2002)

"If a male athlete does that, it's not even a headline."

> —Martina Navratilova, on the media frenzy over Jennifer Capriati's brushes with the law for possession of marijuana and shoplifting (2001)

"When I helped run the Pacific Southwest, which always had a top female field, I watched carefully and saw the truth: namely, that people get up and go get a hot dog or go to the bathroom when the women come on."

—Jack Kramer. From his 1979 book, *The Game: My 40 Years in Tennis*

"I couldn't have caused more of a stir if I had walked out there naked."

—"Gorgeous Gussie" Moran, on her sexy lace panties, which scandalized Wimbledon in 1949

"You have put sin and vulgarity into tennis."

—A member of the Wimbledon committee, attacking Ted Tinling for creating Gussie Moran's titillating outfit. From Tinling's 1983 memoir, *Love and Faults: Personalities Who Have Changed the History of Tennis in My Lifetime*

"They are unnecessarily attracting the eye to the sexual area."

—The All-England Club committee's ruling on Gussie Moran's lace panties, which resulted in a thirty-year Wimbledon ban for their creator, Ted Tinling

"It used to bother me a lot that they didn't write up the tennis. All they wrote about was Gussie's panties."

—All-time great Louise Brough, on "Gorgeous Gussie" Moran's famous sexy lace panties that caused a furor at straight-laced Wimbledon in 1949

"Ten years from now it won't be enough that we, as ladies, only play tennis. The public wants to see more. We are the possession of the public. They make us stars and let us earn money. In about ten years every woman will play topless."

—Russian sex symbol Anna Kournikova (1998)

"I never felt like an athlete. I was just someone who played tennis matches. I still thought of women athletes as freaks, and I used to hate myself, thinking I must not be a whole woman."

—Chris Evert, early in her career, doubting whether beauty and athleticism could co-exist

"Everyone always looked upon me as the bad guy—as the woman with big muscles. That hurt."

>—Martina Navratilova, saying she just wanted to be loved by the public (1991)

"My femininity is always something I've tried to preserve in this dog-eat-dog world."

>—Margaret Court, the tall and powerful Australian great, who took spells from the circuit for marriage and motherhood

"Tennis fashion is a mirror of society. What women could and could not do was always dictated by their dress. Now you can hardly tell the girls from the men, which saddens me."

>—Famed designer Ted Tinling, who dressed the biggest names in women's tennis for fifty years (1984)

"I don't know why they have the women dolled up in these skintight outfits. You don't see them primping the men players. Why is it so necessary for women athletes to prove themselves as women?"

>—Martina Navratilova, on the marketing of women's tennis (1999)

"My manager wants me to dress like a nun and I want to dress like a teenager."

>—Anna Kournikova, then a teenager

"I don't accept it. I rail against it. I'm upset about it. Women are judged on a much harsher level. We're judged on our looks rather than our accomplishments. It's peculiar. You really should be judged on who you are, not what you look like."

>—Martina Navratilova, upset about the obsession with female competitors' physical appeal (2003)

"You'll be good because you're ugly."

>—What a male coach told sixteen-year-old Billie Jean King (1959)

"The most beautiful thing I have ever seen is Helen Wills [Moody] playing tennis."

>—Charlie Chaplin

"People automatically assumed I had it because I wanted to win more money. I don't need any more money. I've made money. I had it because women should have choice over their futures."

—Billie Jean King, on why she had an abortion in 1971, in a 1972 *SPORT* magazine article

"People go to Laver to talk about tennis—they come to me to talk about abortions."

—Billie Jean King

"What's normal behavior for the guys is unusual for the girls. You're supposed to win but you have to be seen as feminine. You can't scream, you can't say what the guys say. But how are you supposed to be feminine when you're trying to win? You're sweaty, you're tired, and it's no different from what they're trying to do."

—Irina Spirlea, known for her infamous bumping of Venus Williams at the 1997 U.S. Open, making no apologies for competitive behavior

"The women may feel clever for turning their cattiness to their own economic advantage. But isn't it just a gender version of Uncle Tom? It plays into a stereotype of sharp nails, stiletto heels, and barbed tongues that the men who run sports love. So we're back to women behaving the way men expect them to behave. Blame, set, match."

—Maureen Dowd, *New York Times* columnist, on why catfights, although a great marketing tool to lure male sponsors and fans, are a losing proposition for women (2001)

"Talk about psychological warfare. You haven't seen it until you've been around a few women's tournaments."

—Virginia Wade, 1977 Wimbledon champion

"We dig the skirts, the clingy tank tops, and bouncy pony tails. We're suckers for the bitchy rivalries, the family dramas, and the glamour."

—*GQ* magazine (2002)

"You cannot just be a great tennis player, or just be a beautiful person anymore to succeed in the game. You have to have it all, the talent, the looks, the brains and the drive."

—Anna Kournikova, holding court at the 1997 Australian Open

PAEANS TO THE CHAMPIONS

"He can hit shots the rest of us can't hit and don't even think of hitting."

—Jim Courier, on Pete Sampras (1991)

"If there's one role model in tennis, it's Pete Sampras. He's behaving perfectly on the court, he's a nice fellow off the court, and he's play-ing great tennis altogether. I think he's extremely good for tennis."

—Boris Becker (1995)

"For me, Sampras was always the most complete player. He has the power, he has the speed, he has the touch. He is the best player ever."

—Boris Becker, in *Sports Illustrated* (1997)

"Sampras, Sampras, Sampras, Sampras, and Sampras."

—Andre Agassi, asked to name the five greatest players of all time (1998)

"Pete is in a different world. He looks like the best player I've ever seen in this sport."

—John McEnroe, who had previously insisted that Rod Laver was the best player he ever saw, writing in the *Sunday Telegraph* (UK) (1997)

"Sampras is the greatest of all time, and I have to give him a pat on the back for getting there, because the tournaments are a little deeper these days."

—Roy Emerson, after Pete Sampras won his seventh Wimbledon and thirteenth Grand Slam singles title, breaking the career record Sampras and Emerson had shared (2000)

"My goal one day is to be in the same sentence as Rod Laver and Ken Rosewall. If I can match them for ten years, I'd be in their company. They were class acts. That's what I'd like to be."

> —Pete Sampras, after winning his third Grand Slam title at the U.S. Open (1993)

"He's the greatest one. He's the best, the best player of all times. Six years No. 1 in the world, thirteen Grand Slams. Just I cannot even talk about him, it's like talking about God, you know? The guy is the best one. He will be the best one. I don't think that there will be another Pete Sampras."

> —Marat Safin, not taken in by talk of a Sampras slump (2002)

"I couldn't think of anyone I'd rather see break it, because Pete is a terrific ambassador for tennis and a terrific ambassador for America. All around the world he's very well respected. This is the type of person you need as a champion for all the young kids to emulate."

> —All-time great Roy Emerson, on Pete Sampras's pursuit of his record twelve Grand Slam singles titles (1997)

"He was one of the most graceful players of all time, one of the most quietly competitive people of all time. I think of him as one of the best pressure players of all time. It seemed like the bigger the match was, the better he played. . . . He didn't really make a big fuss. He just made his name by winning."

> —Andy Roddick, on Pete Sampras's legacy (2003)

"It's a sure sign of our moral decay that Pete Sampras has been considered boring all these years. There is nothing boring about such depthless ambition or utter all-time greatness. Nor is there anything boring about a guy who so stubbornly bucks his times and the prevailing culture, to remain an understated champion in this era of inflated reputations and surpassingly crude behavior."

> —*Washington Post* columnist Sally Jenkins (2002)

"You know what the name Lendl means to me? Dedication, hard work, overcoming everybody although he maybe didn't have the tennis talent of a lot of guys. I admire him immensely."

> —Pete Sampras, after beating aging, former superstar Ivan Lendl at the 1994 Australian Open

"For sheer genius and perfect technique, Lenglen was the greatest woman star of all time."

—Bill Tilden. From his 1948 memoir, *My Story*

"Where has there been so quaint a personality, so magnificent a game and so representative a specimen of American womanhood in the annals of American tennis as are combined in this young schoolgirl? It is the wholesomeness of Helen Wills [Moody], the honesty, sincerity, and charm of her that is far more interesting than her tennis, great as it is."

—Bill Tilden. From his 1924 book, *The Common Sense of Tennis*

"Whenever a great player comes along, you have to ask, 'Could she have beaten Maureen?' In every case the answer is, I think not."

—Lance Tingay, Hall of Fame tennis correspondent of the *Daily Telegraph* (UK), on American teenager Maureen Connolly, who won nine straight Grand Slam titles from 1951 to 1954

"Serena's got great body strength, she has a strong mind. There's no weakness, really. She's got everything. Forehand, backhand, serve. She's very fluid. To be a great performer, a great athlete, you've got to really enjoy the limelight, like [Michael] Jordan, and that's one of her biggest pluses."

—Tennis legend and U.S. Fed Cup captain Billie Jean King, on Serena Williams (2003)

"She's like the old Green Bay Packers. You know exactly what she's going to do, but there isn't a thing you can do about it."

—Arthur Ashe, on Martina Navratilova

"She seems a freak of nature, the perfect tennis player."

—Virginia Wade, on Martina Navratilova

"Martina is the best athlete I've seen in tennis, and probably the best ever. I think if you combine strength and quickness and agility, she is the best athlete, without a doubt."

—Chris Evert, on archrival and superstar Martina Navratilova (1986)

"For me she is the uncontested No. 1; she has left a mark on the sport like no one else."

—Steffi Graf, naming Martina Navratilova as the greatest player in history (1999)

"Martina is a legend in every town and village across the globe. She doesn't only stand for our sport, she stands for mankind. Her athleticism, her [essence] as a human being, her character to do things her way, is just fantastic."

—Leander Paes, on Martina Navratilova whom he partnered to the 2003 Wimbledon and Australian Open mixed doubles titles (2003)

"Frankly, she's the greatest singles, doubles, and mixed doubles player that has ever lived."

—Billie Jean King, on Martina Navratilova, in *USA Today* (2003)

"Billie Jean is the greatest competitor I've ever known."

—Margaret Court, on archrival Billie Jean King

"On the court she's an evil, merciless bastard. Totally ruthless. She'll do everything and anything within the rules to win."

—Referee Frank Hammond, on fiery champion Billie Jean King, in a 1972 *SPORT* magazine article

"Undoubtedly, Marg was the most athletic woman tennis player I've ever seen. Stronger than most men."

—John Newcombe, on all-time great Margaret Court, holder of a record sixty-two Grand Slam titles (1976)

"Whenever you talk of great women tennis players, you have to start with Margaret. She should go down as the finest woman player of all times."

—Marty Riessen, on 1960s and '70s superstar Margaret Court, his partner in six Grand Slam mixed doubles titles (1970)

"To my mind, it's Borg who's abnormal. I just don't know how he does it."

—John McEnroe, praising Bjorn Borg for his exemplary temperament (1981)

"They should send Borg away to another planet. We play tennis. He plays something else."

—Ilie Nastase

"He's a robot from outer space—a Martian."

> —Ilie Nastase, after losing in straight sets to Bjorn Borg in the Wimbledon final (1976)

"He's almost a perfect tennis machine, because he never stopped oiling his parts."

> —John Newcombe, on six-time French Open and five-time Wimbledon champion Bjorn Borg

"Nastase is so good that I actually can get inspired watching him play."

> —Arthur Ashe

"Shaq, [NFL rushing leader] Emmitt Smith, [baseball star] Ken Griffey Jr., Marion Jones, Andre Agassi, and Pete Sampras. I like the way they come back every time. One wins, then the other wins. They are true competitors."

> —Roy Jones Jr., WBA heavyweight and light heavyweight champion, on his favorite athletes to watch (2003)

"I've never played against anyone who hit the ball so hard, so often, and so accurately."

> —John McEnroe, after beating seventeen-year-old Andre Agassi at Stratton Mountain (1987)

"When Andre's on, forget it. He does practically everything better than anybody else."

> —Pete Sampras

"Agassi has qualities nobody has ever had before, in return of serve and hitting the ball pure and early. . . . He's obviously one of the top two or three players ever."

> —Mats Wilander, holder of seven Grand Slam titles (1995)

"Not just in tennis but in all of sports, he's as great a competitor as you'll ever see."

> —Andre Agassi, on retiring rival Michael Chang (2003)

"I can see famous people at tournaments and not get star struck, but when I see Agassi and Sampras walking around, I just kind of sit still and my jaw drops."

—Andy Roddick (2001)

"Arantxa plays every point like it's the last. She fights hard no matter what the score."

—Steffi Graf, after relentless Arantxa Sanchez Vicario upset her 1–6, 7–6, 6–4 in the 1994 U.S. Open final to seize the No. 1 ranking

"Tilden always seems to have a thousand means of putting the ball away from his opponent's reach. He seems to exercise a strange fascination over his opponent as well as the spectators. Tilden, even when beaten, always leaves an impression on the public mind that he was superior to the victor. All spectators seem to think he can win when he likes."

—Rene Lacoste, assessing archrival Bill Tilden. From his 1928 book, *Lacoste on Tennis*

"Tilden is the only player in the world. The rest of us are second-graders."

—1920s Australian star Gerald Patterson

"Tilden was more of an artist than nine-tenths of the artists I know. It is the beauty of the game that Tilden loves; it is the chase always, rather than the quarry."

—Franklin P. Adams, American newspaperman and parodist

"I do not think any player I have seen between that youthful Davis Cup experience of 1914 and the late 1960s could have beaten the best Tilden."

—Al Laney, distinguished American sportswriter. From his 1968 book, *Covering the Court—A Fifty-Year Love Affair with the Game of Tennis*

"I do not think any tennis player has given me more genuine pleasure than Jack Crawford."

—Al Laney, on the immensely popular Australian who won more overall Grand Slam titles (seventeen) than any pre–World War II male champion and was renowned for his stylish strokes and gentlemanly behavior

"Kramer had an air about him, a type of aggression that is hard to define. There was nothing personal about it, but he played every point as though it was a life-and-death situation."

> —Australian star Adrian Quist. From his book, *Tennis: The Greats 1920–1960*

"There was one time in his life when he was the best tennis player in the world. There was another time in his life when he was the world's greatest golfer."

> —Fred Perry, on 1930s pro and amateur tennis champion Ellsworth Vines. From the 1985 book, *Once a Champion: Legendary Tennis Stars Revisited*

"Emmo closed more bars and practice courts than anybody I've ever met."

> —Arthur Ashe, on 1960s champion Roy Emerson, whose partying and work ethic were second to none

"One, he is the fittest player who ever lived. Two, he is the most popular."

> —Arthur Ashe, on Roy Emerson

"He is probably the classiest fellow I've ever known. He has integrity, loyalty, plus he's always honorable and always good company."

> —Jack Kramer, in praise of Arthur Ashe. From his 1979 memoir, *The Game: My 40 Years in Tennis*

"She gave to us—to all the players in the world—a lesson in how athletes must behave in sport."

> —Juan Antonio Samaranch, president of the International Olympic Committee, on exemplary champion Steffi Graf (1999)

"Steffi is the best all-around player of all-time, regardless of the surface."

> —Martina Navratilova, in praise of Steffi Graf (1996)

"I'm always fascinated to pick the brain of a champion."

> —Andre Agassi, on one benefit of dating Steffi Graf (1999)

"Had she played like this ten years ago when I was dominating, she would have beaten me. At her best she's as good as anybody I've played in twenty years."

> —Martina Navratilova, after Monica Seles routed her 7–5, 6–3, 6–1 in the season-ending Virginia Slims Championships (1992)

"She had presence. She had that fantastic body and feline grace on the court and you were left with a fabulous memory. Her tennis presence really came from her heart. It's like when Nureyev stands on the stage. You can't take your eyes off him. It's physical but it's the soul out there as well."

> —Virginia Wade, on 1960s champion Maria Bueno of Brazil

"Evonne plays tennis the way black people dance."

> —Chris Evert, complimenting Evonne Goolagong Cawley, the most graceful champion since Maria Bueno a decade earlier (1973)

"The incredible thing about playing her is if I hit a winner I will hear 'Good shot!' I keep saying to myself, 'Is this girl real?' She is."

> —Chris Evert, on playing Evonne Goolagong Cawley

"She plays Wimbledon and the other big tournaments as though she were a kid playing in a meadow. Her naturalness in beaming her humanity—the smile, the good-natured shrug, the tiny 'Oops, I've made a booboo' shriek, her obvious feeling that it's really only a game—wins love from an audience that deals out admiration to others."

> —Bud Collins, Hall of Fame journalist and broadcaster, on Evonne Goolagong Cawley. From the 1979 book, *Famous Women Tennis Players*

"He was a bad sonofabitch. He'd do anything, stand there for six hours, to win a match."

> —Jimmy Connors, on why he most admired Pancho Gonzalez

"Next to Jackie Robinson, Pancho Gonzalez was the most competitive athlete I've ever known."

> —Legendary sports broadcaster Howard Cosell. From his book, *Cosell*

"If earth was on the line in a tennis match, the man you'd want serving to save humankind was Ricardo Alonso [Pancho] Gonzalez."

> —*Sports Illustrated* (1999)

"He is the greatest natural athlete tennis has ever known."

> —Amateur champion Tony Trabert, on pro tennis king Pancho Gonzalez (1955)

"Pancho gets fifty points on his serve and fifty points on terror. The great champions are always vicious competitors."

> —Jack Kramer, on old rival Pancho Gonzalez

"Gonzalez was my toughest opponent, a notch above Lew Hoad, but Lew is the greatest when he is on."

> —Ken Rosewall, comparing his archrivals, Pancho Gonzalez and Lew Hoad

"Pancho was one of the fiercest competitors to walk onto a court. . . . He was armed with one of the best serves I've ever faced, was an agile net player, and displayed great touch with his volleys. . . . In his day, he would have eaten John McEnroe for breakfast."

> —John Newcombe, 1960s and '70s Australian star, in *RACQUET* magazine (1994)

"When Lew's game was at its peak, nobody could touch him."

> —Pancho Gonzalez, on Lew Hoad, whom Gonzalez called his toughest opponent during their pro primes

"When you sum Hoad up, you have to say that he was overrated. He might have been the best, but day-to-day, week-to-week, he was the most inconsistent of all the top players. Overall, he lost to Rosewall, to Gonzalez, to Segura, to Trabert. . . . Generally he is held in higher esteem than he deserves. . . . But when Hoad felt like getting up, boy was he something."

> —Jack Kramer. From his 1979 memoir, *The Game: My 40 Years in Tennis*

"Ken Rosewall plays every match his best tennis."

> —Chilean pro Luis Ayala. From the 1973 book, *The Return of a Champion: Pancho Gonzalez' Golden Year 1964*

"It is like hitting against a brick wall."

> —Rod Laver, on playing against unerring Ken Rosewall

"I've played them all, and I never saw anybody hit the ball so hard for so long as Jimmy did."

> —Arthur Ashe, after twenty-year-old Jimmy Connors upset him in five sets for the U.S. Pro singles title (1973)

"A metaphor for life . . . a victory over mortality."

> —Broadcaster Ted Koppel, heaping praise on Jimmy Connors for reaching the U.S. Open semifinals at age thirty-nine (1991)

"No one ever made a tennis court come alive more."

> —Chris Evert, one-time fiancée of Jimmy Connors, on Jimbo's love affair with the U.S. Open, in *USTA Magazine* (2003)

"Connors is a killer. He's got timing, guts, he knows just when to come in and dig. He would have made a helluva fighter."

> —Angelo Dundee, famed trainer of Muhammad Ali

"Looking back from the early 1990s, with Connors still playing well, I see that he was the greatest male tennis player, bar none, in the two and a half decades since the Open era began in 1968."

> —Arthur Ashe. From his 1993 book, *Days of Grace*

"Alice was so special because she played like a man. At that time there was no woman who played anything near like a man. They played a ladies' game—darn good, but it didn't have the pressure or the pace that Alice could put on the balls."

> —All-time great Don Budge, on the unique benefits of pairing in mixed doubles with 1930s champion Alice Marble

"She had more will to win, more drive and guts than anyone else."

> —Alice Marble, on 1930s star Helen Jacobs. From the 1979 book, *Famous Women Tennis Players*

"Never be willing to settle for second best, but keep achievement in proper perspective, and recognize that qualities of spirit have far greater value than personal accomplishments."

> —Helen Jacobs

"There is no doubt in my mind that Mo was the greatest player who ever lived, and I've seen them all except Suzanne Lenglen."

> —Doris Hart, Maureen Connolly's chief rival, on "Little Mo" in *World Tennis* magazine (1978)

"Norman Brookes is the greatest tennis player and genius of all time."

> —Bill Tilden, on the "Wizard" of Oz, the first Australian to win a Wimbledon singles title

"I can assure you that nobody, but nobody, hit the ball harder than Ellsworth Vines."

    —Adrian Quist, on the 1930s American champion (1991)

"The most charming, interesting, and intriguing personality that tennis has known for many a long day is my good friend Baron Gottfried von Cramm of Germany. Here is a player of transcendent skill, a player who can produce tennis that for periods will sweep any player in the world from his path."

    —Bill Tilden. From his 1938 memoirs, *Aces, Places and Faults*

"Cramm was of the old German nobility. . . . But his real nobility was in his human qualities, rather than his lineage; he was one of the finest sportsmen in the world and perhaps the most popular of all the players."

    —Don Budge. From his 1969 book, *Don Budge: A Tennis Memoir*

"More than anything, Chris is a star. Some champions are simply winners; some are heroes; some are leaders. Above all, though, Chris has been a star. In fact, she's the best star tennis ever had."

    —Billie Jean King, on Chris Evert. From her 1982 autobiography, *Billie Jean*

"Chris was like a perfect blonde goddess who was stalking Billie Jean and Virginia and Evonne. Before I even met her, she stood for everything I admired in this country: poise, ability, sportsmanship, money, style."

    —Martina Navratilova, relating that she, as a young girl in Czechoslovakia, knew all about Chris Evert from tennis magazines her cousin sent her from Canada. From her 1985 autobiography, *Martina*

"I feel fairly confident in saying that Budge was the best of all. He owned the most perfect set of mechanics and he was the most consistent. I also feel just as safe in saying that, on his best days, Vines played the best tennis ever."

    —Jack Kramer

"I consider him the finest player 365 days a year that ever lived."

    —Bill Tilden, in praise of 1930s superstar Don Budge. From the 1948 edition of his autobiography, *My Story*

"Playing against Don Budge was like playing against a concrete wall. There was nothing to attack. There was no weakness. When he was in his prime, no player, past or present, could have beaten him."

> —1931 Wimbledon champion Sidney B. Wood Jr., in a 1960 *SPORT* magazine article

"You need to be like Don Budge. You need to look like a champion, act like a champion, and try to play like a champion."

> —The message Perry T. Jones, czar of Southern California tennis, gave to aspiring players

"The most devastating and impressive player I have ever seen."

> —Bobby Riggs, on Don Budge, in a 1960 *SPORT* magazine article

"I put Don Budge right at the pinnacle. If it weren't for the prohibition against the pros at Grand Slams and the interruption of World War II, he would have won so many major titles that you wouldn't have been able to count them."

> —Jack Kramer

"In my opinion, we had Vines, who for one year was the best player ever, and we have Budge, who for the three best years of his life, nobody could hold a candle to. For the best five-year period, I give it to Jack Kramer. The best ten-year period, I give it to Laver. The best twenty-year period, I give [it] to Gonzalez. The best twenty-five to thirty-year period, I give it to Rosewall."

> —Bobby Riggs, ranking the greatest players of all-time (1985). From Paul Fein's *Tennis Confidential*

"In these inspired moments of his, Cochet is the greatest of all Frenchmen, and in my opinion, possibly the greatest player who has ever lived."

> —Bill Tilden, praising Henri Cochet, who beat him in the 1926 U.S. Championships, the 1927 Wimbledon, and the 1928–30 Davis Cup Challenge Rounds (1928)

"He was the genius—shrewd, analytical, superb in technique."

> —Bill Tilden, on Rene Lacoste, one of the "Four Musketeers" who led France to six Davis Cup titles from 1927 to 1932 (1948)

"Boris [Becker] has virtually no weaknesses. He's really a modern Laver—bigger serve, bigger guy."

—1940s and '50s star Pancho Segura (1987)

"[Boris] Becker is by far the greatest sportsman Germany has ever had—bigger even than Max Schmeling."

—Soccer legend Franz Beckenbauer (1990)

"[Boris] Becker is by far the greatest sportsman Germany has ever had—bigger even than Max Schmeling." —Soccer legend Franz Beckenbauer (*Fred Mullane/Camerawork USA, Inc.*)

"He was the most clean-cut diamond of them all. He represented a new generation, not just of Germany, but of humanity, of everything. He was so clean, so pure, so normal, he made everybody a better person. Whenever he talked, people listened. He developed the tennis industry in Germany—in one of the world's greatest economies—totally redirecting the game to Europe."

> —Ion Tiriac, once Boris Becker's manager, on the one-time *wunderkind* (1996)

"In terms of tennis talent, I have never seen anyone better than John."

> —Arthur Ashe, extolling John McEnroe

"Against Connors and Borg you feel like you're being hit with a sledgehammer. But this guy is a stiletto. Junior has great balance and he just slices people up. He's got a ton of shots. It's slice here, nick there, cut over here. Pretty soon you've got blood all over you, even though the wounds aren't deep. Soon after that you've bled to death."

> —Arthur Ashe, explaining the genius of John McEnroe after losing to the nineteen year old, rising star at the Grand Prix Masters in January 1979

"Venus is awesome, that's all. Awesome. She reminds me of Althea Gibson—tall, black, fast, powerful, ambitious, confident. Venus will be the Althea Gibson of the twenty-first century."

> —Billie Jean King, on Venus Williams

"Venus Williams is the best thing that has happened to American tennis for the last twenty years."

> —United States Tennis Association president Harry Marmion (1997)

"She has enormous physical skills. And her mind for the game is about to catch up with her breathtaking athletic skills. She looks like a gazelle on court. I've never seen anything like it. And I may never see anything like it again."

> —Former president Bill Clinton, in praise of Venus Williams, after watching her in action at the French Open and Wimbledon (2001)

"Sports tend to reach their greatest popularity during periods of either a great rivalry or a dynasty. With Serena and Venus Williams, tennis gets both."

    —Associated Press (2002)

"They're the biggest thing to happen to tennis since Billie Jean King beat Bobby Riggs in the '70s."

    —Pam Shriver, on Venus and Serena Williams (2001)

"Venus and Serena are to tennis what the Yankees are to baseball; what the Lakers are to basketball; what Tiger Woods is to golf. Only in our sport it's come in a pair."

    —Arlen Kantarian, United States Tennis Association chief executive officer (2003)

"Ted and women's tennis were synonymous for six decades. He was our historian, our measuring stick, and our conscience. We have come a long way. We could not have done it without you."

    —Chris Evert, in her eulogy at Ted Tinling's memorial service at St. James Church in Piccadilly, England (1990)

"She speaks four languages, plays tennis like a dream, and knows the value of family. I'll always love Martina Hingis."

    —Chris Evert (1997)

"Rod Laver is my tennis God. He's such a humble, nice man who doesn't say anything bad about anybody, even if you try to get him to do it. He's our Babe Ruth. He was the first guy who did everything, came over the ball, served and volleyed, hit from the baseline and sliced."

    —John McEnroe, in *Tennis Magazine* (2002)

"I think he's proven that he can play great in big situations, there's no question. He's doing everything great. He's a great mover, great striker of the ball off both sides. He's a factor from the back of the court, when he comes to the net. His serve is very effective. He knows the game real well, knows court position. As good as it gets out there."

    —Andre Agassi, lavishing praise on Roger Federer, after the twenty-two-year-old Swiss sensation won all five matches, including a 6–3, 6–0, 6–4 final rout of Agassi in the Tennis Masters Cup (2003)

"Pete has the most complete game of anyone I've ever seen. Andre has made a complete turnaround in the last five, six months and is on the same level as Pete. I think these two guys would beat the pants off anybody in the past."

—All-time great Pancho Gonzalez, assessing No. 1 Pete Sampras and No. 2 Andre Agassi (1995)

"He plays every point as if it's World War II."

—Roy Emerson, men's recordholder with twenty-eight Grand Slam titles, on compatriot and world No. 1 Lleyton Hewitt (2003)

FOR THE LOVE OF THE GAME

"When I was forty, my doctor advised me that a man in his forties shouldn't play tennis. I heeded his advice carefully and could hardly wait until I reached fifty to start again."

> —Supreme Court Justice Hugo Black. From *Treasury of Modern Quotations* (1963)

"Ask Nureyev to stop dancing, ask Sinatra to stop singing—then you can ask me to stop playing tennis."

> —Billie Jean King

"Well, one player in the junior draw here, I played against her mother. . . . Her *mother*."

> —Martina Navratilova, still playing and winning on the pro tour at age forty-six, in *Newsday* (2003)

"I love this game. You can't go to Kmart and buy the feeling you get in front of a packed house."

> —Jim Courier

"The only possible regret I have is the feeling that I will die without having played enough tennis."

> —Jean Borotra, the most flamboyant of France's "Four Musketeers," who continued to play and even take tennis lessons into his nineties

"Tennis is my life. I need the fabulous emotions playing tennis gives me."

> —Steffi Graf, announcing she would play the pro tour in 1999

"I'm married to the game of tennis."

—Guillermo Vilas, on his perennial bachelor status (1986)

"The great thing about playing tennis is that you forget your troubles for two hours and when you're finished, everything you do is better. Even the beer tastes better."

—Bill Talbert, U.S. doubles champion, U.S. Open director, and author

"My goal is to be the No. 1 player in the world, and I wasn't getting a chance to do that. I wanted my freedom."

—What Czech Martina Navratilova, eighteen, told the Immigration and Naturalization office in New York when asking for political asylum (1975)

"I love the sport. I'll be back here [Wimbledon] every year."

—Boxing great Sugar Ray Leonard, who says he plays three to four hours a day (1987)

"I love this sport. It's an amazing test of individual human endeavor."

—Actress Faye Dunaway, in *USTA Magazine* (2003)

"I'd rather play tennis."

—Bianca Jagger, on the joy of sex

"If I'm in the middle of hitting a most fantastic cross-court backhand topspin and someone says 'Can you stop now and have sex?' I'll say, 'No thanks!'"

—Sir Cliff Richard, British pop singer and an avid tennis fan

"I was lucky enough to be a ball boy [at the Davis Cup]. I thought I had died and gone to heaven, and that really sparked my lifelong love for the sport."

—Former president George Herbert Walker Bush, in *Sports Illustrated* (2003)

"What makes the game so much fun is knowing that whenever I'm in China, Australia, Pakistan, Jordan, or Sweden, I always have something that transcends language barriers, all cultural or political differences. I have my tennis."

—Former president George Herbert Walker Bush, in *USTA Magazine* (2003)

"I love watching Andre play. I love watching all these guys play. I'm a tennis name-dropping freak."

> —Former president George Herbert Walker Bush, while watching ageless Andre Agassi play three thrilling matches at the Tennis Masters Cup in Houston (2003)

"I'm through with school. All I want to do is to play tennis. From morning to night. My whole life long."

> —Pancho Gonzalez, then a teenager whose disdain for school and poor academic record prompted Perry T. Jones, the czar of southern California tennis, to suspend him from competition. From Gianni Clerici's 1976 book, *Tennis*

"To me, there is a cycle in sports: The more you enjoy it, the more you practice; the more you practice, the more you improve; therefore, you enjoy it more."

> —Pancho Gonzalez

"My greatest high was to hit a ball well, to try to do it perfectly, to try different things with my shots whether they came off or not. I can think back to matches I lost where I played one or two points perfectly, and that gave me a thrill. The most exciting match I ever played was the 1974 U.S. Open final against Billie Jean, and I lost it."

> —Evonne Goolagong Cawley, 1970s champion from Australia

"I would rather play beautiful tennis than win. In fact, if I'm playing really well, really hitting the ball, I can lose track of the purpose behind it all."

> —Virginia Wade. From the 1975 book, *Carnival at Forest Hills: The Anatomy of a Tennis Tournament*

"I've been run ragged, my back is stiff, and I feel like shit. But, boy it was fun. To get a stadium rocking like that is a kick you can't believe."

> —An exhausted Jimmy Connors, thirty-eight, after retiring against Michael Chang, nineteen, in the fifth set at the French Open (1991)

"I wish I had the love of the game he's got."

> —John McEnroe, after thirty-nine-year-old Jimmy Connors's energetic charge to the U.S. Open semifinals (1991)

"Tennis will never end for me because I love it so much. When my professional career is over, I will continue to play all my life."

—Monica Seles

"I love the winning, I can take the losing, but most of all I love to play."

—Boris Becker

"We know what will happen in the world, more or less, don't we? But we don't know what will happen in tennis, and I can hardly wait to find out."

—Tennis historian and maven Ted Tinling, in a 1984 *Sports Illustrated* article

"I'm so excited about next year that I can't even stand it. I've never been bored on a tennis court. The ball always comes over the net differently. There's always something different about it. Life is as exciting as you make it."

—Fired-up, forty-seven-year-old Martina Navratilova, after teaming with Lisa Raymond in Philadelphia to win her seventh women's doubles title of 2003

"I can live without the crowds and publicity. But I have to play, and I always will, even if it's at a public park with nobody watching."

—Billie Jean King. From the 1997 book, *The Tennis Lover's Book of Wisdom*

"A sunny day, white balls, tight racquet, fresh white tennis clothes, a good-natured opponent, and a brisk game—this spells heaven for the one who loves tennis."

—All-time great Helen Wills Moody. From her 1929 book, *Tennis*

"The feeling of playing a great match is unbelievably exciting. Everyone knows how hard it is to find such an intense feeling in real life. Look at Michael Jordan who is planning a comeback again. It's like an addiction."

—Pete Sampras, on why retirement is the most difficult decision for many athletes (2001)

WHAT A RACKET!

"It is indispensable to have a good racket, else the game may not be fully enjoyed, and as that article is rather expensive, many who would otherwise be active players are simply lookers-on."

> —The *Paris Tribune*, advising its European and American readers (1889)

"No matter how intricately or how well manufactured, no two wood frames are alike. There is a different feel or balance. With steel it is possible to make rackets that conform to the most minute specification."

> —Rene Lacoste, former Wimbledon and twice U.S. champion and one of France's famous "Four Musketeers," on why the steel racket that he invented—and which made its debut as the Wilson T2000 in 1967—is superior to wood

"As to the outcome of the so-called battle of the rackets, steel versus wood, I predict a secure and happy future for both. Human nature being what it is, there will always be plenty of tennis players who will want to own either or both."

> —Sarah Palfrey, who captured eighteen Grand Slam titles in singles, doubles, and mixed from 1930 to 1945. From her 1968 book, *Tennis for Anyone!*

"Within five years the standard frame will be a Prince-size frame. Conventional-size rackets will look funny and small."

> —Howard Head, who revolutionized racket design with Prince heads that were 50 percent larger than traditional, in *World Tennis* magazine (1979)

"The best material for a racquet always was, and still is, wood."

—Jack Kramer in *Tennis* magazine (1980)

"The big joke—although it wasn't funny at the time—was that the metal rackets Chemold was giving us were nothing but junk. Mine used to snap off at the throat, and they couldn't string them properly. I still don't know how I was able to win three of the four Grand Slam tournaments with them—in France, England, and the United States."

—Margaret Court, in her 1975 book, *Court on Court: A Life in Tennis*

"I've worked too long and too hard to get the kind of aggressive style that I have, and I'd like to keep it. As for those new over-sized rackets, they're for women, old people, and sissies."

—Jimmy Connors, on why he was the only top player to stick with a steel racquet, the small-headed Wilson T2000 (1982)

"I have played with both wood and metal, and I have won major tournaments with both, but I prefer wood by far. It is my feeling that a player who learns the game with a metal racquet never really learns how to hit the ball correctly."

—From Billie Jean King's 1978 instruction book, *Tennis Love: A Parents' Guide to the Sport*

"I remember my first racket. It was a grey Donnay. I can still picture it now. I loved tennis so much from the minute I first tried it . . . from that moment on, I wouldn't let go of my racket."

—Justine Henin-Hardenne, 2003 French and U.S. Open champion from Belgium, as was her first racket (2003)

"We have a favorite racket even if twenty-four have been made from the same mold. It's all psychological and when we get to the point when we don't have a favorite then we've matured."

—Alice Marble, 1930s champion, on a common tennis superstition, in the 1974 book, *The Encyclopedia of Tennis*

"It's the steel racket—it has improved my game 25 percent."

—Clark Graebner, after reaching the final of the U.S. Championships with his new Wilson T2000 (1967)

"All the skill is going out of the game. Players like Rod Laver and Bjorn Borg could do wonderful things with a wood racket. Now it's boom, boom, boom."

—Ilie Nastase, stylish 1970s star, advocating the banning of large graphite rackets used by most pro players (1995)

"It is so easy to play with the new rackets; all you need is a flick of the wrist. Don't misunderstand me. I've got one, too, but it's just like Ping-Pong. Something is wrong when you hit the ball as hard as you can for ten shots in a row and every one goes in. And everybody plays the same style."

—Budge Patty, winner of the French and Wimbledon championships in 1950, unimpressed with the modern game (1997)

"I am where I am because I grew up with wood. I think kids ought to play with wood racquets until age fourteen or so. It's the only way to master strokes. The graphite, the power, that comes later."

—Pete Sampras, in *GQ* magazine (2000)

"Becker would never have won Wimbledon at the age of seventeen with a wood-framed racket. The guy has wonderful talent and was unbelievably strong for a teenager, but it was the racket that made the difference."

—John McEnroe, an advocate of a return to wood rackets. From the 1988 book, *Open Tennis: The First Twenty Years*

"If you give him a smaller-headed, wooden racket, he'd be an average player."

—Pat Cash, on countryman and world No. 1 Lleyton Hewitt (2002)

"High-powered rackets are destroying tennis and making it really boring. When you saw McEnroe and Connors play at Wimbledon, that was real tennis. With the wide-bodies, it will get worse. If it was up to me, I would go back to the old wooden rackets and play real tennis."

—Michael Stich, who upset Boris Becker in the terribly dull 1991 Wimbledon final, in which the ball was in play for only nine minutes in the two-and-a-half-hour match (1991)

"Something needs to be done. The power has destroyed the essence of the sport. It is no longer necessary to hit the ball properly because you can just whale away with loads of topspin, knowing the ball will stay in court."

—John Barrett, former British Davis Cup captain and technical expert at Slazenger, and current BBC tennis commentator, insisting that the future prosperity of tennis lies in reducing the width of racket frames to 22.8 cm (2003)

"The materials are so ridiculous now, it's too easy. I would rather see them go back to smaller rackets and take away the sweet spots. Something needs to be done. The game's too easy with these rackets. You see pictures in the locker-room of Ken Rosewall and Roy Emerson, Margaret Court—all the great Australians and the rackets they were playing with. The sweet spot was tiny."

—Tennis legend Martina Navratilova, en route to Grand Slam title No. 57, the Australian Open mixed doubles, at age forty-six (2003)

"The first time I played with a metal racket, I thought it was a joke because it was so easy. The sweet spot has to be made smaller to bring back finesse. You want to level the playing field so skill can win over brawn."

—Martina Navratilova, one of several former champions who signed a petition to the International Tennis Federation to decrease the width of racket heads (2003)

YOU'VE COME
A LONG WAY, BABY!

"Women have but one task, that of crowning the winner with garlands."

> —Baron Pierre de Coubertin, founder of the modern Olympic Games (1902)

"When people ask me who founded the tour, I always say Jack Kramer."

> —Gladys Heldman, who in 1970 hosted her own tournament, the Virginia Slims of Houston, after Kramer announced his Pacific Southwest tournament would offer the men's champion $12,500 and the women's champion only $1,500. Heldman then founded the highly successful Virginia Slims tour.

"For two decades, right into the 1970s, Gladys was the most powerful tennis voice in America. She is also the smartest kid I ever ran into anywhere."

> —Jack Kramer, former all-time great player and later pro promoter, tournament director, TV commentator, and founder and first executive director of the ATP (the players' union), on Gladys Heldman, who crusaded for open tennis and women's rights, as founder/director of the authoritative *World Tennis* magazine. From Kramer's 1979 autobiography, *The Game: My 40 Years in Tennis*

"Without Gladys there wouldn't be women's professional tennis as we know it. She was a passionate advocate and driving force behind the start of the Virginia Slims tour, and helped change the face of women's sports. Because of her vision women's tennis was changed forever."

> —Billie Jean King, in a Bud Collins appreciation piece (2003)

"There was no way you could convince me that watching women play tennis would be a business success."

—Jerry Diamond, before he became executive director of the women's pro tour between 1974 and 1985 (1971)

"Bobby's just fighting for money. I'm fighting for a cause."

—Feminist champion Billie Jean King, before she took on Bobby Riggs in their famous "Battle of the Sexes" match (1973)

"I'm playing Billie Jean for all the guys who are gonna get married, whose wives won't let them play poker on Friday night or go fishin' on the weekend. I've gotta do it, an old guy fifty-five years old with one foot in the grave. There wouldn't be any world problems if women had stayed in the kitchen and the bedroom."

—Crowing chauvinist Bobby Riggs, before he lost to Billie Jean King (1973)

"People were just having a great time around this match. They really got into it. Because it wasn't about tennis. It was about emotions and sexism and all the things, preconceived ideas, that people have lived with for centuries."

—Billie Jean King, recalling her celebrated match against Bobby Riggs (1992)

"The operation was a great success, a beautiful promotion. The only thing is, me, the patient, got killed. But, hey, a happy ending. I cried all the way to the bank."

—Bobby Riggs, with his hustler's view of the "Battle of the Sexes" (1992)

"Ridiculous as this may sound, her victory helped validate the idea that women could hang in there, not just on the tennis court, but on the job or in the home. It was proof not so much of physical prowess but of mental toughness. Feminists had not yet reached out to the masses. Billie Jean reached out, grabbed them by the hair, and made them take notice."

—Grace Lichtenstein, former executive editor of *World Tennis* magazine. From the 1995 book, *The Sports 100*

"On campuses people were hanging out of their dorm windows celebrating. The match had enormous symbolic importance."

> —Feminist leader Gloria Steinem, on the landmark "Battle of the Sexes" match

"Women should never be allowed on center court."

> —Jack Kramer, after his match was delayed by a long women's singles match

"After the Hopman Cup [mixed doubles matches], I changed my mind a lot about women's tennis. Hingis and Rubin—they returned my serve like a piece of cake. It is unbelievable. I couldn't hit an ace. They were returning better than the guys."

> —Rocket-serving Goran Ivanisevic (1996)

"I was impressed by the speed of her shots. I do understand that other players have problems against her because she has a slice shot which is incredible, incredible. I can tell you, she doesn't have to envy anybody on the men's tour"

> —Marc Rosset, 1992 Olympic gold medalist, after practicing with Steffi Graf at the French Open (1997)

"When you look at men play, they don't hit as hard from the baseline."

> —Chris Evert, tennis champion turned TV analyst, in praise of women players (2001)

"The whole point of women's tennis in the last generation has been that women are free to be powerful, competitive, sweaty, noisy jocks, just like the men."

> —*New York Times* sports columnist George Vecsey, defending Monica Seles who was hounded at Wimbledon by sexist British tabloids who measured her decibels with "grunt-o-meters." The *Sun* even set up a telephone "groanline" and invited its readers to call in and listen to a recording of Seles's noises (1992)

"The male players usually have actresses or models. Sampras, Agassi, Krajicek; they want pretty girls, Barbies. I don't like that. They have the money, so they get the pretty ones."

> —Martina Hingis (1998)

"Men are doing this [playing tennis] for a living now. They have families, and they don't want to give up money just for girls to play."

—Arthur Ashe, on prize-money allotment at pro tournaments (1970)

"It was tough. You stayed in fleabag hotels and just scraped by. . . . I often say I wish players today could go through a couple of weeks of that and just experience what we did. I'm really happy for today's players to be able to make a lot of money. I just wish it had come along a little sooner."

—American star Nancy Richey, whose sixty-nine singles titles, including the French and Australian Opens, stretched from 1960 to 1977, in *ACE* magazine (2003)

"It has been my experience during eighteen years of tournament tennis that women are no more given to tears in defeat than men, nor is their enthusiasm in victory more excessive. To claim, even facetiously, that it is, is to lessen public regard for the important place that women have achieved, against immeasurable disadvantages."

—Helen Jacobs, 1930s American star. From her 1949 book, *Gallery of Champions*

"The current players hit the ball harder, but is it as good to watch? No, I do not think so. Personally, I prefer watching the women these days."

—Henri Leconte, former world top tenner, who describes himself as "[Anna] Kournikova's No. 1 fan" (1998)

"They need to wake up and smell the coffee. The women are pulling in the crowds. But, you know, women have to struggle. Then again, we could be in Afghanistan."

—Martina Navratilova, on unequal prize-money at Wimbledon and the French Open (2001)

"Almost every day for the last four years, someone comes up to me and says, 'Hey, when are you going to have children?' I say, 'I'm not ready yet.' They say, 'Why aren't you at home?' I say, 'Why don't you go ask Rod Laver why he isn't at home?'"

—Billie Jean King, talking to a reporter. From the 1984 book, *In Its Own Image: How Television Has Transformed Sports*

"Margaret is women's lib in action, even though she doesn't seem to realize it. She earns the bread and her husband baby-sits."

>—Billie Jean King, on Australian champion Margaret Court, who twice took time off to have children, resumed her career, and traveled the world with her husband and family

"She is constantly criticizing [my husband] Barry and me in public. . . . She also won't let up on women's lib and me. . . . In some stupid way she thinks I'm playing only because of the big money in the game. I'd probably still be playing if tennis were strictly amateur because I enjoy the game. Barry understands this. Despite what Billie Jean says, he has a full-time job."

>—Margaret Court, setting the record straight in her 1975 book, *Court on Court: A Life in Tennis*

"Venus and Serena are providing another benchmark for women's sports. I was thinking about 1973, and how women couldn't even get a credit card back then. Can you imagine Serena and Venus without a credit card?"

>—Billie Jean King, pioneer of the professional Women's Tennis Association thirty years ago, on the Williams sisters playing for equal prize money before a prime-time TV audience in the U.S. Open final (2002)

"Women's sports is in its infancy. It's a $1 billion economy internationally. Men's sports is a $25 billion economy. Do you think we have a long way to go? Hello? But it is going to change. The twenty-first century will be a women's century."

>—Billie Jean King, in *USTA Magazine* (2003)

LIFE ON THE TOUR

"Our life is a combination of excitement beyond words and tedium beyond words."

—Pam Shriver (1985)

"Living on the road sounds great. People think you're out partying all the time, drinking and chasing [tail]. What they don't know is mostly you're just in your room alone."

—Mel Purcell, saying the toughest opponent is constant travel. From the 1983 book, *Short Circuit*

"Tennis is a game that calls for lots of discipline, hard work, and practice. . . . There are playboys in tennis today, just as there have always been, but they don't win the big ones."

—Bobby Riggs, triple Wimbledon champion in 1939 and 1946–47 pro champion. From his 1973 autobiography, *Court Hustler*

"It's a real grind. It's not as glamorous as people think. You do travel the world but you are stuck in a hotel room. There's more to life than tennis."

—Patrick Rafter (2000)

"Women's tennis is a very lonely world, especially when you are at the top. You do not have that many friends. There is a lot of jealousy out there."

—Martina Hingis

"I don't know what better teenage life you could get than going around the world doing what you love to do."

> —Anna Kournikova

"It's easier to have enemies than to have friends—especially if your friends happen to be fellow professional tennis players and you're on your way to being number one in the world. It may be a cliche that it's lonely at the top, but just because it's a cliche doesn't mean it's wrong."

> —John McEnroe. From his 2002 autobiography, *You Cannot Be Serious*

"It's not as much fun when we women are all by ourselves. It's better for our tennis but socially it's not fun. If you want to be a tennis player, dating is secondary."

> —Val Ziegenfuss, on the loneliness of the women's tour, in the 1974 book, *A Long Way, Baby—Behind the Scenes in Women's Pro Tennis*

"Being a woman tennis player—particularly one who's six feet tall—is not the greatest insurance for an enhanced social life. You're insulated and isolated much of the time, and if you meet a young man he's liable to wonder if you're a lesbian. If he doesn't, all he offers you is a quick sexual relationship—as a big favor to you, of course."

> —Pam Shriver. From her 1986 book, *Passing Shots: Pam Shriver on Tour*

"Personally, I don't care what Martina chooses to do in her private life as long as she's healthy and happy. But in the back of my mind, I think about her meeting the right guy and being swept off her feet. Martina is extremely sweepable, so I think it's only a matter of time before she gets married and has kids."

> —Pam Shriver, on her close friend and doubles partner, Martina Navratilova. From her 1986 book, *Passing Shots: Pam Shriver on Tour*

"Now women players don't care how they dress. There are no men around and the girls never seem to have dates. Playing one-week tournaments is obviously not conducive to forming lasting relationships. The big thing instead is money. And that makes the girls tougher and harder. All they care about is winning. I hate to think what the tour will be like ten years from now."

—All-time great Margaret Court. From her 1975 book, *Court on Court: A Life in Tennis*

"All the draws were fixed, except in the major tournaments. If you were seeded, you'd play the local club secretary in the first round and the No. 3 local junior in the second. . . . If you were not a 'name' player and you were about to beat one of the 'ticket-sellers,' the tournament director would literally run out on the court and order you to lose. If you went ahead and beat him despite the warning, you simply wouldn't get an invitation back."

—Barry Phillips-Moore, a mid-level Australian, on the way it was on the European tour in the pre–Open Era days. From *World Tennis* (1978)

"The hardest thing on the tour is coping with losing. You're alone in a strange place and it's easy to get discouraged."

—Tim Wilkison. From the 1983 book, *Short Circuit*

"There's nothing like knowing that if you don't win you don't eat that night to make you practice and play harder. If it's handed to you on a plate, like it is with some of the younger players, where's the motivation? It's not a disaster if they lose. It was for me."

—Canadian-turned-Englishman Greg Rusedski, then world-ranked No. 4, on his earlier dog-eat-dog days on the satellite circuits without the financial help of a tennis federation (1997)

"Tennis makes you grow up fast. You could be eighteen, nineteen, or even younger, competing in a challenger [tournament] in Turkey or Asia and you don't have any buddies with you. If you turn pro and you're not doing well, it's not a 'I'm-feeling-sorry-for-you sport.' There are no salary guarantees like in baseball or football."

—Brad Gilbert, former world-ranked No. 4 and later coach of Andre Agassi and Andy Roddick, in the *San Francisco Chronicle* (2004)

"A typical tour day schedule was like this: get up, eat breakfast, practice, eat or play your match, shower, play doubles, shower again, eat dinner, go to bed. That is the basic routine. It doesn't vary much."

—Arthur Ashe. From his 1981 book, *Off the Court*

"I'll be honest—beer and women hurt us a lot."

> —Australian Rod Frawley, on why he and some of his countrymen never fulfilled their potential (1980)

"Tennis unfortunately doesn't encourage any kind of intellectual development. It actually discourages that. The dumber you are on the court, the better you're going to play."

> —Former world-ranked No. 1 Jim Courier (1999)

"The sad fact is that tennis players don't develop as all-round human beings. They might be very good at catching airplanes and booking hotels, but that's it."

> —Pat Cash. From www.hickoksports.com

"The tour is something inside me. . . . I suffer when I lose, but I want to be where the show is. I know people say I should retire, but what do I do then? To tell me to retire tomorrow is like saying I must die tomorrow. And I don't want to die."

> —Ilie Nastase at thirty-five, in the twilight of his career, in *World Tennis* magazine (1981)

"Of course, I know from experience that men's professional tennis, for all its white, upper-class associations, is also a haven of promiscuity and easy sex, as perhaps all male professional sports are."

> —Arthur Ashe. From his 1993 memoir, *Days of Grace*

"You take the hit during the tournament and you crash afterwards. You have guys who have played super during one tournament and who you've never seen again. . . . Never heard anybody talk about again."

> —Yannick Noah, talking about cocaine and amphetamines, in an interview with French magazine, *Rock & Folk* (1980)

"It will probably add five or ten years to his career because it's so convenient. As far as I'm concerned, being a [pro] tennis player is not on-court. It's dealing with the dead days and all the [traveling] hassles."

> —Luke Jensen, after accompanying Andre Agassi on his ten-seat Lockheed JetStar plane from Las Vegas to Scottsdale

"Our life is showering and changing. I change clothes five times a day and wash my hair every day. It's a tough role to play, so you don't see many *femmes fatales* in tennis dresses."

—Billie Jean King

"Top 10 players have no friends at their level on the tour. It isn't done, because it isn't smart tennis."

—Monica Seles. From her 1996 autobiography, *Monica: From Fear to Victory*

"In the end losses don't put you over the edge, for your young mind can straighten that out. But dinner for one, that's what breaks your heart."

—Laxmi Poruri, a Stanford graduate who quit the women's tour after two years, in a *New York Times* essay

"I was all by myself then and I was so happy, but I had no one to hug. I hugged a light pole. An aluminum light pole."

—Martina Navratilova, vividly remembering her first tournament victory in her adopted country in 1974 at the Virginia Slims event in Orlando (1992)

"One thing I've learned is that it's tough to have success without someone to share it with. I'd like to have someone to share it with but still retain my independence. I'm beginning to wonder if that's possible."

—Chris Evert, in 1978. From the 1979 book, *Famous Women Tennis Players*

"The thing about Chris is she always handles herself with class, but she has nastiness in just the right way."

—Pam Shriver, on Chris Evert. From her 1986 book, *Passing Shots: Pam Shriver on Tour*

"I was in the locker room recently with five top ten players. Not one word was said in twenty minutes. As I walked out, I said, 'It was a pleasure talking with you fellows.' "

—Jimmy Connors, lamenting the lack of camaraderie in men's tennis (1994)

"I know nuns with better social lives than me."

—Wendy Turnbull, former top tenner (1979)

"If you do strike a friendship with a man, you are immediately confronted with another dilemma: does he like me, or is he more attracted by the fact that I earn a considerable amount of money and get my photograph in newspapers and on the television?"

—Hana Mandlikova. From her 1989 autobiography, *Hana*

"They get it too easy. The men on their circuit often have a lot of groupie women chasing after them. Life on their circuit is much easier than ours. We can't just go to a bar and pick up somebody, especially if we're decent."

—Australian standout Dianne Fromholtz (1980)

"Overall, dozens of sources said they knew of coaches who made suggestive remarks, fondled girls, gave massages that weren't welcome, and had sex with players when they could get away with it. Some players admitted that it happened to them. None wanted to be quoted by name, both because of embarrassment and because they fear repercussions from coaches who were still on the tour."

—Michael Mewshaw. From his 1993 exposé of the women's professional circuit, *Ladies of the Court: Grace and Disgrace on the Women's Tennis Tour*

"It used to be that you would see people running towards you and think, 'Oh, they want autographs.' But now you wonder, 'Oh, my God, are they carrying a pen or a knife.' "

—Martina Navratilova, who hired a burly full-time security guard after Monica Seles was stabbed (1993)

"I'm always telling myself, 'Don't get involved with a tennis player.' When players date other players, everyone on the circuit talks."

—Austrian beauty Barbara Schett (2001)

"In the tennis world, nobody really bothers to sort out the wives as people; they are just tolerated as appendages. It's not right, but that's the way it is. It will change in time."

—Arthur Ashe. From his 1975 book, *Portrait in Motion*

"It takes a special kind of woman to be the wife of a top-class tennis player, especially these days. It's a horrible life, and not glamorous at all. You are constantly living out of a suitcase, packing and unpacking, with no privacy. Your life is ruled by the demands of sponsors, coaches, and fitness trainers. It is far from easy."

> —Carol Seheult, a clinical and sports psychologist who works with elite athletes and their partners (2002)

"Among the women it's all bitchiness and cattiness. They say, 'How dare this person be No. 1 when she is only eighteen years old?' They feel the same about Jennifer Capriati. They smile to Monica's face, but behind her back they are sticking in the knives."

> —American multimillionaire Jim Levee, a former Steffi Graf loyalist who travels to tournaments with the Seles family, claiming that a locker room hate campaign is being waged against Monica (1992)

"I hate the falseness and jealousy of tennis players. They say one thing to your face and something else behind your back."

> —Arantxa Sanchez Vicario (1993)

"So many of the girls are horrible. You begin to feel hated. I have learned that every time you walk on court they want to kill you. Why? Because they don't want me to get ahead. Because they don't like the attention I get. Because I have a personality. Because I smile."

> —African American Alexandra Stevenson, who described her rookie year on the pro tennis tour as "tougher than anyone can prepare you for" (2000)

"I've learned what it feels like to be No. 115 in the world and have everyone treat you really badly. When you start winning, everyone loves you."

> —American pro Alexandra Stevenson (2002)

"The juniors prepared me well for the pros. I'm used to girls acting like that. It's just as catty in the juniors. I didn't expect them to like having me on tour. They didn't want to lose to someone so young. I had my mother there to support me, and that was all that mattered."

> —Martina Hingis, reflecting on her first pro match as a fourteen-year-old, in 1994

"We used to be pals, but because of a minor disagreement we are no longer. . . . That's what the tour does to you. . . . It's a tough world."

> —Mary Joe Fernandez, after former close friend Lindsay Davenport crushed her 6–1, 6–1 in the Indian Wells semifinals (1997)

"Tennis has made me grow up. Believe me, I feel older than my age. I've seen the world, the good guys and the bad guys. Yes, I've lived many lives through tennis."

> —Paradorn Srichaphan, a twenty-three year old, rising star from Thailand (2003)

"I always felt that these guys turned to more partying than playing because they found out they could not win, and not the other way around."

> —Don Budge, from his 1969 book, *Don Budge: A Tennis Memoir*

"I don't know anybody on the circuit who uses drugs. These guys are athletes."

> —Vince Van Patten, actor turned pro tennis player, who recorded wins over John McEnroe, Vitas Gerulaitis, and Jose Luis Clerc. From the 1983 book, *Short Circuit*

"The U.S. is the only country in the world where people open up their homes to house tennis players. This never occurs in Europe."

> —Derek Tarr, a South African living in Birmingham, Alabama (1987)

"That's the good thing about sports. Everybody comes together. You can't bring other things to interfere. It's what keeps all the countries together."

> —Aisam-ul-Haq Qureshi, a Pakistani Muslim, who is paired with Amir Hadad, an Israeli Jew, in men's doubles at the 2002 U.S. Open

"Our game's nothing about politics or religion. I hope people will see that two people who are supposed to be enemies can get along. We play well together, and we both think we have a good chance."

> —Amir Hadad, on the unlikely doubles partnership of him, an Israeli Jew, and Aisam-ul-Haq Qureshi, a Pakistani Muslim, at the 2002 Wimbledon

"We're not here to change anything: politicians and governments do that."

> —Pakistan's Aisam-ul-Haq Qureshi, answering criticism back home for having an Israeli partner, Amir Hadad, in the 2002 Wimbledon doubles

"The pro tour has created a great opportunity for all of us: to win money and destroy our bodies at the same time."

> —Billie Jean King, whose brilliant career was interrupted by several knee surgeries

"I saw the entertainment world is like the tennis circuit. When you win, you are the most beautiful, smart person in the world. When you lose, though, you are nothing."

> —1997 French Open champion Iva Majoli, after a week's social swirl in Cannes, France

"I think the reason I've won so much is that I've kept my distance from most of the women players."

> —Chris Evert (1976)

"Almost to a man the players will tell you they don't trust agents. Just as quickly, the agents will tell you not to trust players. In truth, both are, for the most part, right."

> —Author John Feinstein. From his 1991 book, *Hard Courts*

"I think it gives me the opportunity to rest my mind in some pretty special ways. Whether you've had a good day or bad day doesn't really matter when you see your little boy."

> —Andre Agassi, on touring with wife Steffi and son Jaden Gil (2003)

"It's like an insane asylum. Someone is throwing a racket, someone crashing a locker door, someone laughing, someone crying. It's terrible."

> —Srdjan Ivanisevic, the father of three-time Wimbledon finalist Goran, revealing locker room secrets at Wimbledon (1999)

"You wouldn't believe some of the things you go through: two-year-old ball kids, hundred-year-old line judges."

> —American journeyman Justin Gimelstob, on the not-so-good life on the pro circuit (2003)

"You live and die by those numbers. For some people, your whole identity is your ranking. I once heard someone ask a player, 'How are you?' He answered, 'I'm No. 29 this week.' Not 'I'm happy' or 'I'm depressed' or 'I'm making it day to day.' Just 'I'm No. 29,' like that said it all."

—Bill Scanlon, on the all-important computer rankings. From the 1983 book, *Short Circuit*

"Tennis opened my eyes to a lot of things. It gave me an opportunity to travel the world and meet some of the nicest people around, so what else could you ask for? It certainly beat milking cows back in Australia."

—All-time great Roy Emerson, in the *Independent* (UK) (2004)

THE MAJESTY OF WIMBLEDON

"You can find out anything you want to know about a person by putting him on Centre Court."

> —John Newcombe, three-time singles and five-time doubles champion at Wimbledon (1995)

"I have a passion for Wimbledon. Even as a little girl I could see how beautiful it was."

> —Steffi Graf (1995)

"I used to have my tennis racket in bed with me as a child. That's how much I dreamed about winning Wimbledon."

> —Billie Jean King, holder of a record twenty Wimbledon titles (1993)

"I love Wimbledon. I could hug Wimbledon. I love the atmosphere. The Centre Court. Everything about it."

> —Billie Jean King, before routing Evonne Goolagong Cawley for her sixth Wimbledon singles title (1975)

"Wimbledon. It's like making love a hundred times to the most beautiful woman you ever saw."

> —John Newcombe. From the 1979 book, *Inside Tennis: A Season on the Pro Tour*

"Finally, I win this son-of-a-bitch tournament, and I take my trophy and go all around the stadium, bowing to the people and giving the finger to everybody. Then I take my rackets and break them up in my hands. I throw them in the river, and I stop to play tennis."

> —Ilie Nastase, two-time runner-up, recounting a dream-cum-revenge fantasy about Wimbledon

"Until I win or die."

> —Ivan Lendl, when asked how long he would keep trying to win Wimbledon. Alas, Lendl, who amassed three French and U.S. and two Australian titles, never achieved his magnificent obsession.

"I never realized what it all meant. Nothing, and I mean nothing, compares with winning Wimbledon."

> —Andre Agassi, after he won the 1992 Wimbledon Championships. From the 1993 book, *Agassi: The Fall and Rise of the Enfant Terrible of Tennis*

"Wimbledon is like the Super Bowl, the World Series, and the NBA Finals all rolled into one."

> —Tony Trabert. From his 1988 book, *Trabert on Tennis: The View from Center Court*

"The British are all such excellent tennis experts that a player's game has to rise simply as a matter of self-defense. The British fans are critics, but they are as fair as they are knowledgeable, and playing at Wimbledon is much like an appearance before a jury."

> —Don Budge. From his 1969 book, *Don Budge: A Tennis Memoir*

"The most knowledgeable tennis audience ever was that at Wimbledon in the 1930s."

> —Tennis historian Ted Tinling, in a 1984 *Sports Illustrated* article

"Forever. I would sleep in a tent."

> —Martina Hingis, when asked how long she would wait in a queue to get into Wimbledon if she were a fan (1997)

"Wimbledon is the greatest tournament in the world. I love the U.S. Open and I was excited by the French Open. But this . . . I mean, there's nothing like it. And everybody knows it."

> —Former president Bill Clinton, after attending Wimbledon (2001)

"It is the tournament every player wants to win above all others."

> —Helen Wills Moody

"I got goose bumps when I was walking out there. It's just kind of majestic."

> —Andy Roddick, after making his Centre Court debut

"To be out there on Centre Court is the greatest feeling in the world."

—Andre Agassi (2003)

"Just walking out there to play on the Centre Court is like being in a magic showcase of the tennis world. . . . I love it."

—Jimmy Connors

"New Yorkers love it when you spill your guts out there. You spill your guts out at Wimbledon, [and] they make you stop and clean it up."

—Two-time Wimbledon champion Jimmy Connors

"To me, Wimbledon stands for prestige, quality, and tradition. It's the most famous tournament in the world, and the Centre Court is the most famous court in the world. When I think of Wimbledon, I think of The All England Club, grass courts, royalty, and ivy on the walls. The whole thing is so dignified."

—Chris Evert

"Queen Mary might not approve."

—The admonition that Wimbledon authorities used for years to pressure players on matters of propriety

"If you say anything during a tennis match, they make it seem like you committed murder or something."

—John McEnroe

"It's what the atmosphere instills here. At Wimbledon things come to a pitch. The best grass. The best crowd. The royalty. You all of a sudden feel the whole thing is important. You play your best tennis."

—Rod Laver, four-time Wimbledon singles champion, on his favorite tournament. From the 1972 book, *Wimbledon: A Celebration*

"Wimbledon is foremost a national phenomenon. . . . Wimbledon captures the imagination of a complete country more so than any other athletic event, simply because it attracts the interest of both sexes in a way that other great competitions do not."

—Arthur Ashe. From his 1975 book, *Portrait in Motion*

"Just walking out there to play on the Centre Court is like being in a magic showcase of the tennis world. . . . I love it."—Jimmy Connors (*Fred Mullane/Camerawork USA, Inc.*)

"You can have a tournament anywhere in the world, and it will never hold the mystique that Wimbledon has."

—Andre Agassi (1992)

"This is so great, to touch the trophy. If I never win another match I don't care. Whatever I do in my life, wherever I go, I'm going to always be a Wimbledon champion."

—Goran Ivanisevic, savoring his triumph as a wild card at age twenty-nine after losing three finals in the 1990s (2001)

"Of all the tournaments, the one I remember most is Wimbledon. . . . They would send a chauffeured limousine to your hotel to take you to the matches. The linesmen walked regally on the court. I'm sure every campaigner would agree that there's no better tournament than Wimbledon; it's the premier, number one, world's greatest event. . . ."

—Bobby Riggs, who captured all three events at the 1939 Wimbledon Championships, the only time he competed there

"You can't be considered a great player unless you win Wimbledon. That's the way it is."

—Mats Wilander, who won seven Grand Slam titles but never Wimbledon (1989)

"I do not believe that any sport possesses anything comparable to Wimbledon. It is a shrine and dripping with tradition, but the memories never dull the present. On the contrary, at Wimbledon the tradition seems to breathe life into the everyday and make it more significant."

—Don Budge. From his 1969 book, *Don Budge: A Tennis Memoir*

"It's like a love affair that grows. I loved Wimbledon from the first time I knew about it, and it's been reciprocated. It's like in a relationship where you love that person more and more. I feel this place in my bones. I feel all those champions out there, dead and alive, when I'm out there. There's no place like it."

—Martina Navratilova, nine-times singles champion, after competing in her eleventh final and twenty-second time at Wimbledon (1994)

"I couldn't see the ball. 'I thought, God, am I this nervous?' Then I remembered, I was so nervous that I hadn't put on my glasses. After that it wasn't so bad."

> —1960s and '70s French star Francoise Durr, during her speech at the induction ceremony at the International Tennis Hall of Fame, recalling her panic when she stepped on Wimbledon's hallowed Centre Court for the first time (2003)

"It's hard to compare anything with the feeling of walking out onto Centre Court, especially if it's for a final. And it's an experience where all the players agree with me—it's one of a kind."

> —Boris Becker, three-time champion and four-time runner-up at Wimbledon (1999)

"Of all the evocative names in sports . . . I do not believe that any has more significance or rings the bells of memory more loudly and clearly than Wimbledon."

> —Herbert Warren Wind. From his 1979 book, *Game, Set and Match*

"Wimbledon is a tournament that if you get a bum off the street and ask him about it, he knows Wimbledon."

> —Zina Garrison, the first African American woman to reach the Wimbledon final since Althea Gibson (1990)

"This is hallowed ground, the field of dreams for tennis players. It's great. It's legendary."

> —African American James Blake, after his singles debut at Wimbledon (2002)

"Ask any tennis player from any corner of the globe who has played there, which is the greatest tennis tournament in the world and unhesitatingly will come the answer, 'Wimbledon!' I have never met a player who considered otherwise."

> —Gardnar Mulloy, 1940s and '50s American star. From his 1959 autobiography, *Advantage Striker*

"You can come over to London as No. 1 in the world, but nobody thinks you're anybody until you've won Wimbledon. They act like they've got the biggest tournament in the world. And they're right, they do. This is the one."

> —Pete Sampras (1996)

POINTS OF CONTENTION

"The women today are huge. They need to leverage that. The top ten have to be willing not to show up unless they get what the men do. Do they have the courage—not only for themselves but for future generations? It's doubtful. They're into collecting money. It's about being a celebrity."

> —Billie Jean King, challenging the current teen queens and veterans Steffi Graf and Monica Seles to fight for equal prize money with the men at the Australian and French Opens and Wimbledon (1998)

"The Grand Slam prize money should be equal. It's irrelevant that women don't play five sets. The price of a theatre ticket isn't dictated by how long the play is. Wimbledon is so stuck in a rut."

> —Virginia Wade, in the *Evening Standard* (UK) (2003)

"In actual figures at Wimbledon, in one hour on the court the women played eight minutes, the men under four. Let me ask you this: Would you rather watch a great two-hour movie or a great four-hour movie? Pavarotti doesn't get less for singing two-and-one-half hours of Verdi instead of four-and-one-half hours of Wagner."

> —WTA Tour CEO Bart McGuire, dismissing the claim that the men players should get more prize money because their matches are best of five sets instead of best of three and generally last longer

"Women need money, too, you know."

> —What USTA president Walter Elcock, who introduced equal prize money to the Grand Slam tournaments at the U.S. Open in 1973, told those who opposed the concept

"It is most undesirable that an organisation should be able to represent a governing body, sponsors, a significant number of top players, negotiate television, cable and satellite contracts, and sell merchandise rights. The situation is pregnant with conflict of interests and cannot carry public confidence."

> —From a report of the Committee of Enquiry into Sports Sponsorship, chaired by former UK Minister for Sport, Dennis Howell. The report examined management companies, such as International Management Group, and their role in sports. (1983)

"Every morning when I get up, I see something I don't like in the game."

> —Philippe Chatrier, esteemed president of the International Tennis Federation from 1977 to 1991 (1992)

"The ace is absolutely contrary to the spirit of the game. Tennis is a conversation, whereas the ace is brute force. It ends the conversation, full stop."

> —Philippe Chatrier, advocating that only one serve be allowed (1992)

"The end result of this is that whether Connors likes it or not he is now in a position, effectively if not literally, where he has sued just about every player in the game. Would you like to have to play people you've sued?"

> —Arthur Ashe, on Jimmy Connors's lawsuit against the Association of Tennis Professionals. From his 1975 book, *Portrait in Motion*

"If you took one hundred of those stories about our being ruthless or shark-like, ninety of them would center on attitudes we have taken on behalf of our clients. I think being ruthless, in the context in which it is applied to me, is really sort of a compliment."

> —Mark McCormack, founder and CEO of International Management Group (IMG), the world's largest sports and entertainment marketing firm

"It's the tournaments [not the players] who should be having the revolt. You find out somebody who supposedly is sick or injured and can't play in a tournament is playing golf and having a great time someplace else. And nobody does anything about it. That's terrible! That's been happening for fifteen years."

—Jack Kramer, "founding father" of the International Grand Prix circuit and first executive director of the Association of Tennis Professionals (ATP), galled at irresponsible players and opposed to the ATP revolt against the governing Men's Tennis Council (1988)

"Appearance money is bad for the integrity of the sport. If a guy is paid $100,000 to show up for a tournament where the first prize is $32,000, it's wrong."

—Marshall Happer, Men's International Professional Tennis Council (MIPTC) administrator (1983)

"I'd never vote to legalize guarantees. That's the day I'd resign. The situation is twice as bad as last year. The top 30 players could get guarantees, depending on the tournament. It used to be only fifteen."

—Arthur Ashe. From the 1983 exposé, *Short Circuit*

"If you're paid before you walk on the court, what's the point in playing as if your life depended on it?"

—Arthur Ashe, denouncing exhibitions and legitimate tournaments in which players receive appearance money

"It's like Willie Mays playing on Tuesday and Saturday and then going off to do home-run derby on the other days."

—Jack Kramer, founder of the Grand Prix circuit, advocating that players support the main tour and forego exhibitions

"If you hire a cleaning lady she must clean your room, otherwise you don't pay. I am raising the flag for world tennis."

—Czech Open tournament director Peter Kovarcik, refusing to pay top two seeds Yevgeny Kafelnikov and Goran Ivanisevic appearance money after their half-hearted efforts in lackluster first-round defeats (1999)

"It's ridiculous. Doesn't anybody have the courage to stand up and do the right thing?"

—Vijay Amritraj, disgusted at the preferential treatment accorded Bjorn Borg, who in 1982 refused to play the qualifying event as scheduled at the Alan King Classic, which delayed the start of the tournament because he was committed to play exhibitions in Japan. From the 1983 book, *Short Circuit*

"I don't know whether his ego got in the way, but a rule is a rule. If he made his choice, he should have stuck to it and not bitched about it. Can't he put himself out just a little bit for the privileges and rewards he's received from the game?"

> —John Alexander, denouncing Bjorn Borg's refusal to abide by the rules and play qualifying events. From the 1983 book, *Short Circuit*

"Tennis has to stop paying guarantees to the players. How bad is it that players take a guarantee, tank a match, and walk away with the money? It should go into prize money, because players have to earn the right to play."

> —Jim McIngvale, Houston multimillionaire and owner of the Tennis Masters Cup (2003)

"It's deceptive, it deceives the public. It's false advertising. There are cases where the loser in a tournament makes more than a winner. I think it's actually illegal what they're doing. If the Justice Department in the United States viewed it as they should, they'd put players in jail."

> —John Alexander, denouncing appearance money. From the 1983 exposé, *Short Circuit*

"Plain and simple, a guarantee is appearance money. A bribe."

> —Tony Trabert, 1950s champion and later a TV analyst. From his 1988 book, *Trabert on Tennis: The View from Center Court*

"It is certainly making players and us a lot of money, but personally it is very hard for me to justify because I think guarantees eventually dampen competitiveness and desire and intensity."

> —Donald Dell, then chairman of ProServ, a leading sports management company (1993)

"We played for tin cups. We would get appearance money. The press said we were tennis bums and were getting money under the table. The players today do the same thing [guarantees], but they're heroes."

> —Gardnar Mulloy, ninety, whose résumé includes three Davis Cup titles for the United States in the 1940s and five Grand Slam doubles titles (2003)

"The MTC [Men's Tennis Council] has failed to control the three biggest problems in the men's game—appearance money, exhibitions, and tanking."

—Gladys Heldman, in *World Tennis* magazine, which she founded (1989)

"Tennis does not need the Olympics. Those who advocate Olympic tennis believe it's an idea whose time has come. In fact, it's an idea whose time has passed."

—Cliff Drysdale, 1965 U.S. Championships finalist and current TV commentator, in *Tennis* magazine (1994)

"This is the greatest accomplishment I have ever had. To win a Grand Slam [title] is the greatest thing in the sport, but to win an Olympics is the biggest thing you can do in all sports."

—Andre Agassi, ecstatic after becoming the first U.S. tennis player since 1924 to win the men's singles gold medal (1996)

"How can you have a lousy half year and still be No. 8? It's a bunch of baloney. We're the only sport where every game doesn't count. You should not be allowed to have fifteen lousy results and they don't count because you have fourteen better ones."

—Ivan Lendl, denouncing the ATP ranking system that counted only a player's best fourteen tournaments (1993)

"Every time you step on the court, it should count. With the 'Best 14' system, that's not the case. You can play twenty-five or twenty-six events, lose in the first round in a number of them and still have a pretty high ranking. That's not good for the game."

—Pete Sampras (1996)

"To me, the ranking system is like giving a professional golfer mulligans. They could hit a bad shot and say, 'You know what, let's not count that one.' But we will count it if you hit a better one."

—Andre Agassi, on the "Best 14" ranking system (1996)

"How can you be No. 1 if you haven't won a Grand Slam?"

—Pete Sampras, on Australian Open runner-up Marcelo Rios's gaining the No. 1 ranking in March 1998, thanks to the defective "Best 14" ranking system (1998)

"You can be dead and still be No. 1."

> —Pete Sampras, on the ATP Tour's badly flawed ranking system (1999)

"Just because you're No. 1 on the computer doesn't mean you're the best player in the world."

> —Pete Sampras, denouncing the flawed ATP ranking system that enabled several players with relatively underwhelming records (like Marcelo Rios, Carlos Moya, and Yevgeny Kafelnikov) to gain the No. 1 spot during 1998–99 (1999)

"The Race really doesn't concern us."

> —Lleyton Hewitt, echoing the disdainful opinion of many players regarding the ATP Champions Race, which is promoted ahead of the rolling twelve-month rankings, now called the Entry System (2002)

"The Atlantic Ocean is the biggest problem we have. The factual power of tennis is in the States, but the theoretical power lies in Europe. That's the conflict. Endless problems arise from not really understanding each other's modes of thought and conduct."

> —Couturier and impresario Ted Tinling, whose international outlook and mediating skills often helped avert political crises in tennis (1983)

"All the credit's going to that Bollettieri. But she spends most of her time here."

> —Natalya Kochetkova, director of The Spartak Olympic Sports School in Moscow, aggrieved at media reports that glamorous teenage prodigy and Wimbledon semifinalist Anna Kournikova owes her success to coaching at the Bollettieri Tennis Academy for the past five years. Spartak coach Rosa Mukhamedzhanova presciently added, "We'll produce a lot more Kournikovas in the future." (1997)

"If we start implementing a tiebreaker [instead of a third set] in mixed doubles, eventually it's going to go to men's doubles and women's doubles, and in the long term, singles as well. And then tennis is no longer a true test of skill, and nothing like we've known it. We have a successful scoring system, and we're changing that. What they're doing to mixed doubles now is the beginning of the downfall of the whole game."

> —Todd Woodbridge, doubles great and president of the ATP Players Council, denouncing the ten-point super tiebreaker used to replace the entire deciding set in mixed doubles at the Australian Open (2001)

"We succeeded because the country's best players went to the battle-ground every day and beat the crap out of each other. Where is that battleground in America today?"

—Noted coach Nick Bollettieri, attributing the dearth of male American tennis stars to youngsters not training at top tennis academies such as his, where Andre Agassi, Jim Courier, Aaron Krickstein, and Jimmy Arias trained in the 1980s (2001)

"I've always said the slow balls favor the big guys, not the small guys. The big guys are strong enough to finish the points. The smaller guys have to hit through the ball a lot more to get the same pace."

—Harold Solomon, diminutive 1970s clay court standout, after Wimbledon used a softer Slazenger tennis ball it claimed was 7 percent slower in an effort to reduce rocket serving and increase the number of rallies (1995)

"I call tennis 'the lazy man's game' now. Guys rely on giant serves and huge groundstrokes, but little thought, strategy, or passion goes into it—or so it seems. That's largely why no one truly dominates the sport now. There's loads of talent out there—just look at players such as Lleyton Hewitt, Gustavo Kuerten, Yevgeny Kafelnikov, and Marat Safin. But does anybody have the fire of Connors, the dedication of Lendl, or the physical presence of Borg? Not that I'm aware of, at least not yet."

—John McEnroe. From his 2002 autobiography, *You Cannot Be Serious*

"More than anything else for a while, [John] McEnroe's antics cost the sport. It cost the administration of the sport its reputation. The idea took hold that the people running the sport were cowards, that they were afraid to put him down for his obviously rude and sometimes obscene behavior."

—From the 1995 book, *Arthur Ashe on Tennis*

"In baseball or football a player gets thrown out and a sub comes in. In tennis the match is over! What's the answer?"

—U.S. Open referee Mike Blanchard, confounded by the dilemma of defaulting a player—such as Ilie Nastase for nearly causing a riot during his turbulent match against John McEnroe—before a live audience of thousands and a television audience of millions (1979)

"Sure. For pluses and minuses, in every sport, bigger-than-life characters help transcend the sport. They create interest, they create writing, must-see TV. So that's important. Like the [New York] Yankees. Whether you love 'em or hate 'em, they're like the eight-hundred-pound gorilla."

—Brad Gilbert, former world-ranked No. 4 and later coach of Andre Agassi and Andy Roddick, when asked in an *Oakland Tribune* interview whether bad boys Connors and McEnroe were great for the game (2003)

"It irks me to hear people say that we didn't try too hard because there was no money riding on the outcome. [Today] the big money cushions the loss. When we played, if you lost, you got nothing. You just waited for the next tournament. So if any players killed themselves trying, *we* did."

—Vic Seixas, 1953 Wimbledon and 1954 U.S. champion. From his 1983 book, *Prime Time Tennis*

"The game is a scandal. But it doesn't get the public attention and scrutiny you'd expect. It's still played under the rug. In the papers and on TV it's rah-rah for tennis. . . . But a lot of hanky-panky goes on that no one knows about or cares about."

—Hall of Fame journalist and TV commentator Bud Collins. From the 1983 exposé, *Short Circuit*

"Beyond any question, the big game as played today far outstrips any all-court game of the past. . . . First, we believe that a Kramer or Gonzalez employing the big game of today would consistently beat a Tilden on grass playing his all-court game of 1920–25. Second, we are convinced that had Tilden lived in the 1960 era, he likewise would have adopted and mastered the big game style."

—From William F. Talbert and Bruce S. Old's 1962 classic book, *The Game of Singles in Tennis*

"If you took the athlete of my time in the 1950s and played him in 1987 under the same circumstances, he would be much stronger, play much harder, and therefore he would play better. If you took the player of 1987 and sent him back to the middle fifties, he wouldn't play any better than the players who were around then."

—Pancho Gonzalez, pro champion from 1954 to 1961

"If you set up a team match—players from the era of Open Tennis versus players from the pre–Open era—Tilden, Budge, Gonzalez, Laver, etc., our top ten versus their top ten . . . why, we'd kill them. Their first two hundred against our top two hundred, we'd get swamped."

> —Gardnar Mulloy, 1940s and '50s American star, contending that men's tennis is deeper than ever but not better at the top. From the 1985 book, *Remembrance of Games Past*

"I pity the neighbors on her wedding night."

> —Sir Peter Ustinov, actor, social critic, and tennisphile, on Monica Seles's eardrum-breaking grunting at Wimbledon (1990)

"When sportswomen make a little noise in the course of their endeavors—as the teenage champion Monica Seles is wont to do— there is something approaching a moral panic among media men. But sportswomen *do* makes noises; they also swear, scratch, spit, and probably *go to the bathroom* for all I know. . . . The only thing they [men] can do is give in and enjoy it. After all, hearing Seles play is about as close to experiencing the female orgasm as any of these stuffed shirts are likely to get."

> —Julie Burchill, in the *Mail on Sunday* (1992)

"In Germany, I ask a kid like Boris Becker to jump and he asks how high? In Britain they ask why?"

> —Ion Tiriac, on one reason the British haven't produced a Wimbledon champion since Fred Perry in the mid-1930s

"Grass tennis is the height of skill, for on grass spin, change of pace, speed, control, placement and steadiness, all play their true part and carry their correct value. Grass tennis may be won by strength, finesse, subtlety or a combination of all."

> —Bill Tilden. From his 1925 book, *Match Play and the Spin of the Ball*

"This is the most difficult to win. You have the crowd here, you have the heat here, you have the noise here."

> —Boris Becker, who won every Grand Slam event except the French Open, contending that the U.S. Open is the most challenging of the four Slams

"They spent $250 million on this incredible facility. They could have spent that money to build a roof over this court—which would have been fantastic. They could have used this [Arthur Ashe Stadium] for year-round events. Now we're sitting twiddling our thumbs."

> —John McEnroe, USA Network analyst, frustrated at the many rained-out matches at the U.S. Open and the low-tech sight of workers on their hands and knees wiping the court dry with towels (2003)

"The silliest of all Grand Slam decisions is playing the semis and finals on Saturday and Sunday. I'll say that until the end of time. You want to see guys play their best on the last day."

> —John McEnroe, who advocates a day of rest between the men's semis and finals at the U.S. Open (2003)

"This is the only competition in the world that I know of where you continue to play once it's over."

> —Australian Davis Cup captain John Fitzgerald, advocating the ITF decree that dead rubbers should no longer be played. He suggests teams substitute young players for an "exhibition" style match against similar opposition for dead rubbers (2003)

"There's no reason when a [series] is over to have to risk injury and losing. . . . You don't see them playing Game 7 of the World Series if it's over after Game 6."

> —Andre Agassi, who suffered a rib injury playing a dead rubber against Australian Darren Cahill in the 1990 Davis Cup final, on why he refused to play in a meaningless match against The Bahamas in the relegation round in 1993, and why Cup matches should end after the outcome is decided

"Why can a student go to college on a music scholarship and play professionally during the summer, but an athlete cannot go on an athletic scholarship and play professionally at all? Athletes are discriminated against. We are the only group who are restricted like that."

> —Billie Jean King, holding court in the press tent during the 1974 U.S. Open. From the 1975 book, *Carnival at Forest Hills: The Anatomy of a Tennis Tournament*

"A guy who goes to college signs away his career."

> —American qualifier Brian Vahaly, twenty-three, who graduated from the University of Virginia with a 3.5 grade-point average in the double major of finance and business management, after upsetting Juan Carlos Ferrero and Tommy Robredo to reach the 2003 Indian Wells quarterfinals

"I don't know any women who know the men's game. At the same time, I'm not sure men can really know the women's game. I mean, how would they know how women are feeling at a certain time of the month?"

> —John McEnroe, at a press conference, early in his tennis broadcasting career, where he suggested that women, including longtime friend Mary Carillo, a highly respected TV analyst, should not commentate on men's tennis. McEnroe later changed his mind and often shared the booth with Carillo and other women.

"Commentators, some popular ones, in fact, just talk too much. They feel it necessary to chatter away constantly. This may be entertaining, but I feel it does a disservice to the game and the viewers. After all, they're interested in the *game!*"

> —Tony Trabert. From his 1988 book, *Trabert on Tennis: The View from Center Court*

"There's no way I could beat Rod Laver, Stan Smith, or Pancho Gonzalez. But I think at some time in the future we may very well have a woman win the world championship of tennis."

> —Billie Jean King. From her 1974 book, *Billie Jean King's Secrets of Winning Tennis*

"The players say they 'make' the tournaments and that's bullshit. The best players in the world were here this week and the revenue to this tournament from TV is 5 percent of what Wimbledon and the others make. Did the top players 'make' Indian Wells? Wimbledon's TV rights are enormous because they have spent years and years making their event important. The last thing the Grand Slams are going to do is hand money over to an organization that's always fighting."

> —Bob Kain, president of IMG's Americas division, talking to a British newspaper (2003)

"The problem is so bad that you might as well just let them use it and when players see people dying on court and exploding, then it's going to change their minds. People are just happy to sacrifice their health for three years of fame."

> —Australian player Andrew Ilie, on the drug problem in pro tennis. Ilie's claims were dismissed by a number of rivals on the men's tour. (2003)

"The bottom line is the promotion of our game sucks. It's like we've evolved into two different tours. One gets everything poured into it and the other one gets table scraps."

> —Doubles standout Sandon Stolle, son of 1960s star Fred Stolle, protesting various ATP tour proposals that diminish doubles

"The lack of attention to press people *by* tennis people is appalling. At most major tournaments, unless you're a byline from the *New York Times* or *Sports Illustrated,* you are treated like a bad smell. In other words, the quicker you can get rid of it, the better. . . . What players, sponsors, and officials can't comprehend is that without the media, there are no players, sponsors, or officials. There's no game."

> —Gene Scott, in an incisive *Tennis Week* column decrying the near-zero status of the media (2004)

"Tennis is a very human game facing a great danger that it will be strangulated in a cat's cradle of unnecessary or inhumane rules."

> —Ted Tinling, involved with the game for more than sixty years as a tennis couturier, impresario, historian, and author (1990)

"Big-time tennis will go on in spite of itself."

> —Bill Tilden

"If I could change tennis, it would be organizing all the bodies of tennis. It's sort of absurd to have so many people, so many organizations, working separately—in some cases, arguably, even against each other—for sponsorship dollars, for air time, for branding. If everybody literally put aside their own agendas and they came together and sold tennis as an entire package, worldwide, all the year, the amount of growth and progress you would see would be incredible."

> —Tennis champion Andre Agassi, proposing the creation of a commissioner as a means of unifying the disparate factions (2003)

"We should blow it up and start all over again. The sport is evolving, but the structure is not. It is the same old scenario. Everybody wants to hold on to their little tournament or little patch, and they are not really looking at what is best for the game. Something needs to be done now."

—Martina Navratilova, with a stark state-of-the-game message (2003)

"Certainly there does not appear to be anything much wrong with the game of tennis itself, although proposals for changing it always are with us. There has been little change since the rules were settled upon and possibly improvement can be had by changing some rules, but a game so stylized as tennis should be treated with great restraint. One of the things wrong may be that so many people keep trying to alter it to suit other people who do not really play it."

—Al Laney, a distinguished tennis writer for the *New York Herald Tribune*. From his 1968 memoir, *Covering the Court: A Fifty-Year Love Affair with the Game of Tennis*

THE EGO HAS LANDED

"I am beautiful, famous, and gorgeous."

> —Anna Kournikova's favorite expression, according to her mother Alla (1998)

"It's just another record for me. I mean, I have so many records already."

> —Martina Hingis, after winning the 1997 Australian Open, asked what becoming the youngest player in the twentieth century to win a Grand Slam singles title—at sixteen years, three months, and twenty-six days—meant to her

"I'm number one in the world. Unless that changes soon, I have a right to be arrogant."

> —Martina Hingis, who owned the No. 1 tennis ranking for eighty straight weeks until Lindsay Davenport dethroned her (1998)

"She's very pretty, but I'm sure she would like to change places with me if she could and have four Grand Slam titles."

> —Martina Hingis, comparing herself favorably with sex symbol Anna Kournikova, in *Sports Illustrated* (1998)

"The era isn't over until I say it's over."

> —Dethroned but proud champion Martina Navratilova, after failing to win a Grand Slam title for the first time since 1980 (1988)

"She's a good athlete; I'm a great athlete."

> —Serena Williams, comparing herself with Steffi Graf (1999)

"I just feel I can make any shot on the court. I always felt that way. I always felt I could beat the men players. My parents never told me that I couldn't."

>—Venus Williams, seventeen and ranked No. 66, after losing to Martina Hingis in the 1997 U.S. Open final

"In my mind, I'm always the best. I can't see anybody better than me."

>—Venus Williams after winning her second straight Wimbledon (2001)

"If I did as well on the court as I do off the court, I'd be No. 1 by now."

>—"Broadway" Vitas Gerulaitis, popular 1970s playboy

"I'm not going to sit here and tell you I'm the greatest ever. Did you ever hear Laver say he was the greatest ever?"

>—Pete Sampras (2000)

"It's all the time, 'Tiger Woods, Tiger Woods.' I am better than he is. I've been on top longer and I am younger. I'm just better."

>—Martina Hingis (1997)

"I had a great year. You know, what can I improve? Sometimes I ask myself."

>—Martina "Hubris" Hingis, after winning three of the four Grand Slams at age sixteen (1997)

"You won, but I'm prettier and more marketable than you."

>—What Anna Kournikova reportedly blurted to Martina Hingis, after the older Hingis embarrassed her 6–0, 6–0 in the junior U.S. Open (1994)

"Martina asked if I thought I was the queen—because the real queen was her."

>—Anna Kournikova, telling a Chilean newspaper about the catfight that caused Hingis to dump her as a doubles partner (2002)

"I'm glad you're doing this story on us and not on the WNBA. We're so much prettier than all the other women in sports."

>—Martina Hingis, in *Detour* magazine (1998)

"I know I am the best tennis coach in the world. I have no doubts about that."

> —Nick Bollettieri. From his 1996 autobiography, *My Aces, My Faults*

"My greatest strength is that I have no weaknesses."

> —John McEnroe (1979)

"I would say tennis needs me more, but I need tennis, too."

> —John McEnroe, returning to the circuit from a break (1988)

"If you believe in someone up above, that person, for whatever reason, wanted me to play tennis. . . . Believe it or not, I think God had an enjoyable time watching my tantrums."

> —John McEnroe, even invoking The Almighty during his long-winded, forty-five-minute speech at his induction into the International Tennis Hall of Fame in Newport, Rhode Island (1999)

"I take things by the throat and shake them and stand by what I do, right or wrong. You'll be sorry when I'm gone."

> —Jimmy Connors (1985)

"Nobody reminds me of me."

> —Inimitable Jimmy Connors, asked if his conqueror in the U.S. Open semifinals, Jim Courier, reminded him of himself (1991)

"This girl must be mad. Does she think she can come and beat me on my home courts?"

> —The incomparable Suzanne Lenglen, who hadn't lost a match in nearly seven years, when she learned rising American star Helen Wills Moody was playing the Riviera circuit and forcing a long-awaited showdown (1926)

"I could go *beyond* No. 1. With the way I play and my height and aggressiveness and courage and no fear, I could change the game. It's like Michael Jordan and the rest of the players in the NBA. He was a step ahead of everyone else."

> —Supremely confident Venus Williams at age fourteen, sounding like the early Ali (1994)

"With the way I play and my height and aggressiveness and courage and no fear, I could change the game."—Venus Williams, at age fourteen (*Susan Mullane/Camerawork USA, Inc.*)

"It's the business that wants this and we're playing the game, me and Anna and Venus. We're the Spice Girls of tennis."

—Martina Hingis, the ever-smiling Swiss Miss at age eighteen (1998)

"No, I don't consider myself to be a representative of my people. I am thinking of me and nobody else."

—African American tennis pioneer Althea Gibson, when a reporter asked if she was proud to be compared to baseball pioneer Jackie Robinson as an outstanding representative of her race after she won Wimbledon (1957)

"Nobody, but nobody, knows more about tennis than I do."

—Bombastic TV sports broadcaster Howard Cosell (1979)

"I'm more of a celebrity than the players. The only players I'm not more of a celebrity than are Venus and Serena, which is really amazing."

—Richard Williams, highly controversial father/coach/manager of stars Venus and Serena (1998)

"I think I would agree on that. It doesn't matter whether you have class. The only thing is what you think of yourself. And right now, I'm the king of tennis."

> —Richard Williams, on being described by Jennifer Capriati as having "no class" (2002)

"I touch everyone. Everyone wants to see me. I don't blame them: Got to get a look at Serena."

> —Serena Williams, whose thrilling 6–3, 7–6 U.S. Open final victory increased CBS's TV ratings by an astonishing 100 percent over the '98 final (1999)

"We're strong, we're very strong. We're making it happen in different ways. We're bringing in new power. We can run fast, we can jump high, we can last. We have it all."

> —Serena Williams, on the many winning attributes she shares with sister Venus (2000)

"I'm really exciting. I smile a lot. I win a lot and I'm really sexy."

> —Serena Williams, unburdened by false modesty, after winning her first Wimbledon singles title (2002)

"I don't like Vic Braden getting credit for rolling a ball to her in the crib and Emerson getting credit for her serve, when it hasn't changed. Maybe it's an ego sort of thing. I've done it and I've done it all. It's like a work of art. An artist would feel robbed if someone else put his name on a painting."

> —Highly regarded coach Robert Lansdorp, on his prize student, Tracy Austin (1979)

"I think I'm one of the toughest guys mentally on the tour. I think I'm one of the quickest guys. You know, passing shots, returns. I think I'm up there with the best of them."

> —World-ranked No. 1 Lleyton Hewitt, not hiding his talents under a bushel (2002)

"When you become a top player, you think that nothing else and nobody else matters. You can tell everybody on earth, 'Listen, I'm playing tennis, I don't have time for you. I'm in the semifinals of the U.S. Open, screw everybody and everything else.'"

> —Former No. 1 Mats Wilander (1995)

"They are trying to turn us into money whores. It's obscene. They say 'a million.' And then you say, 'No.' And then they offer— because they think everybody has his price—three million. And then you say, 'No' again. It feels good to know that I don't come cheap."

> —Boris Becker, whose personal worth was then estimated at $30 million but could have been several times more if he didn't reject most of the commercial opportunities he was offered, in *Esquire* magazine (1992)

"I'm like an expensive menu. You can look at it, but you can't afford it."

> —Anna Kournikova (2001)

"A copy is never as good as the original."

> —Anna Kournikova, on the media comparing rising young players with her through nicknames, such as "the new Anna" and "the American Anna" (2002)

HOMOSEXUALITY

"What kind of a game can it be if the best player of all time was a fag?"

> —A comment Bud Collins heard many times during his first fifteen years as a sportswriter—which he labeled "the Tilden Turnoff." From his 1989 book, *My Life with the Pros*

"Martina is a poor role model for young players like my daughter because she is a lesbian."

> —Margaret Court, recordholder for career Grand Slam titles (62), blasting Martina Navratilova (1990)

"It is very sad for children to be exposed to homosexuality. Martina is a nice person. Her life has just gone astray."

> —Margaret Court, a born-again minister living in Perth, Australia (1990)

"If someone wants to be a homophobe, that's their right. I can't change them. I feel sorry for people like that because what scares them is the unknown. . . . I've always tried to educate people by example, by being a good person. That's all I can do."

> —Martina Navratilova, responding to Margaret Court's public criticism (1990)

"Martina has been a role model for me. . . . We should judge her on what she did on the court, not on her private life."

> —Chris Evert, defending Martina Navratilova (1990)

"I'd rather you slept with a different man every night than sleep with a woman."

—Mirek Navratil, Martina Navratilova's stepfather in Czechoslovakia, on learning of her homosexuality. From Navratilova's 1985 autobiography, *Martina*

"I've asked a lot of writers this: 'Have you ever asked male athletes if they were gay?' None of them have, but many of them ask women athletes if they are gay. They treat male athletes differently. Even when they know there are some gay guys out there, they protect them."

—Champion and gay-rights activist Martina Navratilova (1996)

"Are you still the alternative?"

—Martina Navratilova's rejoinder to a male reporter who asked, "Are you still a lesbian?"

"Wouldn't you want me in the front lines?"

—Martina Navratilova, a muscular 5'8½" and 145 pounds, on whether gays should serve in the military

"It happens in the best of families."

—Message on the gay pride T-shirt worn by Martina Navratilova in post-match conferences at Wimbledon (1993)

"Who in their right mind would choose to be gay and be ostracized? It's not a choice."

—Martina Navratilova, the world's most prominent gay athlete (2003)

"However, even more harmful to the sport's reputation is the widespread suspicion that the game attracts homosexuals of both sexes more than other sports do. As far as men's tennis goes, I know from forty-four years of exposure to hundreds and hundreds of players that the suspicion has no foundation in fact."

—Bobby Riggs. From his 1973 autobiography, *Court Hustler*

"I don't see any evidence of homosexuality among the men. Maybe it's in reaction against the Tilden era, which was impregnated with it. Tennis has become a very macho, young-lion situation. They growl and they bark. It's a fine breed of guys, very fine."

—Ted Tinling, tennis couturier and historian. From the 1983 book, *Short Circuit*

"If you don't date a lot, you're thought of as a lesbian. Most of us are uptight about talking about it because we're always accused of it, and because most of the time when we're approached about it, it's like 'Ho, ho, that's perverted.' For myself, I wouldn't be interested, but I don't think anyone has a right to put somebody down for it."

> —Attractive tour player Kris Kemmer. From the 1974 book, *A Long Way, Baby—Behind the Scenes in Women's Pro Tennis*

"She travels with her girlfriend, she is half a man."

> —Martina Hingis on openly gay Amelie Mauresmo, her victim in the Australian Open final (1999)

"Hingis was stupid for what she said. She was out of line. I don't have a lot to say about it. It is her problem."

> —Amelie Mauresmo's reply to Hingis's "half a man" remark (1999)

"Unfortunately, you guys love to write the worst line possible. You've probably hurt a very nice girl. She's an incredible player, and I'm sorry all this happened. I learned my lesson. I'm not going to say anything at all about anything anymore. And you guys can have the most boring press conferences ever. And I don't think any player will give a crap."

> —World-ranked No. 1 Lindsay Davenport, angry that newspapers implied she had criticized the gayness of her powerfully built Australian Open conqueror, Amelie Mauresmo, when Davenport said, "A couple times I thought I was playing a guy" (1999)

"I couldn't stand it if Jelena turned out to be one of them. I'd kill myself."

> —Damir Dokic, the bizarre father of world top tenner Jelena Dokic, who claims that more than 40 percent of women players are lesbians (2002)

"They're homophobic. They know very little about it. . . . I think being labeled by your sexuality is shocking. You should be talked about as a person. You shouldn't have discrimination because of your sexuality."

> —Billie Jean King, who came out near the end of her tennis career, criticizing the media for its poor handling of Amelie Mauresmo's announcement that she is a lesbian (1999)

"It's an absolute jungle out there. A big, bad place. It just isn't a normal place for a young girl. As her mother, I want to make sure she's okay. The biggest threats to girls her age are the other girls on the tour. I always chaperone her. I never let her alone for a minute."

> —Samantha Stevenson, minus any proof, alleging that predatory lesbians on the tour endangered her daughter Alexandra (1999)

"There's no such thing as a predatory lesbian. It doesn't exist. I mean, in the locker room there's never ever been anything inappropriate done or said in my presence. This is just a stereotypical view based on old prejudices that has nothing to do with the truth. It's an insult to me."

> —Martina Navratilova, angered at Samantha Stevenson's contention that she has to chaperone her daughter Alexandra everywhere for fear of lesbian approaches in the locker room (1999)

"I've been on the tour for eighteen years and I've never seen anything."

> —Chris Evert, rebutting allegations that lesbianism is a major problem on the women's circuit (1989)

"In all my years on the tour, I was never, even in the remotest possible manner, approached by another player for sexual reasons. The lesbians I know would never think of proselytizing younger players, in a shower or anywhere else."

> —Billie Jean King. From her 1982 autobiography, *Billie Jean*

"Female athletes are stereotyped by the general population—and usually as homosexuals. And that is our bond. No, not that we are homosexuals, but that we are stereotyped. . . . All female athletes feel that we are treated unfairly in this regard by the public."

> —Billie Jean King. From her 1982 autobiography, *Billie Jean*

"Subaru was a big breakthrough for the gay community. I don't think being gay is going to stand in the way anymore for athletes."

> —Martina Navratilova, the world's most well-known gay athlete, after belatedly appearing in her first major TV commercial, for Subaru vehicles (2001)

"Women tennis players have always maintained that there were more gay men than women on the tour, and that mostly male sportswriters would never question a male player's sexuality or write sly innuendo."

—Robert Lipsyte and Peter Levine. From the 1995 book, *Idols of the Game*

"The female player's way of life rapidly begins to militate against her cultivation of traditional heterosexual relationships. . . . Many women who may not be biologically programmed as lesbians make their lives complete, if not necessarily whole, by becoming gay. This decision represents a total surrender to the demands of the profession."

—Peter Bodo. From his 1995 book, *The Courts of Babylon: Tales of Greed and Glory in the Harsh New World of Professional Tennis*

"The tour lifestyle is too tough for a woman alone. That's when some of the homosexual relationships start. What happens is a girl who's been out on the tour for a few years gets depressed. She's probably had a steady boyfriend, but the distance or something broke that up, and she's vulnerable."

—Pam Shriver. From her 1986 book, *Passing Shots: Pam Shriver on Tour*

THE GOD SQUAD

"I would have won six Wimbledon titles, instead of three, if I'd known then what I know today about the study of the word of God and the power of it."

—Margaret Court, holder of a record sixty-two Grand Slam titles and now a minister in Perth, Australia

"I guess the Good Lord was not on my side that day."

—Margaret Court, on her 6–2, 6–1 "Mother's Day Massacre" at the hands of Bobby Riggs in 1973. From her 1975 book, *Court on Court: A Life in Tennis*

"I will not play any more tournament tennis. If I had been meant to play tennis again, God would have led me to it."

—Margaret Court

"My only regret in a life filled with many 'firsts' is that I did not make Jesus the Lord of my life until I almost retired from tennis. Losses would have been rare had I had His presence within me, knowing how to renew my mind to God's scriptures to control and reject fear and concern, bringing peace and security, self-confidence and self-esteem by knowing who I really was in Christ."

—Margaret Court, in *Tennis Life Magazine*, South Africa

"Jesus Loves You! M. Chang"

—How Michael Chang signs autographs

"I've realized that no matter what, I'm never alone, because He's with me. If you don't have faith in Jesus, it's difficult to deal with things. When I don't know what to do, I say, 'Okay, God, it's Yours—You take care of it!' "

—Nicole Arendt, in *Sports Spectrum* magazine

"If tennis is all you have, if it's all you live for, then you're bound to get hurt. . . . I don't like to go around preaching about it, but my faith has become my foundation. It helps me to keep everything in perspective, and it helps me to see that the bad times are as much part of the ultimate plan as the good times."

—Mary Joe Fernandez, who was raised a Catholic. From the 1995 book, *The Courts of Babylon: Tales of Greed and Glory in the Harsh World of Professional Tennis*

"If I know a call is wrong, I would rather correct it. I do it because of my Christianity."

—Camille Benjamin (1987)

"I am playing for God."

—What 1976 French Open champion Sue Barker once announced on the court

"God is on our side."

—Message emblazoned on a sweater worn by Pat Cash at Wimbledon (1992)

"Wouldn't it have been amazing if I hadn't played on Sunday? It would have made a huge impact on tennis, and maybe the world."

—Stan Smith, 1971 U.S. Open and 1972 Wimbledon champion and a devout Christian, in the *Naples Daily News*

"I like to go to church. It's so nice and peaceful inside. You come out and you feel clean. Everything dirty is gone."

—Anna Kournikova

"The tour breeds a selfishness, where everything is focused on the player. The Lord had to deal with me about this aspect, and show me the servant's attitude of following Him, of allowing Him to use me to minister to others. This is a constant struggle, for the flesh is still present, the human, selfish nature that wants to fulfill itself."

> —Camille Benjamin, 1980s and '90s player, in the Tennis Ambassadors Christian Ministry *Love to Serve* Newsletter (2000)

"Tennis has followed most of the other sports in terms of the pressure of increased prize money, the intensity, the parental involvement and everything. Often it's not even fun anymore. It's just too tough—the pressures and the temptations are too great. More than ever, if a young person is going to go in that direction, they need to have such a solid foundation in the Lord. There's no other way to keep your life on track."

> —Betsy Nagelsen, 1978 Australian Open finalist and wife of IMG founder Mark McCormack, in the *Love to Serve Newsletter,* Tennis Ambassadors Christian Ministry (2000)

"My interest in life is personal growth. Faith in God is the strongest part of my life."

> —Andre Agassi (1993)

"I am blessed with a talent, and I have an obligation to the Lord to make the most of it."

> —Andre Agassi. From the 1997 book, *The Tennis Lover's Book of Wisdom*

"It all starts with the Lord and ends with the Lord. I'm not interested in material gifts."

> —Gloria Connors, mother/coach of superstar Jimmy Connors, on becoming a born-again Christian after her mother died in 1972, in a 1978 *SPORT* magazine article

"I go out there and do my best, but whatever happens is the Lord's will."

> —Gene Mayer, who prayed for fifteen minutes before the 1977 Stockholm Open final and then played brilliantly to beat Ray Moore

"If, with God's help, I cannot beat my opponent, I accept defeat as something that was ordained."

> —Althea Gibson, 1950s champion. From the 1997 book, *The Tennis Lover's Book of Wisdom*

"I do not believe that because we cannot scientifically and objectively prove the existence of God, we can therefore dispense with religion and the Bible. I know that I turn my back on God only at my peril. This I shall never do."

—Arthur Ashe. From his 1993 memoir, *Days of Grace*

"It's number one in my life. If it weren't for God, I wouldn't have anything. Religion has helped me realize who I am. It's helped me not to get ahead of myself and not to get bombastic. It keeps me humble."

—Serena Williams, a devout Jehovah's Witness (1998)

"Vengeance belongs to God. . . . I am just here to play tennis."

—Serena Williams, before her victorious Australian Open semi-final with Kim Clijsters who had beaten the American in their last big match (2003)

"I'm a Jehovah's Witness, we don't really vote. No matter what happens, we'll be all right."

—Venus Williams (2001)

"God will protect us. I trust in God and not in people. People make mistakes. God is watching over us."

—Venus Williams, telling Belgium's *De Morgen* newspaper she is not afraid of the impending war in Iraq (2003)

"Why is it always expected that you have to hate your sister? That's not normal. Jealousy isn't normal, either. The Bible says jealousy is rottenness to the bone. It is. It will get you crazy."

—Venus Williams, dismissing the notion that her sibling rivalry with Serena is harming their relationship, in the *Telegraph* (UK) (2003)

"My game is better suited to grass. I don't think Borg can stay back and be effective. God is my guru."

—Sandy Mayer, before losing in straight sets to Bjorn Borg in the Wimbledon quarterfinals (1978)

"I feel that every match should be played as if Christ were the only one in the audience. And what you should do is to play the match as He would want you to, carry yourself in a way that is Christ-like."

—Former world-ranked No. 4 Gene Mayer, in *Tennis* magazine (1980)

"I pray, but I don't pray to win. I pray for the inspiration to give my best."

> —Althea Gibson. From the 1997 book, *The Tennis Lover's Book of Wisdom*

"My relationship with God is basically very simple. I put everything in God's hands. I don't worry. That's made a huge difference in my tennis game, as it has in my life."

> —Mary Pierce, attributing her more relaxed attitude to having "God in my life" (2000)

"I had a better relationship with Jesus Christ."

> —The reason Michael Chang once gave for winning a close match

"I have always held a strong feeling that God granted me a measure of on-court success because that allowed me the chance to tell others about Jesus Christ. That's why I have seen myself as an evangelist with a tennis racket ever since I won the French Open."

> —Michael Chang. From his 2002 autobiography, *Holding Serve*

"I know every time I bring up the Lord Jesus' name everybody nods. I know you're becoming sick of it, but it's the truth. He gets all the credit."

> —Michael Chang, after hearing some boos in his victory speech after the French Open final (1989)

"The link between sports and Christianity is tenuous at best. The athlete talks in generalities about 'glorifying God,' but is there anything noble about the brushback, the intentional foul, or a blindside hit? Yet these are all a part of sports that we accept, and even embrace."

> —Ted Kluck, American sportswriter (2002)

PERSONALITY CULT

"The player owes as much to the gallery as the actor owes the audience."

> —"Big Bill" Tilden, voted the best tennis player of the first half of the twentieth century in a 1950 Associated Press poll

"It's the people out here who make or break you. The priority is to entertain them."

> —Andre Agassi, eighteen-year-old rising star (1988)

"To be a great performer, a great athlete, you've got to really enjoy the limelight, like [Michael] Jordan, or any of us, and that's one of her biggest plusses."

> —Billie Jean King on Serena Williams (2003)

"They've been probably the best thing that's happened to tennis. Everything they say or even dad [Richard] says . . . you guys have a heart attack about and write it all over the place. They give us so much exposure. They create all this drama for the sport."

> —Lindsay Davenport on the importance of Venus and Serena Williams (2001)

"You've got to have all types of people in the game. Like Connors and McEnroe who people either hate or love. But a guy like Borg can be boring. It's fine for him to be self-controlled and private, but this game is still a show. You've got to realize that."

> —Pancho Gonzalez, charismatic 1950s champion (1980)

"If all players behaved like me, nobody would come to watch tennis."

> —Brian Gottfried, quiet former No. 5. From the 1983 book, *Short Circuit*

"It's like all of my press conferences at the moment are about Venus and Serena. I would really appreciate it if they were about my tennis or something."

> —Cheerful but uncontroversial Kim Clijsters, then ranked No. 1 (2003)

"With his talent and emotion, [Gonzalez] deserves to be on a pedestal with the most flamboyant celebrities—Babe Ruth, Arnold Palmer, Joe Namath, among others."

> —Pulitzer Prize–winning journalist Dave Anderson. From his 1973 book, *Return of a Champion: Pancho Gonzalez' Golden Year 1964*

"Everybody had a different game back then—and their own personality. Gerulaitis was the New Yorker. Nastase was the crazy Romanian. Newcombe the beer-drinking Australian. Panatta the spaghetti-eating Italian. Me. McEnroe. Borg. Today you see one, you've seen them all."

> —Jimmy Connors, in the *San Jose Mercury News* (1994)

"When there are 10,000 people in the stands and the television cameras are there, we are all actors. There is the serious one, the one who always screams at the umpire, the one who never says a word, the one who is a clown."

> —Yannick Noah, tennis champion and entertainer (1988)

"I do have a personality. The people that know me know that."

> —Pete Sampras (1995)

"To have someone tell me that I ought to make an effort to be more exciting is just the biggest load of garbage. We're all different."

> —Pete Sampras, replying to John McEnroe's suggestion that he try to be more colorful (1995)

"Large numbers of so-called sports fans all over the civilized world attend events to be entertained, and neither superb execution nor sportsmanship satisfies them. These oafs sit in the stands in anticipation of vulgarity, brutality, and embarrassment. . . . After cringing over the deplorable conduct of my countryman, McEnroe, I take heart in Sampras' manners and his colossal achievements. Possibly, the long decline in manners that began in American athletics with Muhammad Ali and Joe Namath is over."

> —Columnist R. Emmett Tyrrell Jr., criticizing the British for complaining that gentlemanly Pete Sampras is boring (1995)

"A little one."

> —Reserved champion Stefan Edberg, on whether he has a personality

"If I'm boring, it's not my fault."

> —Stefan Edberg, exemplary sportsman and formerly ranked No.1

"I don't go to tennis matches to watch personalities. I go to watch tennis and I judge players by their abilities. You can go to Sea World if you want personalities."

> —Roy Emerson, in *Tennis Week* magazine (1994)

"The worse I play, the people they like me more, I don't know why."

> —Goran Ivanisevic (2000)

"They're the least accessible athletes that I know of. You can't get to them. They spend very little time talking to the press. That hurts them, hurts the game, because you don't get to know them as well."

> —Hall of Famer Tony Trabert, on today's tennis pros (2002)

"He's very evolved, more than in his linear years. He's very in the moment."

> —Actress/singer Barbra Streisand, in praise of Andre Agassi

"They [John McEnroe, Ivan Lendl, and Jimmy Connors] weren't the nicest people in the world, they were the most selfish tennis players, but they were great for the game. Tennis needs players who don't care about pleasing the sponsors, who don't care about being nice."

> —Mats Wilander, a nice guy himself as a 1980s star (1999)

"I think we're the last of our kind. Guys who know tennis is not just sport but a form of entertainment. Character, showmen, eccentrics, or whatever."

—Jimmy Connors in the *Daily Telegraph* (UK) (1992)

"We are professionals. The crowd must be allowed to participate. New Yorkers want blood."

—Jimmy Connors, on involving the rowdy U.S. Open spectators (1976)

"The characters like myself, Nastase, McEnroe, and Gerulaitis don't exist anymore. When you had the characters, you didn't appreciate them. Now you don't have them and you're begging for them."

—Jimmy Connors (1999)

"There is a 'demand' for 'personalities,' because that's the kind of age we're living in. Laver, Rosewall, Ashe: these were dynamic and exemplary figures; they didn't need 'personality' because they had character."

—Martin Amis, in the *New Yorker* (1994)

"I wish I was playing in the Connors-McEnroe-Borg era, when they had more personalities. They had the rivalries, and there are times I wish I was part of that. At other times I wish I was part of the Laver-Rosewall era, because image and society and media were different then. They just cared about the tennis."

—Pete Sampras (1997)

"I didn't always think of myself as an entertainer until I realized, when I started playing in bigger venues, that it's my job. When I fill out a job application, expect 'entertainer.'"

—Serena Williams (2002)

RACE MATTERS

"He [Arthur Ashe] took the burden of race and wore it as a cloak of dignity."

—Andrew Young, former U.S. delegate to the United Nations

"Through whatever combination of factors, black Americans today make up a substantial proportion of America's top athletes in most of the major sports. But that has not been true in tennis because the sport has been organized in ways that have discouraged black participation."

—Arthur Ashe (1988)

"We faced a lot of problems because of racial discrimination in those days. When we traveled to play Purdue or Indiana, we used to send our white teammates into restaurants to get sandwiches and we'd eat in the car."

—Robert Ryland, the hero of young Arthur Ashe and a Wayne State University standout, who in 1946 was one of the first two blacks to compete in the NCAA Tennis Championships

"Given the same chance as others have had, blacks could dominate tennis in as little as ten to fifteen years just as they have dominated in other sports."

—Arthur Ashe (1988)

"It [black domination] will create problems because their behavior, speech, and dress is just a completely different culture. Tennis is a

162

very conservative game with deep roots in Victorian English moral codes and traditions. Minorities—in particular, inner-city minorities—have cultural norms that are diametrically opposite those of upper-middle and upper-class white American standards."

—Arthur Ashe (1988)

"Obviously blacks have walked into basketball, baseball, and football, and they are tremendous athletes. If tennis is anything like other sports, whites won't be able to compete with them."

—John McEnroe (1990)

"The next black Grand Slam winner is more likely to be a woman than a man. . . . The best male black athletes are still playing basketball and running track."

—Arthur Ashe. From the 1992 book, *Tough Draw*

"It remains to be seen if blacks have what it takes to adapt to the rigors of tennis. We are always hearing about how blacks are so good at jumping and sprinting, but apart from [Arthur] Ashe and [Althea] Gibson, there hasn't been any who has risen to the top. Maybe it has something to do with nature."

—ITF President Philippe Chatrier (1982)

"You can't compare tennis with baseball, basketball, or football. When Jackie Robinson broke the color line in 1947 with the Brooklyn Dodgers, dozens of good baseball players in the Negro leagues were waiting to follow. When Althea Gibson, the first prominent black in tennis, won national grass-court titles at Forest Hills in 1957 and 1958, there was no reservoir of black talent waiting to walk in if the door ever opened. Blacks had no identification with the sport—on or off the court."

—Arthur Ashe. From his 1981 book, *Off the Court*

"If Noah were white and had short hair, he would be [ranked] No. 50."

—Boris Becker on highly athletic but groundstroke-deficient Yannick Noah, in *World Tennis* magazine (1990)

"What we need is an American Yannick Noah. In many respects, I wasn't a very good role model. We need someone who's got flair and can play in-your-face tennis. And he should comport himself like Julius Erving."

—Arthur Ashe (1987)

"Nobody has ever walked up to my daughters and said hello. They look the other way. They want them to be their Stepin Fetchit."

—Oracene Price, mother of Venus and Serena Williams

"In the field of sports you are more or less accepted for what you do rather than what you are."

—Althea Gibson, first black champion in tennis. From Ashton Applewhite's *And I Quote* (1992)

"When you look at it, I heard something [racist] once or twice in all the matches I've played in my life. It wasn't very often. People in the heat of battle might say something they might not ordinarily say."

—African American Rodney Harmon, 1982 U.S. Open quarterfinalist and then Director of Multicultural Development for the United States Tennis Association, who grew up in Richmond, Virginia, and was an All-American at Southern Methodist University in Texas, in a Reuters story (2001)

"It takes money to be a tennis player, sweetheart, simple as that, and black folks don't have that kind of money. Lessons, racquets, balls, shoes, travel expenses—the black family just can't afford it the way whites can. Then the white kids who don't have money can get sponsors. But if you're black, forget it. Who wants to sponsor a black unless he's Arthur Ashe?"

—Tour player Sylvia Hooks, on the dearth of blacks in pro tennis. From the 1974 book, *A Long Way, Baby—Behind the Scenes in Women's Pro Tennis*

"The cover-up is the USTA's superficial interest in discovering tennis talent in America. . . . From appearances, it seems like a blatant plan to lock out, shut out, and close the doors on inner-city kids. . . . The NJTL (National Junior Tennis League) needs to become more serious because for a certainty the USTA has failed. It seems that the USTA has made a complete example of how not to embrace poor people in America."

> —Richard Williams, charging that whatever the USTA has done at the grassroots and elite levels for African American players with its $2.2 million Multicultural Development Program (out of its whopping $160 million budget), it amounts to little short of a cover-up (2000). In *Florida Tennis* magazine (2002)

"Blacks are athletically stronger because they are naturally built like athletes and do not require much physical training at all. They also learn sports quite easily. Thousands of African athletes have never taken lessons from a teacher or coach to develop their natural talent, yet they still perform at an impressive level."

> —Nicolas Ayeboua, executive director of the Confederation of African Tennis and ITF Development Officer for Africa (2000). From *Tennis Confidential: Greatest Players, Matches, and Controversies* (2002)

"Since the first known study of differences between black and white athletes in 1928, the data have been remarkably consistent: in most sports, African-descended athletes have the capacity to do better with their raw skills than whites."

> —Jon Entine. From his 2000 book, *Taboo: Why Black Athletes Dominate Sports and Why We're Afraid to Talk About It*

"If Africans have a third of what Europeans or Americans have, they will dominate tennis for sure."

> —Nicolas Ayeboua (2000). From *Tennis Confidential: Greatest Players, Matches, and Controversies* (2002)

"A lot of people think that black people can't rally and just think they're athletes and can't think. As you can see, that's not true. I can rally. Venus can rally."

> —Serena Williams, after being asked how she rallied so successfully from the baseline against Martina Hingis

"Hi, racist."

> —How Ilie Nastase used to greet South African pros in the 1970s

"It's a terrible thing. When I play, 99 percent of the time, I'm the only black male out there. It seems almost normal. But it's not normal because tennis is the perfect sport for black people. There is a lot of athletic ability needed to play tennis now, and I think blacks would make it so much more entertaining."

—Ronald Agenor, in *Black Tennis* magazine (1991)

"Dr. Johnson [patron of aspiring young African American players] told us no matter what happened, no matter what went against us, we should always show no emotion around whites. I guess that's why I seem so emotionless on the court. You'll never know how I really feel inside. You'll just see nothing, or you'll see me politely smiling. Then again, the training was so thorough, I may never know what's really going on inside me either."

—Arthur Ashe. From a 1974 *SPORT* magazine article

"There were also maxims meant only for little black Southern boys: when in doubt, call your opponent's shot good; if you're serving the game before the change of ends, pick up the balls on your side and hand them to your opponent during the crossover. Dr. [Robert Walter] Johnson knew we were going into territory that was often hostile and he wanted our behavior to be beyond reproach. It would be years before I understood the emotional toll of repressing anger and natural frustration."

—Arthur Ashe. From his 1981 book, *Off the Court*

"A few years ago, Rev. Jessie Jackson told me, 'Arthur, you're not arrogant enough.' I told him, 'I'm *not* arrogant.'"

—Arthur Ashe, in a 1974 *SPORT* magazine article

"You sometimes wonder, why make all those sacrifices if those coming behind you don't want to step up to the plate and take a big swing?"

—Arthur Ashe, on taking a position against apartheid in 1960s South Africa (1992)

"Ashe once told me, 'Every day I close my eyes and pray that people won't be as cruel to my children as they have been to me.'"

—Roy Firestone. From his 1993 book, *Up Close*

"What infuriated me most was having a white Richmond type come up to me somewhere in the world and say, 'I saw you play at Byrd Park when you were a kid.' Nobody saw me at Byrd Park, because when I was a kid it was for whites only."

—Arthur Ashe. From his 1981 book, *Off the Court*

"Here I am, the toast of a club I'd never be admitted into as a member."

—Arthur Ashe, after winning the National Amateur title at Longwood Cricket Club (1968)

"It is eleven years since Althea Gibson won at Wimbledon and Forest Hills. But it is shockingly obvious that those who run many American country clubs do not yet know the score."

—From an editorial in the *New York Times*. It decried the fact that three Washington, D.C., area country clubs dropped out of a women's tennis league rather than play another club that had a black player, the wife of Carl T. Rowan, the American ambassador to Finland (1968)

"It's a burden all right. But AIDS isn't the heaviest burden I have had to bear. No question about it. Race has always been my biggest burden. Having to live as a minority in America. Even now it continues to feel like an extra weight tied around me."

—Arthur Ashe. From his 1993 book, *Days of Grace*

"All of a sudden, I wasn't a tennis player anymore. I was black and I was a nobody and the reactions of people were completely different. Nothing bad, nothing that could start a fight, just different. In fact, I've never had any problems being black here. It's like Larry Holmes says: When you're black and you have money, then you are not black."

—Yannick Noah, recalling how he became unrecognized in France when he started wearing Rastafarian dreadlocks, in a 1983 *Sports Illustrated* article

"Because we don't ever want to forget where we're from . . . the ghetto."

—Richard Williams, controversial father/coach of black sensations Venus and Serena, on why he keeps a piece of concrete in his pocket

"People have been treating them with kid gloves because they're African American. If they were white, they would have been told off and more."

—Tennis legend Martina Navratilova, on Venus and Serena Williams (2001)

"It's very difficult for a young, black kid to identify with a white tennis player. I mean, who are they going to relate to, Michael Jordan and Walter Payton or Boris Becker and Ivan Lendl? If you're talking about exposing young, black athletes to tennis, you can't underestimate the importance of having black role models."

—MaliVai Washington, in *Black Tennis* magazine (1991)

"When I played basketball, they would go, 'Hey, here comes Arthur Ashe.'" .

—Levar Harper-Griffith, a black satellite player from Brooklyn, New York, telling *USA Today* how he was teased by friends for his passion for tennis (2000)

"What if Michael Jordan had chosen tennis instead of basketball? Or Carl Lewis or Sugar Ray Leonard or Walter Payton or Ken Griffey Jr.?"

—Arthur Ashe

"Maybe it's over for me, but to South Africa I say there will be more after me and more after them. I pity South Africa in its use of apartheid because discrimination never has and never will permanently become the modus operandi anywhere in the world. Human beings will just not subjugate themselves to discrimination very long."

—Arthur Ashe, after being refused a visa by South Africa for the third time on the grounds that he was "still persona non grata"

"Apartheid is wrong. . . . What bothers me is that people around the world judge me not for who I am but for where I'm from. I don't think that's fair."

—Christo van Rensburg, world-class South African player (1990)

"I have never had a problem being black, but the Cameroon [Tennis] Federation never supported me. The reason? My mother was white."

—1983 French Open champion Yannick Noah, on reverse discrimination in Cameroon as a boy

"To me, that's a racist comment—'They're bad for tennis.' They're the best thing that's ever happened to women's tennis."

—Billie Jean King, on criticism that the domination of Venus and Serena Williams hurts interest in tennis (2002)

"It's the worst act of prejudice since they killed Martin Luther King."

—Richard Williams, father/coach of Venus and Serena, on the jeers and boos the angry Indian Wells crowd directed at Serena Williams before and during the final because of the last-minute (knee injury) semifinal default of Venus the day before. Spectators also booed Venus and her father, Richard, when they arrived as spectators, and Richard accused them of making racist remarks. (2001)

"I don't know what the deal on that is: I guess it's because the environment of tennis has mostly been white. Especially over here in a culture where you see that people have conquered other people who were indigenous to this country. And the same thing in the United States."

—Oracene Price, mother/coach of Venus and Serena Williams, attributing the American and Australian public's lukewarm reaction to her daughters to racism (2003)

"I don't think it had anything to do with color. Australian crowds respect ability, and the problem in the final was they didn't know which sister to support."

—Former Grand Slam winner Margaret Court, on the subdued crowd for the all-Williams Australian Open final, which ended with a four-Slam sweep for Serena (2003)

"I know Arthur would be very disappointed if he knew a ground pass now costs $40 and that it's [$53] to get a terrible seat the first week in Arthur Ashe Stadium."

—Distinguished tennis journalist Bud Collins, on the paucity of African American spectators at the U.S. Open (2001)

"I never believed something like that existed in Germany. It is not worse here than anywhere else in Europe, but we have a different past and that's dangerous. Some people keep on asking me why I am going out with a dark-skinned girl. What's that supposed to mean?"

> —Boris Becker, when some people at the rowdy Cologne carnival celebrations shouted racial insults at Barbara Feltus, Becker's then girlfriend, and a German whose father is black (1992)

"I experience the best and worst of life now, sometimes within fifteen minutes. I am someone who cannot get served because I'm black; I get talked to in pidgin German—'You money have?'—and my banknotes get held up to the light to see if they're genuine. Then the next minute I'm Frau Becker, treated like a queen, people all over me, first-class service. Sometimes I find both awful."

> —Barbara Feltus, Boris Becker's fiancée, on the double-edged life of a black girl at the top, in Germany's *Stern* magazine (1993)

"I'm not an ambassador for any race or any country. My mother is white; my father is black. So inside me I don't feel like I'm black or white. I think I do more for people by winning Roland Garros than I could by going to South Africa and having meetings. Maybe when I'm thirty-five I'll change, but I don't think so."

> —Yannick Noah, in a 1983 *Sports Illustrated* article

"What better symbol for open tennis could there be than a black hero, signifying that the closed days of country-club tennis were over?"

> —Jack Kramer. From his 1979 memoir, *The Game: My 40 Years in Tennis*

"Shaking hands with the queen of England was a long way from being forced to sit in the colored section of the bus going into downtown Wilmington, North Carolina. Dancing with the Duke of Devonshire was a long way from not being allowed to bowl in Jefferson City, Missouri, because the white customers complained about it."

> —Althea Gibson, recalling the culture shock of her incredible 1957 Wimbledon title adventure. From her 1958 autobiography, *I Always Wanted to Be Somebody*

"Who could have imagined? Who could have thought? Here stands before you a Negro woman, raised in Harlem, who went on to become a tennis player . . . in fact, the first black-woman champion of this world."

—Althea Gibson, a sports pioneer who broke tennis's color barrier in 1950 as the first black entrant at the U.S. Nationals (now U.S. Open), as she presented her 1957–58 Wimbledon trophies to the Smithsonian Institution (1988)

"I am not a racially conscious person. I don't want to be. . . . I'm a tennis player, not a Negro tennis player."

—Althea Gibson. From her 1958 autobiography, *I Always Wanted to Be Somebody*

"I was just sitting with Zina. And I told her, 'You couldn't make this up.' Two young girls like this, from where they came from, entering Arthur Ashe Stadium past choirs of kids and Diana Ross, into an Open final on prime-time national television. I could never have dreamed this up."

—Former tour player Leslie Allen-Selmore, referring to Zina Garrison, another African American who made it all the way to the Wimbledon final, on Venus and Serena Williams playing the first all-black final at a Grand Slam tournament (2001)

DOUBLE YOUR PLEASURE

"You either go to bed with someone or you play tennis with them. But don't do both."

— Humor columnist Art Buchwald, on mixed doubles

"The moment that stands out most in my mind is when Karen Hantze and I won our first Wimbledon doubles championship in 1961. . . . We started winning our matches and found ourselves in the final! And then when we took the final, I couldn't believe it. Today I cherish that Wimbledon championship as much as any. I know that people always think that singles matter more, but doubles matter just as much to me."

— Tennis legend Billie Jean King who won a record twenty Wimbledon titles (six singles, ten doubles, and four mixed doubles). From the 1986 book, *Athletes Tell Their Unforgettable Moments in Sport*

"People enjoy doubles more than singles, because they have less work, have a partner to blame for defeat, and have someone to listen to their gripes as they play."

— Bill Tilden

"I've always loved doubles. I love playing on teams, I love working with a partner and trying to figure things out. I always loved the talking."

— Martina Navratilova, the greatest female doubles player in history, in *Tennis* magazine (2004)

"For sheer enjoyment, thrills, and satisfaction, you can't beat a good game of doubles between two evenly matched teams of the first rank. There is more fun in doubles, both for the players and the spectators."

> —1930s great Don Budge. From his 1939 autobiography, *Budge on Tennis*

"The theoretical game is for all four players to be forward at once and all volleying. The game resolves itself into a question of which side will miss or lose its position first."

> —Dr. James Dwight, considered the father of American tennis, in 1893. From the 1956 classic book, *The Game of Doubles in Tennis*

"Doubles is mainly a matter of getting a service break, then hanging on for dear life."

> —George Lott, 1920s and '30s doubles champion

"I am as proud of my doubles record as anything I did in singles."

> —John Newcombe, who captured seven Grand Slam singles titles and seventeen Grand Slam doubles titles (1990)

"There's no question in my mind that for the future good of the game, doubles should be compulsory if you enter an ATP Tour event."

> —John Newcombe, in *North Carolina Tennis Today* magazine (1994)

"The more doubles I play, the better I am in singles."

> —Martina Hingis, winner of five singles and nine doubles Grand Slam events (2001)

"A sound tip in doubles: do not play an angle unless you can make a sure placement. An angle is a risk, so why take unnecessary risks? When in doubt, low down the center is the safest method of gaining success."

> —John E. Bromwich, the shrewd Australian who captured seventeen Grand Slam doubles and mixed doubles titles and racked up a 20–1 Davis Cup doubles record. From the 1956 classic book, *The Game of Doubles in Tennis*

"Okay, I'll serve first and take the overheads."

> —What doubles star Darlene Hard told Rod Laver when they walked on court to play mixed doubles together at Wimbledon (1959)

"If tennis is going to grow exponentially, we are going to have to be intelligent and give doubles its due."

> —Gene Scott, former world-class player, tournament promoter, and publisher of *Tennis Week* magazine (1992)

"I get annoyed when players bad-mouth doubles. People who aren't good at it play down its importance. The only basis for bad attitude is that the prize money is lower. It's ridiculous that you don't win any money in mixed doubles unless you qualify for the semifinals. They should be encouraging people to play doubles here instead of discouraging."

> —Straight-talking Australian Owen Davidson, who amassed ten mixed doubles and two doubles Grand Slam titles, at the 1974 U.S. Open. From the 1975 book, *Carnival at Forest Hills: The Anatomy of a Tennis Tournament*

"Doubles is a scandal in tennis today. Borg and Connors never play. Some tank artfully, some make a joke out of it. There have been times when *both* teams in a match have been trying to lose."

> —Jack Kramer. From his 1979 autobiography, *The Game: My 40 Years in Tennis*

"The way tournaments treat doubles reminds me of a grocer who has a good product but won't put it out on the shelf. The people would buy the product if they saw it, but most of them aren't even aware it's available because of the way it's hidden from view."

> —Doubles champion Frew McMillan (1991)

"If that doesn't marginalize mixed doubles, I don't know what does."

> —John McEnroe, former champion and current TV analyst, denouncing the use of tiebreakers in lieu of legitimate, full-length deciding (third) sets in mixed doubles at Grand Slam events (2003)

"You need to be a more capable tennis player to be great at doubles."

> —Martina Navratilova, in *Tennis* magazine (2004)

"A more complete player might evolve if everyone [on the pro tour] had to play singles and doubles."

> —Doubles great Mark Woodforde, in *Tennis Week* (2000)

"John McEnroe and anyone."

—Peter Fleming, who partnered McEnroe to seven Grand Slam doubles titles from 1979 to 1984, nominating the best doubles team in history (1982)

"With twenty-eight titles I have a record that no one's going to break because no one plays doubles anymore."

—Australian great Roy Emerson, who racked up sixteen Grand Slam titles in doubles, in the *Independent* (UK) (2004)

"This is when doubles becomes a big deal. You don't get that elsewhere anymore."

—Yannick Noah, French Davis Cup captain, after the 1996 final in which France won the pivotal doubles match and went on to edge out Sweden 3–2. From 1972 to 2003, the country that captured the Davis Cup final also triumphed in the doubles every time but twice.

"Nothing can ruin the morale of a team more quickly than where one player shows by word or manner his dissatisfaction with a shot by the other. It not only gives rise to an undercurrent of feeling between the two members and ruins their coordination, but it gives comfort and encouragement to the opponents. Be helpful to one another, be self-sacrificing, and be generous to a fault or to as many faults as your partner makes."

—From John Hope Doeg and Allison Danzig's 1932 instruction book, *Lawn Tennis*

"Mixed doubles are always starting divorces. If you play with your wife, you fight with her. If you play with somebody else, she fights with you."

—Sidney B. Wood Jr., 1931 Wimbledon champion

"If you remember only one thing, remember that doubles is a little like marriage: nothing destroys the partnership faster than a lack of communication."

—Harry Hopman, captain of fifteen winning Australian Davis Cup teams from 1950 through 1969, in his 1975 book, *Lobbing into the Sun*

"Playing doubles with somebody sets up a strange relationship, in which you are friend, teammate, and competitor."

—Martina Navratilova. From her 1985 autobiography, *Martina*

"Nothing is more spectacular than a first-class doubles match; even more than singles play, the doubles game provides a test of generalship and resourcefulness that challenges the utmost concentration and ingenuity of the player."

> —Vincent Richards, who won three U.S. doubles championships with Bill Tilden and two with Dick Williams. From the classic 1956 book, *The Game of Doubles in Tennis*

"A good doubles match can be one of the fastest and most exciting of all sports events."

> —John Newcombe, in *World Tennis* magazine (1977)

STYLES AND STRATEGIES

"Perfect back play will beat perfect volleying. It is always possible to pass a volleyer with the court as it is at present; and I know that when I lose a stroke by being volleyed it is my own fault."

> —Herbert Lawford, who beat Ernest Renshaw in the 1887 Wimbledon final, from distinguished British journalist Lance Tingay's article, "When the Wind Blew in 1883"

"Before many years taking the ball off the ground will be quite the exception; and in its place there will be far finer and more exciting rallies in the volley than have ever been up to the present."

> —Ernest Renshaw, who beat Herbert Lawford in the 1888 Wimbledon final, from Tingay's article, "When the Wind Blew in 1883"

"Perfect style, inexhaustible stamina, and the best strokes are of no avail, if the brain that governs the hand is not able to plan moves by which winning strokes may be achieved."

> —Anthony Wilding, the 1910–13 Wimbledon champion from New Zealand. From Josef Brabenec's 1980 book, *Tennis: The Decision-Making Sport*

"I began to study tennis from the standpoint of geometry and physics, began to work out carefully a strategic and psychological approach to the game. Thus my first real pupil, and my most successful, was myself."

> —Bill Tilden, in his 1948 book, *My Story: A Champion's Memoirs*

"In no other sport are the strategic possibilities so numerous, the ways to outwit your opponent so rich and varied within the accepted sportsmanlike bounds."

>   —Sarah Palfrey, a clever strategist who captured eighteen Grand Slam titles in singles, doubles, and mixed doubles from 1930 to 1945. From her 1968 book, *Tennis for Anyone!*

"Tennis was quite different then. Ballet was the model for the woman athlete, and Suzanne [Lenglen] epitomized balletic grace in sport. Now, the model is the running track and weight room. I must say I preferred the old one."

>   —Ted Tinling

"When I started to play tennis, I fell into the use of the chop stroke—something that I hope every junior steers clear of, for I can truthfully say that it retarded my progress in the game for at least two years."

>   —Vincent Richards, a 1920s American standout, in *Country Life* magazine (circa 1930)

"Too many players play the game the way they *think* it should be played, not as they should play it."

>   —Wayne Sabin, noted teaching professional and former U.S. Davis Cupper. From the 1969 instruction book, *Inside Tennis: Techniques of Winning*

"There are no hard and fast rules for learning to play tennis or for developing your game, and there is no one style which could be laid down as the 'correct' way to play."

>   —Harry Hopman. From his 1972 instruction book, *Better Tennis*

"The use of two hands not only weakens your strokes but robs you of confidence and gives your opponent a psychological advantage."

>   —Jack Kramer. From his 1949 book, *Winning Tennis*

"Even the top stars who play with two hands never recommend it to anyone else. . . . A club player who learns to play with two hands is limiting himself terribly."

>   —Dennis Van der Meer, famed teaching professional and founder of the Professional Tennis Registry (PTR). From his 1974 book, *Tennis Clinic*

"It shouldn't be taught to kids. The trouble with it is that it establishes a weakness."

> —Billie Jean King, critical of the two-handed backhand after seventeen-year-old Chris Evert used it effectively to reach the 1972 U.S. Open semifinals. From the 1979 book, *Famous Women Tennis Players*

"Chris, Jimmy, and other top players are talented enough to make the two-handed backhand work well for them. But basically it is an unsound shot. It's a limited shot. . . . But I think the two-handed craze is passing now."

> —Margaret Court, in her 1975 book, *Court on Court: A Life in Tennis*

"I don't like the two-fisted shot, except with Chris Evert. She has a way of making it look beautiful."

> —All-time great Helen Wills Moody (1977)

"I like the two-handed stuff, or more accurately, I like what it represents. We've been so damned hidebound in tennis that I think it's beneficial any time the game gets some variety."

> —Arthur Ashe. From his 1975 book, *Portrait in Motion*

"She's a great role model—for the image she projects and for her backhand. I think there must be a million kids playing who wouldn't have played if they had defensive backhands. All the kids can attack on both wings now, and that wouldn't exist if it hadn't been for Chris."

> —Tennis historian Ted Tinling, on Chris Evert

"I didn't teach the two-hander to her. She started that way because she was too small and weak to swing the backhand with one hand. I hoped she'd change—but how can I argue with this success?"

> —Jimmy Evert, father/coach of 1970s and '80s champion Chris Evert, advising against teaching the two-handed backhand. From the 1997 book, *Bud Collins' Tennis Encyclopedia*

"If I had advice to give a youngster today, I would say play your backhand with two hands. You cannot have a very good backhand with one hand; you need a strong wrist, a strong arm."

> —Rene Lacoste, eighty-two, one of France's famed "Four Musketeers" during the late 1920s and early 1930s, in a 1987 interview in *World Tennis* magazine

"I didn't teach the two-hander to her . . . but how can I argue with this success?"—Jimmy Evert, on his daughter's trademark (*Fred Mullane/Camerawork USA, Inc.*)

"My two-handed backhand was not only a good shot, it was my *best* shot. Abandoning my best shot was frustrating, controversial, and risky."

> —Pete Sampras, who at age fourteen was ordered to switch to a one-handed backhand by coach Pete Fischer, who presciently called it "a move for the long run," in *Tennis* magazine

"I am a great believer in practice, but above all in intensive practice. My idea of intensive practice is to pick out one stroke and hammer away at that shot until it is completely mastered."

> —Bill Tilden. From his 1925 instruction book, *Match Play and the Spin of the Ball*

"Strokes are the weapons with which you fight your tennis battles. The better the weapon, the greater the chance of victory."

> —Bill Tilden, 1920s superstar, who did not win major titles until he revamped his defective backhand

"You're only as good as your second serve and first volley."

> —Australian champion John Newcombe, who amassed twenty-five career Grand Slam titles in singles, doubles, and mixed doubles

"The great beauty of tennis is the inexhaustible variety of playing methods to which one may make recourse."

> —Don Budge, from his 1939 book, *Budge on Tennis*

"The difference between men's tennis and women's tennis as played by the best of both sexes has lain only in strength and endurance, and doesn't affect the variety of stroke equipment that can be developed. . . . There is proof of it in every tournament at the present time, and proof grows stronger every year."

> —Helen Jacobs, in her 1933 instruction book, *Modern Tennis*

"The stroke is perfectly concealed and accurate, and McGrath may play through a set without netting or outing more than three or four balls."

> —H. G. Barwick, praising Australian teenager Vivian McGrath, the first world-class player with a two-handed backhand, in *American Lawn Tennis* magazine (1933)

"The finest backhand in the world is possessed by Vivian McGrath. However, the shot is one that I cannot recommend as a model, for he uses two hands on the racket to make it. I doubt if one person in a thousand could learn to make such a stroke more efficiently with two hands than with one."

> —Wilmer Allison, 1935 U.S. champion. From the instruction book, *How to Play Lawn Tennis*

"It never bothered me that others were using different grips and strokes. I was stubborn."

> —Bjorn Borg, whose Western forehand and two-handed backhand inspired a generation of imitators

"In five years tennis is going to be very boring, and we'll have a draw with 128 Borgs."

> —Vitas Gerulaitis, decrying the top-spinning baseline clones that Bjorn Borg inspired. From the 1983 book, *Short Circuit*

"Nobody is so bad that he or she cannot enjoy tennis. In all my years of experience, I never found a person who couldn't play."

> —John Newcombe, former Australian star and operator of a tennis ranch in Texas. From the 1975 instruction book, *The Family Tennis Book*, written by him and his wife Angie

"If you can walk to the drinking fountain without falling over, you have the physical ability to play tennis well."

> —Noted instructor and tennis innovator Vic Braden

"The art of lawn tennis is control and restraint and putting the ball where the other guy ain't."

> —Harry Hopman. From his 1972 instruction book, *Better Tennis*

"Charlie summed it up when he said, 'Short blokes can't hit flat balls. Big men don't need spin, but the little runts like you do.'"

> —Rod Laver, on the wise advice his renowned Australian coach, Charlie Hollis, gave him as a youngster. From Laver's 1964 book, *How to Play Winning Tennis*

"I consider wall practice the best way to learn strokes."

> —Henri Cochet, one of France's "Four Musketeers" of the 1920s and early 1930s, renowned for hitting the ball on the rise

"A match is more easily won by a judicious combination of driving and volleying than by using one of these methods to the exclusion of the other."

> —Henri Cochet. From the 1937 instruction book, *How to Play Lawn Tennis* and reprinted from *Tennis, Its Technique and Its Psychology*, published by Societe Parisienne D'Edition, Paris

"How many times does a player considered the weaker beat an opponent of higher reputation! It is because the 'weaker' has shown himself the more intelligent, the more subtle, the deeper."

> —Henri Cochet. From the 1937 instruction book, *How to Play Lawn Tennis* and reprinted from *Tennis, Its Technique and Its Psychology*, published by Societe Parisienne D'Edition, Paris

"I'm always asked, 'Shouldn't I play with someone better to improve my game?' That's a real fallacy. Playing someone better than yourself does make you try harder and improve match-playing ability. But to improve yourself as a tennis player, you need sound strokes. People of average skill should know that the best way to improve strokes is actually to play with a weaker opponent."

> —Dennis Van der Meer, famed teaching professional and founder of the Professional Tennis Registry (PTR). From his 1974 book, *Tennis Clinic*

"The whole point of intensive practice is to get to a stage in your tennis when you're not thinking about the mechanics of stroking during a match, only where you want to put the ball."

> —Roy Emerson, all-time men's leader in Grand Slam titles with twenty-eight. From the 1976 book, *Tennis for the Bloody Fun of It*, which he co-wrote with Rod Laver

"Don't forget about practicing service returns. This is one stroke that hardly anybody in tennis practices enough, and yet you hit it almost as often as you hit a serve."

> —Roy Emerson. From the 1976 book, *Tennis for the Bloody Fun of It*

"Tennis is a difficult game to learn. Very difficult. You have to be a generalist. You can't be a specialist and excel in tennis. You have to become adept in about four or five different sets of exercises, none of which are the same. Physiologically, serving a tennis ball is nothing like hitting a forehand; they're two completely different actions. Hitting a volley is not like hitting an overhead; they too are two completely different functions. You must learn how to do all of them."

>—Arthur Ashe. From his 1981 book, *Off the Court*

"It takes five years to make a tennis player, and ten years to make a champion."

>—Bill Tilden

"When you are thinking about the thrill of going after winners, just calm yourself by remembering that tennis matches are always lost on errors and never won by placements."

>—Bill Tilden. From his 1950 instruction book, *How to Play Better Tennis*

"I was never satisfied if I did not play beautifully. I was always going for the impossible shots."

>—Maria Bueno, 1960s champion from Brazil

"Volleying has destroyed much of the beauty of the game. Long rallies are rarely witnessed."

>—The *Field Magazine* (UK), commenting on the state of the game after Willie Renshaw volleyed relentlessly to overwhelm John Hartley 6–0, 6–1, 6–1 in the 1881 Wimbledon final

"In any match between the perfect baseline player and the perfect net rusher, I would take the baseliner every time."

>—Bill Tilden

"Today, every outstanding player in the game is a volleyer."

>—Don Budge. From his 1939 book, *Budge on Tennis*

"It always burned me up that grass players were dismissed as serve-and-volley. A clay specialist is a much more limited type. He can only hit defensive groundstrokes."

>—Jack Kramer. From his 1979 book, *The Game: My 40 Years in Tennis*

"I'm the last serve-and-volleyer, it seems. But with the way Monica [Seles] and Jennifer [Capriati] are hitting the ball, there's just not much variety."

> —Martina Navratilova, after losing the U.S. Open final to Seles (1991)

"If Connors used that two-handed stuff on Bill Tilden, he'd be lucky to get two games a set."

> —George Lott, 1920s and '30s doubles star (1979)

"When kids get to a certain age, their parents have to sit them down and explain, 'If you want to go anywhere in this sport, you have to get rid of that two-handed backhand.'"

> —Jack Kramer (1987)

"But that won't give me a free hand to hold the beer."

> —What Billy Carter, the late brother of former U.S. president Jimmy Carter, said while being taught a two-handed backhand

"No matter how many adjustments you might make in your swing, a proper grip will last for the rest of your life."

> —Vic Braden. From the 1997 book, *The Tennis Lover's Book of Wisdom*

"I have broken every rule recommended by instruction books over the past fifty years."

> —Bjorn Borg

"Orthodoxy does not mean being restricted; on the contrary, it is the foundation that offers the greatest scope for future development. When coaches find a natural strength already developed in a player, they usually encourage it, whether it is strictly orthodox or not."

> —Paul Metzler. From his 1968 instruction book, *Advanced Tennis*

"What a dull game lawn tennis would be if it didn't change! Part of its charm and fascination lies in the continual development of new methods, tactics, and technique."

> —Tony Mottram, English Davis Cup player from 1947 to 1955, and Joy Mottram, English Wightman Cup player from 1947 to 1952. From their 1957 book, *Modern Lawn Tennis*

"You try to predict how a sport will be ten, fifteen, twenty years from now. . . . I used to lay awake thinking of how tennis was going to be played when Andre was twenty-two or twenty-three. Speed is the key—power forehand, power backhand, no weaknesses. The most important thing is to be inside the court, to hit the ball on the rise and not let the other guy hit the ball."

> —Emmanuel "Mike" Agassi, Andre's father and first coach, in the 1997 book, *Agassi and Ecstasy: The Turbulent Life of Andre Agassi*

"Andre moves faster between points than some players do *during* points. He could be the poster boy for the caffeine industry."

> —Brad Gilbert, on Andre Agassi's energy. From his 1993 book, *Winning Ugly*

"She plays tennis like she's double-parked."

> —TV commentator Mary Carillo, on hyper teen star Andrea Jaeger

"The minute you think you know all there is to know about tennis is the minute your game starts going down the tubes."

> —Jimmy Connors. From the 1997 book, *The Tennis Lover's Book of Wisdom*

"Most weekend players are brain-dead on the tennis court. They go out and run around with no plan, no thought, no nothing. And that's why they can be had."

> —Brad Gilbert, a canny strategist as a player and coach, on the difference between the pro and recreational ranks. From his 1993 book, *Winning Ugly*

"The firmness of the grip at impact is the single most important factor in hitting a tennis ball."

> —Stanley Plagenhoef, associate professor of physical education, University of Massachusetts, and director of the Bio-Mechanics Laboratory. From his 1970 book, *Fundamentals of Tennis*

"The volley is in grave danger of being driven from the game."

> —Pat Cash's warning about the slowing of balls and courts (1998)

"He always told me that if I wanted to be a great player I would have to hit over the ball."

—Australian legend Rod Laver, whose topspin groundstrokes were instrumental in his winning a record two Grand Slams, on boyhood coach Charlie Hollis

"To me, tennis was more of an art than a sport. I was a very natural player. Everything was done by impulse or intuition. I could never be programmed like most of the players are today."

—Maria Bueno, graceful 1960s champion from Brazil

"At the present time the young English star, Betty Nuthall, uses an underhanded serve. Some critics have said that it is a bad way of serving. I am rather inclined to believe that it is far better than the onlooker realizes. It is certainly unique, and individual, and it is to her the most natural and logical way of serving."

—Helen Wills Moody. From her 1929 book, *Tennis*

"Everybody says be natural. . . . Nearly everything I've seen about tennis that's natural is wrong."

—Noted coach Vic Braden

"Maximum results with the minimum effort."

—Australian great Ken Rosewall, summing up his compact game

"Never allow a player to play the game he prefers if you can possibly force him to play any other. Never give a player a shot he likes to play."

—Bill Tilden's authoritative and time-tested advice. From his 1925 classic, *Match Play and the Spin of the Ball*

"Never change a winning game. Always change a losing game."

—Bill Tilden, with the most famous tennis maxim

"In singles the main error of many players is the lack of knowledge of when to defend and when to attack."

—Bill Tilden. From his 1925 classic, *Match Play and the Spin of the Ball*

"Do not be caught in the territory between the service line and the baseline, for there you are neither in suitable position to volley or drive effectively."

—From John Hope Doeg and Allison Danzig's 1932 instruction book, *Lawn Tennis*

"Tennis to me is just like a chess game. You have to maneuver, you have to know your opponent's strengths and weaknesses."

> —Althea Gibson, 1950s champion

"Has any player come out of Bollettieri's academy a more complete player than when he or she went in? I can't think of one."

> —Tony Trabert, 1955 Wimbledon, French, and U.S. champion and TV tennis analyst. From his 1988 book, *Trabert on Tennis: The View from Center Court*

"He was suspicious and cagey, and these characteristics came out in his tennis. He was The Wizard who thought two shots ahead. At every change of ends he planned a little scheme. He was like a general without an army. . . . He saw more in the strategy of the game than he did in the strategy of actual living."

> —Dame Mabel Balcombe Brookes, wife of Norman Brookes, great Australian player of the early twentieth century

"Tennis is like football. You must set up the plays. If you set it up right, all you have to do is execute."

> —Martina Navratilova

"Good footwork nearly always means sound strokes; bad or poor footwork prevents your hitting the ball correctly. . . . By far the greatest majority of errors originate through incorrect footwork."

> —Tony Mottram, English Davis Cup player from 1947 to 1955, and Joy Mottram, English Wightman Cup player from 1947 to 1952. From their 1957 book, *Modern Lawn Tennis*

"When you play a better player, don't try to hit harder. Play your own game, but try to be faster on your feet."

> —Pancho Gonzalez. From the 1997 book, *The Tennis Lover's Book of Wisdom*

"The difference between a great player and a good one is that the great player misses fewer easy shots."

> —Jack Kramer

"The great part about tennis is you can't run out the clock. You can't just get a lead for yourself and slow down. You have to find a way to finish."

—Andre Agassi, who rallied from two sets and a break down to overtake Frenchman Paul-Henri Mathieu at the French Open (2002)

"I've always tried to get in my opponent's face."

—Feisty world-ranked No. 1 Lleyton Hewitt (2002)

"Major matches are won by a combination of three factors. One needs the technical skills to guide and control the ball, the tactics to probe the opponent's weaknesses, and the nerves to hit the strokes and carry out the plan when the pressure is on."

—Pancho Segura, astute player and coach (1976)

"Some very valuable things of the past have been lost in the wild scramble for speed and power."

—Bill Tilden (1950)

"Brute force is taking over from strategy, from intelligence, from psychology."

—Philippe Chatrier, former ITF president, averring that men's tennis has changed for the worse (1992)

"Foot-and-eye coordination is more important in tennis than hand-eye coordination. . . . Anybody can swing a racquet. It's the great feet that win Grand Slam titles."

—Arthur Ashe. From his 1981 book, *Off the Court*

"It's weird that at her age Hingis knows so much about all the shots and strategies and nuances of the game. When I played doubles with her, I learned so much."

—Tour veteran Mary Joe Fernandez, on sixteen-year-old phenom Martina Hingis (1997)

"Martina plays two strokes ahead in every rally. To her, tennis is a game of chess."

—Former doubles superstar and current TV analyst Pam Shriver, on the cerebral style of Martina Hingis (2001)

"The player must develop his own strategy on the court. If he is intelligent, alert, and open-minded enough to recognize his mistakes and profit by them, he will learn more of the science of the game in a few seasons of competition than all the textbooks can teach him."

　　—From John Hope Doeg and Allison Danzig's 1932 instruction book, *Lawn Tennis*

"Men's tennis needs to be played on the slowest surface possible. The tennis we saw in Shanghai and the Davis Cup final in Paris, you can't play better tennis than that. When you have guys hitting great groundstrokes, sometimes fifteen in a row, that builds character. If it's one serve and no volley, that builds no character."

　　—Mats Wilander, who won seven Grand Slam titles in the 1980s, mostly from the baseline (2002)

"It's hunt and kill tennis. It's like a children's computer game: Zap! Splat! Kapow!"

　　—Ion Tiriac, former Romanian Davis Cupper and head of Elite Management, describing the rocket serves of former recordholder Greg Rusedski (149 mph) and Taylor Dent (2001)

"It began with [Maurice] McLoughlin. A hard serve and speed of foot that get you to the net, that's the American game. Australia adopted it. Laver plays the same way they played fifty years ago."

　　—Walter Merrill Hall, who nearly beat Bill Tilden in the quarterfinals of the 1918 U.S. Nationals at Forest Hills. Interviewed in the 1975 book, *Forest Hills: An Illustrated History*

"I ran to the net behind every service until the day I retired."

　　—Oliver Campbell, an American star who won the U.S. singles title in 1890–92 and U.S. doubles title in 1888 (with Valentine Hall) and 1891–92 (with Bob Huntington)

"I played the game the way it ought to be played."

　　—Martina Navratilova

"I played the game the way it ought to be played." —Martina Navratilova (*Fred Mullane/ Camerawork USA, Inc.*)

"If there is a hole in your game, plug it by intensive practice. Do not worry about the defeats you must bear during the time your game is developing. Go out to make of yourself the greatest player that lies within the range of your natural abilities and your opportunities. . . . There is far more pleasure to tennis if you have no fear about your strokes."

 —Bill Tilden. From his 1925 book, *Match Play and the Spin of the Ball*

"If you have slow courts, you've got to have fast balls. You can't have slow and slow, or the attacking player has no chance. Serve-volleyers are a dying breed and, unfortunately, it's now the nature of the game to discourage attacking players."

 —Pat Cash, serve-volleying 1987 Wimbledon champion (2002)

"I believe the next truly great player is going to be a serve-volleyer because as a tactic, it's a massive advantage."

 —Pat Cash (2003)

"In the future, classic serve-and-volley tennis will become pretty much extinct."

 —Pete Sampras, winner of a record fourteen Grand Slam singles titles as an awesome serve-volleyer (2002)

"It would be a tragedy because stylistically to lose serving and volleying would be awful for the sport. I'd miss it like hell. Some great baseline matches still intrigue me, *maybe* as much as serve-and-volley matches. But in the end, I want to see styles clash. I want to see strategies clash. The best matches I've ever seen have all of that going for them."

 —Mary Carillo, distinguished TV analyst and former French Open mixed champion with John McEnroe, on the prospect that Pete Sampras and Martina Navratilova would make history in a way they never intended, as the last serve-and-volley champions (2003)

LOVE AFFAIRS

"I don't know, but I've heard rumors that it's wild."

—Mark Philippoussis, at age nineteen, on the subject on love (1996)

"I've never been in love. I'm looking forward to it. It must be a great feeling, but it hasn't happened to me yet."

—Gabriela Sabatini, the divine Argentine, in the *Daily Telegraph* (UK) (1993)

"I would love to have someone special who really loves me for myself rather than who I am."

—Gabriela Sabatini, in the *Daily Telegraph* (1993)

"I will do everything possible not to lose him. What woman wouldn't want to be in my shoes? The truth is that when I'm by Borg's side, finally I feel like a woman. A man like this only comes along once."

—Loredana Berte, Italian singer and sex symbol, and for a time, Borg's second wife, in *Oggi* magazine (1988)

"We were kids. Neither of us really knew how to give."

—Chris Evert, explaining why her fairy-tale romance with Jimmy Connors did not survive their stardom. From Peter Bodo's 1979 book, *Inside Tennis: A Season on the Pro Tour*

"I still carried a torch for him. I went out with other men, but I thought about him for two or three years after we broke up. I saw him at tournaments, and we went out in between his girlfriends and my boyfriends. He was still number one with me right up until I met John. It's hard to get that first love out of your system. I still hoped something would happen and Jimmy and I would get back together again."

> —Chris Evert, on her feelings for Jimmy Connors after they broke off their engagement. In 1979 Connors married Patti McGuire and Evert married John Lloyd. From the 1985 book, *Lloyd on Lloyd* by Chris and John Lloyd with Carol Thatcher

"Let me put it this way: being with Tatum took me to a whole new plane. Until I met her, I'd never been in the *National Enquirer*."

> —John McEnroe, on his comely actress-wife, Tatum O'Neal, in *Esquire* magazine (1987)

"John represented everything I wanted. He wasn't an actor. He was a really big success. He was young. He had money. He totally turned me on."

> —Tatum O'Neal, recalling what first attracted her to husband John McEnroe (1990)

"She was successful even younger than me, and I felt she could help me to navigate what it would be like to be in the public eye, which I was having some troubles with."

> —John McEnroe, explaining that finding a kindred soul in child actress Tatum O'Neal was what attracted him to her. From the 2003 book, *On Being John McEnroe*

"I've had a lot of experience with men who are bullies. Taking on John McEnroe was the biggest struggle of my life."

> —Tatum O'Neal, recalling her turbulent marriage with John McEnroe, in *Entertainment Weekly* (2002)

"You want to know what McEnroe is? He is a cruel, cruel man. He seems to think he's God. . . . He's a sociopath, he treated people so badly—little people who earn in a year what he makes in one day.

He would push past kids at the airport and his rackets would hit them in the face."

> —Tatum O'Neal, on her ex-husband, John McEnroe (2002)

"Once you throw girls in the mix, that really messes everything up."

> —Jim Courier, four-time Grand Slam champion and former No. 1, who was renowned for his grueling training sessions

"My former girlfriend."

> —Karol Kucera, commenting on his toughest opponent so far. From www.crestwoodtennis.au.com

"The worst part is it's keeping the other girls away. They think I'm about to get married."

> —Lady-killer Vitas Gerulaitis, fuming over false reports that he was secretly engaged, in *Tennis* magazine (1980)

"Whatever happens on court, I'm No. 1 to her and that's all that really matters."

> —Jimmy Connors, on the diamond-studded "No. 1" necklace that his wife Patti gave him (1979)

"My marriage moved me more than my two Wimbledon triumphs put together."

> —Stefan Edberg, after wedding Annette Olsen (1992)

"My husband, seven times Wimbledon champion, Pete. . . . Remember this. You are truly the best player ever to pick up a tennis racket."

> —From the loving letter that Pete Sampras's wife, Bridgette, put inside his bag at the 2002 Wimbledon to encourage her slump-ridden husband. Pete read it at every changeover, but still suffered the worst loss of his career to No. 145–ranked George Bastl.

"If I could ask anything of God, it would be, 'How can I love him more?'"

> —Actress Brooke Shields, Andre Agassi's fiancée (1996)

"She is the sweetest, kindest, warmest, strongest human being that I know, and without her, life would take on a new meaning for me. I cannot even imagine the thought of living life without her."

> —Andre Agassi, expressing his love for Brooke Shields (1996)

"When there is love, you're inspired, you can write poems, you can write music, you can play good tennis."

> —Romantic Andrei Medvedev, after reuniting with fellow pro Anke Huber and breaking a prolonged slump to reach the French Open final (1999)

"With Sergio, I know I can be myself. Before, I always tried to be something better. I wanted to give guys too much."

> —Martina Hingis, on her relationship with golf star Sergio Garcia, in *Sports Illustrated* (2002)

"Totally betrayed. My failure is that I don't love her anymore. Well, should you pay for that? . . . I don't have that kind of money. I mean, I give her that and I'm broke. I might just as well start all over again, eighteen years of tennis down the drain."

> —Martina Navratilova, when asked on the *20/20* program how she felt about Judy Nelson, who recently had filed a multimillion dollar palimony suit against her after their seven-year relationship ended (1991)

"Jessica means something special to me. She is being pestered day and night. I have already lost two or three girlfriends. Now I am scared I could lose Jessica too. To prevent this I would rather give up tennis."

> —Michael Stich, the 1991 Wimbledon champion, on Jessica Stockmann, his lovely actress/girlfriend whom he would marry a few months later (1992)

"My only good result in 1997 was marrying Brooke Shields."

> —Slump-ridden Andre Agassi, whose marriage to actress Shields ended in divorce in 1999

"Boyfriends have to understand me, and my needs . . . and my strict regimen. I go to bed at ten at night, and no later, unless I'm playing in a tournament. And I shower four times a day, after training and matches."

> —Anna Kournikova, with something she wanted to get off her chest

SEX AND THE SINGLES PLAYER

"I know they are silently looking me up and down. I always react in the same embarrassed way. I bend down and tie my shoelaces although it's unnecessary. They don't only want to see you—they want to have you."

> —Boris Becker, on the "eroticism" he sensed between himself and the fans (1992)

"Sex gets in the way of winning."

> —World-ranked No. 1 Jim Courier, after dumping French heiress Morgane Fruhwirth (1993)

"Sex doesn't interfere with your tennis; it's staying out all night trying to find it that affects your tennis."

> —Andre Agassi, on sex before matches

"I feel like I'm a little lighter in my shoes, it makes me kind of run a little bit quicker because I feel like a stud."

> —Andre Agassi, on connubial bliss with Steffi Graf (2002)

"I like it. I'm a big fan of women. I don't know what my girlfriend Lara thinks about it all, but it's a positive thing. I'm very lucky."

> —Patrick Rafter, 1997–98 U.S. Open champion, on being regarded as one of the world's sexiest athletes

"I soon learned it was not a good idea to beat a boy I liked. It's amazing how losing to a girl can turn a guy off. Most fellows consider the girl who is a better athlete a threat. The only men who don't think this way are, in my view, the real men; these are the men who have their own thing, too, and no one can take that away from them."

—Billie Jean King. From her 1974 book, *Billie Jean King's Secrets of Winning Tennis*

"I'd rather have mine—36-26-36—than be No. 1. I have more fun than any No. 1 I know."

—Curvaceous Pat Stewart, lingerie model and top twenty American player in the late 1950s, when asked her ranking number

"I'm not as innocent as I seem."

—Message on a T-shirt worn by Chris Evert in the late 1970s

"I am still a virgin. I do not let anyone have even a peep in my bed."

—Sex symbol Anna Kournikova at eighteen, with an apparent compulsion to set the record straight (1999)

"I don't want a girlfriend now. They're hard work and they're very dangerous."

—Tall, dark, and handsome Mark Philippoussis, at twenty-two (1999)

"Would you complain if the chicks wanted to go after you? It's nice having that image. I remember when women wouldn't look twice at me."

—Patrick Rafter, on his sex-symbol status (1999)

"I could have sex with many women. The same thing happens to me that, unfortunately, frequently happens to women: I am being chased like game. But it's like with many things: If you can have it all, you're no longer tempted."

—Boris Becker (1990)

"I honestly have no idea what makes me so sexy. I am neither an Adonis, nor is my weenie hyper-dimensional."

—Controversial tennis great Boris Becker. From his 2003 best-selling autobiography, *Wait, Stay a Moment Longer*

"It's like chasing a girl; the chase is the fun part."

> —Former world-ranked No. 1 Jim Courier, on going for the No. 1 ranking

"Take me home! Take me home!"

> —What girls used to scream when flamboyant playboy Vitas Gerulaitis left the court in the 1970s

MONEY TALKS

"If I can't play for big money, I play for a little money. And if I can't play for a little money, I stay in bed that day."
—Court hustler Bobby Riggs, in a TV interview with Mike Wallace (1973)

"The final triumph of the computerized one-dimensional man in the deadly serious tennis business. . . . Today's well-behaved automatons, in the third pro generation, have apparently had little education or fun in the process of their being programmed, almost from their cradles, to make money out of tennis."
—E. Digby Baltzell. From his acclaimed 1995 book, *Sporting Gentlemen: Men's Tennis from the Age of Honor to the Cult of the Superstar*

"Maybe Borg had the right idea—to cut the cord quickly and leave when people were still going to miss him. I chose a different route. I chose mediocrity for the last five or six years of my career. I just couldn't walk away from that kind of money."
—John McEnroe. From his 2002 autobiography, *You Cannot Be Serious*

"It's easy for parents to say they'd never let their son or daughter play [the pro tour] at fourteen or fifteen. But when some sponsor puts an envelope in front of them and says, 'Here's a million dollars, Mr. and Mrs. Smith.' Now, their attitude is, 'Let me think about this.'"
—Nick Bollettieri, in the *Ft. Lauderdale Sun-Sentinel* (1993)

"Being a champion is all well and good, but you can't eat a crown."
—Althea Gibson, who retired from amateur tennis in 1958 with five Grand Slam singles crowns (1968)

"I was always motivated to win at the U.S. Open because they pay a lot. This year, it will probably be $950,000. Who wouldn't want to win that?"

> —Serena Williams, tennis queen and admitted shopaholic (2003)

"I put sin into tennis. Tennis couldn't finance itself purely as a sport. It had to turn into a spectacle, and you must pay your debts to the spectators who keep it alive."

> —Ted Tinling, on the sexy lace panties he made for "Gorgeous Gussie" Moran, which created a sensation in 1949

"Here at the home of tennis no player with true feeling for the game played for money."

> —Insouciant Evonne Goolagong Cawley, with a view of Wimbledon that conflicted with feminist advocates of equal prize money (circa 1974)

"Money is what people respect, and when you are a professional athlete, they want to know how much you have made. They judge you on that."

> —Billie Jean King, who in 1971 became the first woman in tennis history to earn more than $100,000 in a year. From the 1975 book, *The Ultimate Tennis Book*

"Each athlete must ask himself or herself what's more important— endorsements, or being true to your beliefs?"

> —Openly gay Martina Navratilova, who often paid a price for her candor (1997)

"I'm worth 40,000 of you."

> —What an angry John McEnroe shouted at a tough crowd (1984)

"It is absurd that a tennis player can go out and make a million dollars a year and teachers are making $25,000, $20,000. I don't think that's fair. If people want to pay for it, that's one thing. But people who influence our lives—for example, firemen and police-men—are so badly underpaid sometimes. You just look at it, it doesn't make sense."

> —John McEnroe (1987)

"I call tennis the McDonald's of sport—you go in, they make a quick buck out of you, and you're out."

    —Pat Cash, from www.tennisontheline.org

"People can criticize me and say I play just for the money, but if they knew what that meant and were in my situation, they would do the same thing."

    —Russian star Marat Safin, who supports his parents and younger sister, Dinara, an aspiring player (2001)

"When I hear people say that you can't make it in tennis if you don't have a lot of money, I know they're wrong. We lived in a socialist country, and we didn't have much money. But I loved the sport, and that was enough."

    —Monica Seles. From her 1996 autobiography, *Monica: From Fear to Victory*

"If I were advising the guys, I'd tell them to take the equal prize money while they can. Fans buy tickets to watch great tennis played by great playing personalities competing for titles in great events. And the women are selling the tickets."

    —John McEnroe (1999)

"Megadollars mean something to everyone. There are players whose incomes went up literally by millions after the attack in Hamburg. Suddenly, rank meant a lot. And you can bet that those players who moved up, who moved closer to number one than ever before, would have preferred me not to return to the tour."

    —Monica Seles, whose lawyers estimated that she lost $10 million in income in the year following her 1993 stabbing. From her 1996 autobiography, *Monica: From Fear to Victory*

"If we don't show up, how are you going to make money? No one really wants to be used as a pawn."

    —Venus Williams, saying female tennis stars deserve appearance fees to play in tournaments (2000)

"I didn't do a good job, so why should I get paid for it?"

    —Australian star Patrick Rafter, explaining why, after losing an early-round match at a tournament in France, he returned his appearance fee (1997)

"If we go on like that, we'll be broke in a little more than a century."

> —Oil tycoon Lamar Hunt, whose WCT Tour lost $100,000 in its first three months, when a reporter asked what would happen as a result (1967)

"Eighty percent of the money that tennis pros make in tournaments comes from sponsors backing them. But most players don't want to believe this. If somebody puts up 80 percent of the money you make, and they ask you to drop by for one hour a week and have a free drink, you've got to be dead crazy not to do it."

> —Arthur Ashe. From his 1975 book, *Portrait in Motion*

"Mark McCormack invented the sports business. It was he who first realized that within the golden triangle of sport, sponsorship, and television, lay vast wealth just waiting to be tapped."

> —*Business Age*, eulogizing McCormack, after he died in 2003. The founder and CEO of International Management Group (which represents more than 1,000 pros) was a masterly negotiator and visionary who created the field of sports marketing and changed the worlds of golf, tennis, and television.

"I'm kind of bitter about people saying I did this to make money. It just isn't so. I was pretty well off as a physician, and I'm pretty poor as a tennis pro."

> —Transsexual Renee Richards, formerly Dr. Richard Raskind, in 1978. She returned to her ophthalmology practice three years later.

"When I was growing up I wanted to be a neurosurgeon. And even though some people think I haven't done much since I turned pro, I'd have to be a damn good surgeon to make what I'm making."

> —Kathy Horvath, the only player to beat Martina Navratilova in 1983

"I came here to play tennis and not to collect that money. I use money like everybody else, but if there wasn't any money in the game, I would still care about tennis and want to play every day."

> —Guillermo Vilas, after collecting $40,000 for winning the season-ending Commercial Union Masters in Melbourne and the $100,000 first prize in the 1974 Grand Prix

"Everybody is talking about money. But it's not so important. I prefer to win Wimbledon to making a million dollars."

> —Bjorn Borg, in *Tennis* magazine (1979)

"No. I would rather be number one and not making any money than number four and making millions. The only thing I *would* resent would be if the men were making the money and the women weren't. But that isn't the case."

> —1940s champion Pauline Betz, when asked if she resented the fact that current tennis players were making so much money while she had received so little. From the 1985 book, *Once a Champion: Legendary Tennis Stars Revisited*

"Just as players of the '50s and '60s had quit the shamateur game as soon as they won a major title that would enhance their income as professionals, Borg had quit the competitive game once it no longer served a purpose. For several years tournament tennis had been a minor aspect of his program, just a form of advertising that kept his price high for endorsements and exhibitions."

> —Michael Mewshaw. From his 1983 exposé, *Short Circuit*

"Definitely, I consider this a business. I'm just grinding out as much money as I can."

> —An over-the-hill Vitas Gerulaitis (1985)

"Dollar language is the only one I know after twenty years in business. And it's also the one used by tennis players."

> —International Tennis Federation president Philippe Chatrier, announcing the $6 million Grand Slam Cup (1989)

"They are trying to turn us into money whores. It's obscene."

> —John McEnroe, a millionaire many times over, referring to the $6 million Grand Slam Cup (1990)

"Money is killing our game. The motivation for true greatness is gone for most players by the time they are eighteen. They win a couple matches as juniors and they are millionaires. Jimmy Connors says when he started playing you had to *win* to get rich. Now, you don't have to win, you just have to have an act."

> —Philippe Chatrier. From the 1992 book, *Tough Draw*

"Big money encourages tanking. In my opinion, tanking is going on even with a lot of the top guys today."

> —Jimmy Connors (1997)

"Those guys play thirty weeks a year, get paid two hundred grand just to show up, and they don't give a shit in the first round. That happens way too much. Half the weeks they don't even care."

—Lindsay Davenport, criticizing the halfhearted play of Yevgeny Kafelnikov, Goran Ivanisevic, Marcelo Rios, and other men players (1999)

"Tennis is going in the wrong direction, and one day it is going to fall apart completely. The money is so great now that it has to stop and I would not be disappointed if it did."

—Boris Becker, in the *Times* (UK) (1992)

"At this stage, money, to me, is more a curse than a blessing."

—Andre Agassi (1991)

"There is too much money in the game nowadays."

—Andre Agassi (2001)

"It was stupid of Andre to say that."

—Nicolas Lapentti (2001)

"When you have one hundred and fifty million in the bank, like Agassi, you're going to say that. People said there was too much money back when [Rod] Laver played at the start of the Open era. Before then tennis was an amateur sport [at the great championships] and any amount of prize money seemed like a lot. People never expected so much money. We said the same thing in my era. So I agree with Lapentti."

—Andres Gomez, 1990 French Open champion (2001)

"The money on the ATP [Tour] is ridiculous compared to what other athletes are making. I've been on the court today [at the 2001 Australian Open] for three hours, ten minutes and, when you look at the prize money check after the tournament is over, it is ridiculous. The golfers make $540,000 a week, which is to the winner. And this is the lowest tournament level they have on the U.S. tour."

—Yevgeny Kafelnikov, 1996 French, 1999 Australian and 2000 Olympic champion (2001)

"My feelings are he should take his prize money when he is done here and go and buy some perspective."

—Andre Agassi, retorting to Yevgeny Kafelnikov's claim that tennis players aren't paid enough (2001)

"Tennis players are unquestionably overpaid, as are pro athletes in general, corporate CEOs and musicians and actors. There's a lot of money out there. Companies are willing to pay big bucks to put their clothes on Anna Kournikova because she gets her pictures in the papers every week wherever she goes. I hope tennis players realize how lucky they are."

—Jim Courier, 1991–92 French Open and 1992–93 Australian Open champion (2001)

"Athletes, in general, are grossly overpaid. The money in tennis, though, compared to other sports like basketball, baseball, and football isn't that great. Our income isn't extravagant. Women's tennis is underpaid in relation to the men. The demand for women's tennis is a lot higher than it used to be. And that should definitely translate into higher prize money."

—Corina Morariu, No. 1 doubles player in 1999 (2001)

"In tennis there are very few guys making huge amounts of money, like people think. For example, I rank 18 and I don't have a clothing deal or any sponsorships. The only money I make is prize money. There is a lot of money but the top five guys get it. The only guys who get guarantees [appearance money] are guys who won Grand Slams or are in the top ten."

—Moroccan veteran Younes El Aynaoui (2001)

"I think we're all overpaid. I mean, we play a sport and we get paid very well. I'm not complaining about the prize money. I don't play for the prize money. I play for the titles."

—Pete Sampras

"My prayer is that I never get to a point in life where I think hundreds of thousands of dollars isn't a lot of money."

—Andre Agassi, told that Serena Williams joked that the Australian Open—where winners received $650,000, lowest of the Grand Slam events—should increase its prize money (2003)

"There is *never* too much money in any sport. And money is not the problem. Money doesn't make guys train less or compete harder. We are obviously earning the money from the television contracts, sponsor contracts, and the tickets we sell at tournaments. We *should* get rewarded more if we are making the sport bigger and more popular. In fact, we should get *more* prize money, a higher percent of the gross income, at the Grand Slam tournaments."

—Andrei Medvedev, 1999 French Open finalist (2001)

"Money is nice, but I came into tennis thinking that if I can buy a two-bedroom home, I'm ahead of 90 percent of the people in the world."

—Patrick Rafter (1998)

"There's too much money in the world. We should be worried about water and oxygen, not money. If you care mainly about money, you're lost."

—Mats Wilander, former No. 1 and winner of seven Grand Slam singles titles (2001)

TRUE CONFESSIONS

"I did things I should not have done. But people make mistakes, especially at my age, when you feel you are so smart, but in fact you are an asshole."

> —Martina Hingis, on behaving like a spoiled brat in the 1999 French Open final (2000)

"Sleeping tablets were my problem. No one knew of the medication I was anaesthetizing myself with. . . . I took the stuff for years."

> —Boris Becker, revealing in his 2003 tell-all book, *Wait, Stay a Moment Longer*, that from early 1987, stressed-out and lonely, he resorted to medication to sleep, and often used whisky and beer. The medication made him melancholy, sleepy, and ineffective in matches, including his 1990 Wimbledon final loss to Stefan Edberg.

"I would have loved it sometimes if an umpire or linesman had just said, 'Look, piss off you little shit.' Maybe they should have had more of a go at me."

> —John McEnroe, older and perhaps wiser, reconsidering his turbulent tennis career (1995)

"I could drink Jack Daniels without stopping. In the [Bollettieri] Academy, it was tougher to get away with, but I enjoyed it because you weren't supposed to. I smoked pot, oh sure."

> —Andre Agassi (1991)

"My accomplishments do not live up to my tennis game. Most people have to work really hard and win some big matches, and then they get money and popularity. For me it has been the reverse of everybody else. The exact opposite."

> —Andre Agassi, two months before his Grand Slam breakthrough at Wimbledon, in *Sports Illustrated* (1992)

"I am really kind of sad. This tournament has offered me and my life so much. It is a shame that I didn't respect it a little earlier."

> —Andre Agassi, who had skipped Wimbledon from 1988 to 1990, after he won The Championships in 1992

"That was my bar mitzvah in tennis, the match that made me a man."

> —Andre Agassi, after beating tenacious Michael Chang in five sets at the U.S. Open (1994)

"I have taken off some years that I have spent a lot of nights regretting."

> —Andre Agassi, still haunted by his past at nearly age thirty-one (2001)

"My only regrets are that I didn't try harder."

> —Louise Brough, who racked up thirty-five major titles in singles, doubles, and mixed doubles from 1942 to 1957. From the 1997 book, *The Tennis Lover's Book of Wisdom*

"I can be my own worst enemy and my best friend. And usually I'm my worst enemy. I rarely think of my good qualities. I have to stop myself sometimes and look at what I've accomplished in my life and tennis."

> —Mary Pierce (1997)

"I had to go through a learning process. It was difficult. I experienced a lot of hard things just to understand life and myself. . . . You could say I had my mid-life crisis in my late twenties. I don't regret any of it, though, except trusting the wrong people."

> —Bjorn Borg, on losing millions in bad business ventures, his two divorces, and being skewered by the Swedish media (1999)

"Listen, it's just a matter of time before I stuff up. It really is. I try to live as normally as I can. Sometimes, you act like a bit of a hooligan. I've got that in my blood a little bit. I'm pretty sensible, but at times, we have our weak points."

> —Patrick Rafter, on his good-guy image (2001)

"Sitting there and watching just about killed me."

> —Venus Williams, on witnessing younger sister Serena, at seventeen, beat her to a Grand Slam title at the 1999 U.S. Open

"I could never have imagined that I would go through a separation and that I could only see the two children and wife whom I love every two or three weeks. That's why I say that I have lost and it's the biggest of all defeats."

> —Three-time Wimbledon champion Boris Becker, on his divorce from German-American Barbara Feltus (2002)

"Over the years I've probably broken the rules more than anyone else."

> —Nick Bollettieri, on his flouting the tour rules prohibiting coaching during matches (1989)

"One of the reasons I wanted to coach Mary [Pierce], I'm sure, was that I hoped she might someday be good enough to beat Monica [Seles], who had turned her back on the academy and me. I've always believed in getting even."

> —Nick Bollettieri. From his 1996 memoir, *My Aces, My Faults*

"If Betty [Stove, her coach] has something to say, I need to be able to digest her coded message. Coaching is an illegal practice during a match, but everyone does it. It's just that some do it smarter than others."

> —Unapologetic Hana Mandlikova, a four-time Slam champion, in her 1989 autobiography, *Hana*

"You may be shocked and I won't name the match, because I don't want to deprive my opponent of anything, but I absolutely tanked the final of a Grand Slam tournament once."

> —Tennis icon Billie Jean King. From her 1982 autobiography, *Billie Jean*

"The act was her punishment for the past three years. It really upset me that Monica Seles was above Steffi Graf in the world tennis ranking. . . . I wanted to help Stephanie."

> —Gunther Parche, on why he stabbed Monica Seles, in his testimony to German police (1993)

"I gotta admit I used to love it, but I got into trouble a lot, got into fights and stuff. Nothing real bad, like with cops or anything. I can't do stuff like that anymore, 'cause I'm fifteen. Now I'm in high school."

> —Andrea Jaeger, then the youngest player to crack the world top ten, saying she used to get into "a few brawls" with boys infuriated that "a girl could do something better than them" in sports. In *Tennis* magazine (1980)

"All I want is to have fun in what I'm doing every day. I don't want to break records. To become the greatest player ever could take me like . . . ten more years and I don't think I'll still be playing at thirty-one."

> —Serena Williams, on pressure to become the greatest (2003)

"I know I've got a problem. When I walk out there on court, I become a maniac. . . . Something comes over me, man."

> —John McEnroe. From the 1990 book, *McEnroe: Taming the Talent*

"I was like a compulsive gambler, or an alcoholic. Anger became a powerful habit. . . . The main reason I took a fair chunk of time off on two occasions was because that anger got out of control. Some part of me began to recognize that a human being should be in control of his emotions, and if I couldn't do that, I shouldn't be out there."

> —John McEnroe. From the 2003 book, *On Being John McEnroe*

"I want to be remembered as a great player, but I guess it will be as a player who got angry on a tennis court."

> —John McEnroe (1991)

"I would like to go out on the court for one match and be a complete jerk. It would be extremely out of character for me, but it would be interesting to experience what it's like."

> —Arthur Ashe

"If I had the mental fortitude of Rod Laver, I would have won twenty more titles. I just don't have the killer instinct."

> —Arthur Ashe

"I was never that cold inside. It was always an act—an act I came to perfect—but an act just the same. It was part of my armory. I felt if my opponents did not know what I was thinking, how I was really feeling inside, then I was invincible."

—Stoic champion Bjorn Borg (1998)

"I never resented the fact that the crowds were for Evonne. But I was envious and wanted to shout, 'Don't you know I'm feeling something inside?'"

—Chris Evert, dubbed "The Ice Maiden," on playing immensely popular 1970s rival Evonne Goolagong Cawley

"The other night I saw myself on TV and ran out of the room. Some people love being a star. I'm not one of those people."

—Lindsay Davenport (1998)

"I can look at myself in the mirror and know I'm a fair competitor on every surface and not a bad guy out there. But people never believe me."

—Thomas Muster, 1995 French Open champion and abrasive personality

"At a cocktail party I was like an olive that found its way into a glass of bourbon. In short, I was a misfit."

—Pancho Gonzalez, pro champion from 1954–61, explaining why he shied away from parties. From his 1959 autobiography, *Man with a Racquet*

"It's always been me and Serena. We just prefer each other's company above anyone else's. We never get tired of each other. Ever. We get tired of other people pretty quick."

—Venus Williams, on why she and sister Serena have no friends on the pro tour and few friends outside their family (2001)

"When I first came into the business, I was very idealistic. I was going to be the agent who really had a positive effect on people's lives, who did more than just make them money. After a while I found out that a lot of it is just bullshit. You make deals for guys, you take a hard line as a negotiator and that's it. That's all they want."

—Dick Dell, client manager for ProServ. From the 1991 book, *Hard Courts*

"I only wish I could have back the years when I was twenty to twenty-four."

—Ivan Lendl, who didn't win his first Grand Slam title until the 1984 French Open (1987)

"If I had one regret, maybe even more than losing the 1984 French Open final to Ivan Lendl, it was that I wasn't able to defuse a tense situation like Jimmy Connors, who could put his arm around someone in the stands and have fans eating out of his hands."

—John McEnroe, in *Tennis* magazine (2002)

"Brad's made a career out of winning matches he was supposed to lose. And I've done just the opposite."

—Andre Agassi, on why he hired Brad Gilbert as coach (1994)

"Except for tennis, I would have been a bag boy in the A&P supermarket."

—Eddie Dibbs, top ten player in the 1970s

"My dad's philosophy was never tell you what you did right, tell you what you did wrong. I think that's what got me to No. 5 in the world. I used to throw up before every match I played. I couldn't stand the thought of losing. When I lost that drive my dad gave me, I was never the same player."

—Jimmy Arias. From the 1992 book, *Tough Draw*

"I really got into tennis so I could get a million dollars. I didn't have the right motives in the beginning at all. I was just like any other [tennis] parent then."

—Richard Williams, controversial father/coach of champions Venus and Serena (1998)

"The parents get *very* involved. I don't care what the other players say. The parents have a lot of expectations with their kids in tennis. If they tell you differently, that's a lot of bull."

—Dr. Paul Berger, father of former top tenner Jay Berger. From the 1992 book, *Tough Draw*

"I ranked No. 8 in the world while I was throwing up twenty times a day."

> —Carling Bassett-Seguso, thirty-five, who had a combination of bulimia and anorexia during her career while playing the tour significantly underweight, commenting on Daniela Hantuchova's alarmingly thin physique (2003)

"I really was not happy with myself, my tennis, my life, my parents, my coaches, my friends. . . . When I looked in the mirror, I actually saw this distorted image. I was so ugly and fat. I just wanted to kill myself."

> —Jennifer Capriati, teenage victim of burnout, in the *New York Times* (1994)

"Every tournament I was playing in 1981, I didn't care."

> —Bjorn Borg, in an article titled "Tanking" in *Tennis* magazine (1993)

"I was never a fighter until this year."

> —Marat Safin, who led the circuit in smashing rackets and was fined at the 2000 Australian Open for not trying, just before grabbing the U.S. Open for his first Grand Slam crown (2000)

"I'm twenty-three and I've had at least sixteen cars. I've had everything you could possibly have. Now I'm a little sick of it, which is good. I got it out of my system. I'm ready to concentrate on tennis."

> —Mark Philippoussis (2000)

"It's not easy for me to live with, knowing that I'm No. 1 because she was attacked."

> —Steffi Graf, on the stabbing of archrival Monica Seles (1994)

"I don't wish to be remembered as the 'grunter' or 'giggler' or even as the girl who got stabbed."

> —Monica Seles

"It's not just my case. I know it's going on with a lot of other players. It's just not right. A lot of other players say the same things happen to them."

—Croatia's Mirjana Lucic, exposing abuse of young players on the women's tour, after fleeing her physically abusive father for America with her mother and her siblings (1998)

"You can look at a men's draw and find maybe three players who have had a [dysfunctional] relationship with their father. With the girls you might find three who don't."

—Sonja Jeyaseelan, No. 1 Canadian player. From the 2001 book, *Venus Envy*

"I had a hard time playing tennis during [the] Vietnam [War]. It really upset me."

—Billie Jean King, whose brilliant career coincided with the war (1999)

"I used to carry a gun with me on tour because of the IRA [kidnap] threat."

—Martina Navratilova, in the *Daily Mail* (UK) (1991)

"First, you play for the glory of China and the Communist Party. Then, for the team. Then, you play for yourself."

—Hu Na, China's No. 1 player who defected to the United States in 1981, when noted coach Vic Braden asked her what she felt when she had gone out to play for China. Braden urged her to start playing for herself. From Braden's 1993 book, *Mental Tennis: How to Psych Yourself to a Winning Game*

"For me, the year since I won the French has been the toughest of my life. I found out that winning in tennis doesn't bring joy, it brings pressure."

—Michael Chang, at age eighteen (1990)

"I would have said it [my main competition] would have been anybody, but not Pete. I played Pete in Rome in 1989 and said, 'The poor guy can't keep a ball in the court. He never should have got rid of his two-handed backhand. I just don't see a good future for him.'"

—Andre Agassi, self-deprecatingly recalling how, as a teenager, he wrongly figured Pete Sampras would never amount to much of a tennis player (2003)

"I didn't find out who were the best [players] until I turned pro and had my brains beaten out for six months at the start of 1963."

> —All-time great Rod Laver, who captured the Grand Slam as an amateur in 1962, on losing nineteen of his first twenty-one pro matches against Ken Rosewall and Lew Hoad

"It does bug me, being No. 2. . . . When you are used to being a champion, it's like a drug—you want to be there again and again."

> —Martina Hingis, eighteen, after losing the No. 1 ranking to Lindsay Davenport (1998)

"Sometimes I feel, been there, done it, now what? What more is there to prove?"

> —Former No. 1–ranked Martina Hingis, sidelined following ankle surgery, at age twenty-one

"To me, it's a little bit more profound because I just know inside what I've really gone through and what it's taken to get to this point. I feel like I've almost been to hell and back."

> —Jennifer Capriati, one-time poster child for premature burnout, on her long and difficult journey to No. 1 (2001)

"I was being given a form of legal steroid they gave to horses until they decided it was too strong even for them. People have to become more aware of what they are putting into their bodies."

> —John McEnroe reacted to Greg Rusedski's admission that he had tested positive for banned steroid nandrolone by admitting he unwittingly took steroids for six years (2004)

"I'm really not a '90s kind of guy. I'm more of a '50s guy."

> —Pete Sampras (2003)

"I have to win the French to be considered the greatest ever. If I don't? It's a strike against me."

> —Pete Sampras (1997)

"I even had to struggle to act human with my mother. Every now and then, she would break down: 'You treat me so badly! Why can't you treat me the way you treat your friends?' And I'd say, 'Because you're my mother!' Then she'd start crying and I'd realize how asinine I was being."

—John McEnroe, fessing up about his meanness. From his 2002 autobiography, *You Cannot Be Serious*

"There are times I'd love to be honest, but most of the time I have
to give the right answer rather than the truthful one. I know you
want more substance, but it has backfired on me before."

—Proper Brit Tim Henman, explaining his media strategy

"The problem is, I don't really have any friends."

—Venus Williams, on her cutlery fetish and why she doesn't show off her
acquisitions to friends (2002)

"I've got to say, what turns me on more than anything is just
making a difference in people's lives. That's one thing I've taken
with me and I'll keep. Probably even more so than the accomplishment[s] itself at the French Open is the fact that somewhere along
the line it gave hope to people."

—Andre Agassi, the altruist, whose college preparatory academy in Las
Vegas has given hope to hundreds of disadvantaged children (1999)

"During the last couple of years of my tennis career, I was suffering, oh, how I was suffering. I would wake up in the morning and
think 'God, I have to go practice and I really don't want to.' I was
miserable but I didn't know what was wrong with me so I consult-
ed a psychologist who told me, 'You either go in this direction,
tennis, or that direction, a new life; it's up to you.' And I realised I
wanted to go in 'that direction,' away from tennis which I had
grown to hate."

—Argentine star Gabriela Sabatini, in the *Telegraph* (UK) (2003)

"Martina claims I tell the dirtiest jokes around—probably as a
semi-revolt against my strict Catholic upbringing. And when I've
become angry in practice, every four-letter word imaginable has
graced these lips."

—Chris Evert, in a Larry Schwartz article on ESPN.com

"I remember when Jimmy [Connors] and I went into confession
and he came out a half-hour later and I said, 'How'd it go?' He
said, 'I wasn't finished. The priest said come back next Sunday.'"

—Chris Evert, on former fiancé Jimmy Connors (2001)

DAVIS CUP

"I thought if men of different nations could get together and compete on the tennis court they would get along and the world would become a better place for it."

> —What Dwight F. Davis, the donor of the Davis Cup, told his grandson, Dwight F. Davis III, when the boy, then eight or nine, asked him why he had given the Davis Cup. From the 1999 book, *Dwight Davis: The Man and the Cup*

"When I started playing tennis I promised my mother two things. One was that I would graduate from college. The other was that I would play Davis Cup."

> —John McEnroe

"I will go anywhere, any time, to play Davis Cup for America."

> —John McEnroe

"When I started to play tennis as a kid, my biggest dream was to represent my country, to be part of the Davis Cup."

> —Bjorn Borg (1999)

"There is a big difference in playing for yourself and playing for your country. When the umpire announces 'Australia' instead of your name and they start playing the national anthem, it's impossible not to get a lump in your throat."

> —Rod Laver

"I still get goose pimples out there with the guys, when I hear the 'Star Spangled Banner' and watch the flag go up."

—John McEnroe (1986)

"The Cup means a helluva lot more to me than winning Wimbledon or the U.S. Open."

—Lleyton Hewitt, after leading Australia to its twenty-eighth Davis Cup title and his second during his five years on the team. The fiery Hewitt pulled out thrilling five-set comeback victories over Swiss star Roger Federer in the semis and No. 3–ranked Juan Carlos Ferrero of Spain in the final. (2003)

"Winning for your country gives you a high that lasts two or three days. You can't go to Kmart and pick that up."

—Jim Courier (1999)

"We have to win. The country will not allow us to lose to the Russians."

—Jan Kodes, star of the Czechoslovakian Davis Cup team, in 1971, three years after Russian tanks had rolled into Czechoslovakia. The Czechs prevailed 4–1 in Prague. From the 1999 book, *The Davis Cup: Celebrating 100 Years of International Tennis*

"It almost means too much. It goes beyond the tennis match. They almost turn it into a war between countries, and I don't agree with that."

—Boris Becker, on German hypernationalism in Davis Cup (1991)

"They say you have the best and worst moments of your career in Davis Cup. This is one of the best moments of my life."

—Patrick Rafter, after dramatically coming back from a two-set deficit to beat Cedric Pioline after four hours and fifteen minutes to help Australia defeat reigning champion France (1997)

"We have a proud tradition. Whenever I get a call to represent my country, I'm there. It's a shame the other guys don't feel the same way. There's nothing better than winning for your country."

—Patrick Rafter, chiding American players for not always playing Davis Cup (1997)

"I personally told every one of them that they're full of crap when they start laying out their baloney excuses about why they are not playing [in the Davis Cup]. They don't care enough is what it boils down to."

> —John McEnroe, on playing for one's country (1997)

"The feeling you get from playing Davis Cup dramatically combines your love for the game of tennis and the country you represent."

> —Vijay Amritraj, who led India to Davis Cup finals in 1974 and 1987. From his 1990 autobiography, *Vijay!*

"Tournament tennis is a wonderful game, but Davis Cup matches are mental torture. Every time I played against those Frenchmen in Davis Cup matches I suffered hell for weeks."

> —Legendary Bill Tilden, who led America to Challenge Round triumphs from 1920–26 before France's "Four Musketeers" dethroned the United States

"I just wish that the average American tennis fan understood how much it takes to play these matches. In 1995, we went to Moscow and won the final on the road and brought the Cup back home. There's no celebration, no trip to the White House. It's a small tidbit in the sports section because it's NFL Sunday. When you give up personal goals for a team goal like this, you should get some accolades."

> —Davis Cup stalwart Jim Courier (1997)

"There is nothing more important to an athlete than to represent his country. You can't really understand the true feeling of Davis Cup until you play in a final."

> —Mark Philippoussis, who won both his singles matches to lead Australia to a 3–2 victory over France in the 1999 final

"The Davis Cup has become impossible—a revolving door. A lot of the countries had to play '74 matches as early as the summer of '73. The Davis Cup nations have to change the format and make it something like the World Cup soccer, with all, or most of the matches played like a huge tournament at one venue."

> —Arthur Ashe. From his 1975 book, *Portrait in Motion*

"The Davis Cup is conducted in an archaic way. It should not be spread out around the world, different venues, different times. It should be patterned after the World Cup of soccer, with the sixteen top nations assembling at one site. It would be fantastic for tennis—a great annual or bi-annual festival of sport—and the TV coverage would carry to hundreds of millions of homes around the world."

—Jack Kramer. From his 1979 book, *The Game: My 40 Years in Tennis*

"It would have been unthinkable when I was starting to get good, back in 1963, that anyone would pass up the opportunity to play Davis Cup."

—U.S. Davis Cup captain Arthur Ashe, referring to Jimmy Connors's sporadic participation in the Cup, in *World Tennis* magazine (1980)

"I want to play in England and on the Davis Cup team. I want to play for my country."

—The tennis goals of twelve-year-old Jimmy Connors (1964)

"It's great to be playing for millions of Americans instead of just Jimmy Connors."

—Jimmy Connors, before making his Davis Cup debut against Venezuela (1976)

"To Mac and me, that silver cup was the Holy Grail. To Jimmy, it seemed that it might have been made of Styrofoam, he had so little sense of, or interest in, Davis Cup legend and lore."

—Arthur Ashe, contrasting John McEnroe's and his love for the Davis Cup with Jimmy Connors's indifference. From Ashe's 1993 memoirs, *Days of Grace*

"I found out about Davis Cup. It's totally different, the pressure that doesn't exist in the tournaments where you're on your own."

—Pete Sampras, on his disastrous Davis Cup debut when he was upset by Henri Leconte and Guy Forget in the final before a roaring French crowd (1991)

"No amount of money can compensate for the loss of ego from a poor Davis Cup performance."

—Mark Cox, 1960s Davis Cup stalwart for Great Britain

"We were playing for the Davis Cup and that was an obsession. Everything else took second or third place and even tournaments took a back seat to the Cup. That should be the case again today."

   —Adrian Quist, 1930s and '40s Davis Cup standout from Australia (1990)

"The Davis Cup could be the single most under-leveraged asset in sports and entertainment today."

   —Arlen Kantarian, USTA chief executive of professional tennis (2000)

"A little cheating is expected in Davis Cup. Not robbery, really, because no one wants to be a thief, but a little help in touchy situations. It is all right because it is for your country, and besides, the other country is doing the same thing when you play there."

   —Italy's Nicola Pietrangeli, on the unstated Golden Rule in some
   countries

"It takes individual character to win Grand Slams. But what you do in Davis Cup is sacrifice for others—it's about sharing and respect for your teammates. That's why the Davis Cup is great."

   —Yannick Noah, French Davis Cup player and captain (1992)

"What I love about Davis Cup is it is not about contracts, schedules and business. This tradition is bigger than dollars."

   —Davis Cup captain Yannick Noah, after France nipped host Sweden 3–2
   in the 1996 Cup final when Arnaud Boetsch outlasted Nicklas Kulti 10–8
   in the deciding set. It was the first time in Davis Cup history that the winner of the Cup was determined in the fifth set of the fifth and final match.

"[Davis Cup is the place to look] if you want to see genuine smiles on the faces of multimillionaires."

   —U.S. Davis Cup captain Tom Gullikson (1996)

"There's an energy in Davis Cup you don't get anywhere else, not even in Grand Slams. If you can't get up for Davis Cup, you'd better check to make sure you're still breathing."

   —Andre Agassi (1999)

"You want to win so much for the people that every shot you miss is like an arrow straight to your heart."

   —Ilie Nastase, on the agony of his famous loss to Stan Smith in Romania's
   3–2 defeat by the United States at Bucharest in the 1972 Davis Cup final

"To me, the greatest thing in the world was playing for my country. It was such a proud moment. My entire country was backing me the minute I stepped out on that court!"

—Fred Perry, who led Great Britain to Davis Cup titles in 1933–36

"What is the most famous sports trophy in the world? You can't have to think twice before the Davis Cup comes to your mind. That highly prized trophy is coveted by tennis teams of all nations. No other competition for any sports prize is as widespread or as far-flung as the competition for the Davis Cup."

—Jack Kramer. From his 1949 book, *Winning Tennis*

"It's for your country. It's for everybody in America. I think it's one of the greatest honors in sports to be asked to participate on behalf of your country. It's been something I've been looking forward to all my life."

—Rising star Andy Roddick, on why he is committed to playing Davis Cup (2001)

"I can't contain the joy I feel when the crowd is behind you. I just love it. Davis Cup is more important in my heart than an everyday Tour event. The juices are flowing as soon as I wake up."

—Hyper, rising American star Andy Roddick, after routing Alberto Martin to clinch a 4–1 Davis Cup victory over Spain and boost his Cup singles record to 7–0 (2002)

"It's obviously great that I'm getting fantastic money playing and going out there and doing something I love. But I'd be playing if there was no money. There's not much money playing Davis Cup. [But] when I set my schedule at the start of the year, Davis Cup is the first thing that I write down."

—World-ranked No. 1 Lleyton Hewitt, who earned nearly $15 million in prize money and endorsements in 2002

"I hope the time will come when we can settle our international differences in courts, just as we settle our tennis differences on a court."

—President Harry Truman, when conducting the Davis Cup draw at the White House, joining President Calvin Coolidge as the only U.S. presidents to conduct the Davis Cup draw (1947)

ALL IN THE FAMILY

"Just do your very best, dear, but make sure you win."

—What the mother of Helen Wills firmly told her daughter before the nineteen-year-old California prodigy lost 6–3, 8–6 to reigning queen Suzanne Lenglen in their historic duel at Cannes, France (1926)

"Good God, how badly you played."

—The mother of Suzanne Lenglen, cruelly chiding her exhausted daughter who had collapsed on a bench and burst into tears following her nerve-wracking victory over Helen Wills at Cannes, France (1926)

"It's you and I against the world."

—What hard-driving mother/coach Gloria Connors often told young Jimmy Connors to instill a tough-guy attitude that reflected their blue-collar roots in Belleville, Illinois

"If a parent is more ambitious than a kid, that's the death of a player."

—Stan Smith, 1971 U.S. Open and 1972 Wimbledon champion, in *Tennis USTA* magazine (1998)

"It's the first time in my life I enjoy tennis."

—Mirjana Lucic, who fled Croatia with her mother and four siblings to Florida after being terrorized physically and mentally for ten years by her father, Marinko (1998)

"I never went to sleep without a prayer, never ever in my whole life. And I never woke up without a prayer. And my prayer was always just to get rid of my father, just for him to leave us alone."

—Mirjana Lucic (1999)

"I could not fight as usual because of all the turmoil. Tennis is a game won with the head, and lately my head has not been on tennis."

> —Steffi Graf, after upset losses at Roland Garros and Wimbledon, referring to sensational front-page stories revealing that her father, Peter, had an extramarital affair with a call girl who, with a boxing promoter, was trying to extort $400,000 from the Grafs (1990)

"The father is often the girl's biggest adversary. There is tremendous ego involved when a man gives up his own work and devotes his life to the career of the daughter."

> —Ion Tiriac, who had to part company with then world-ranked No. 5 Mary Joe Fernandez, after repeated interference from her father, Jose (1996)

"They say my dad just thinks I'm a money-making machine. I wonder how they'd like it if someone wrote something hurtful like that about their family."

> —Fifteen-year-old Jennifer Capriati, on public criticism of her abrasive father, Stefano, in the *New York Times* (1992)

"The excitement, the endorsements, the money, the prestige, the pride. There it all is, and you get caught up in it, and you're not thinking of what your child is missing, and if this is what's best for them. I believe in my heart that she did love tennis, and still does, but I beat myself up later for not stopping things from getting so out of hand back then. I let the whole thing control them."

> —Denise Capriati, confessing the dilemma in handling the career of her daughter Jennifer, who burned out during the mid-1990s (1997)

"I've had a pretty nasty childhood. My mom wasn't with me, so he'd destroy my toys when he got mad. He'd get upset and I'd be scared. I'd just go into my room and hide."

> —Sonya Jeyaseelan, then eighteen, whose father Reggie doubled as coach early in her career, in *USA Today* (1994)

"I'm not ashamed or proud. If I didn't do things like that, she wouldn't be where she is today. She's a little child, young and innocent. There are certain things you can only learn out of fear."

> —Reggie Jeyaseelan, after being told of his daughter's accusations, including his smacking balls at her at the net if she missed two shots in a row, in *USA Today* (1994)

"It sounds strange, but I've been working so hard on just loving myself. I really did hate myself growing up because tennis was everything to my dad, and if I won, I was great. If I didn't, I was nothing."

> —Ann Grossman, on her late father/coach, Bill, who verbally abused her as a teenager (1994)

"I'm very happy my father has not contacted me since my [French Open] victory. . . . At last [my brothers and father] are giving me the respect I asked for, the space to lead my life. . . . They refused to understand my ambitions and determination to become a top player. They could not understand the time and dedication it takes, and they hurt me very much."

> —Justine Henin-Hardenne (2003)

"For a few years my whole life was tennis and Jimmy [Connors], and then there was a void there—no Jimmy. After that, I started thinking about myself, my morals, my life, my future. Until then, my dad had made all the decisions, and I had agreed with everything. Now we have occasional outbursts, but we're closer as a result of them."

> —Chris Evert, in an interview with Julie Heldman. From the 1979 book, *Famous Women Tennis Players*

"Nothing I ever did was good enough for him. I'd beat a kid love and one in a final, and all Dad would say was, 'How did you let him get a game?'"

> —Jimmy Arias, who turned pro at fifteen, won the 1983 Italian Open and ranked a career-high No. 5 in 1984, on his demanding father, Antonio. From *Tennis* magazine (1994)

"If I didn't leave Las Vegas, either my dad was going to pop me or I was going to pop him, and I was probably going to quit tennis."

> —Andre Agassi, then fifteen and on the verge of being kicked out of the Bollettieri Tennis Academy, telling Bollettieri about his dysfunctional family life before leaving Vegas at thirteen. From the 1996 book, *My Aces, My Faults*

"The hardest part about traveling on the tour would be keeping perspective when the whole world is kissing your ass."

> —Tami Agassi, on her brother Andre's early pro years as the *enfant terrible* of tennis, on *ESPN Sports Classic*

"By having kids, I got my humanity back. I'd been like some tennis dude, No. 1 in the world and not happy with it."

> —John McEnroe, in *Sports Illustrated* (1996)

"No, I'm thrilled about being a very good mother."

> —Evonne Goolagong Cawley, when asked in 1978 if she were thrilled that her comeback had gone so well. From the 1979 book, *Famous Women Tennis Players*

"The great high of winning Wimbledon lasts for about a week. You go down in the record book, but you don't have anything tangible to hold on to. But having a baby—there isn't any comparison."

> —Chris Evert, whose eighteen Grand Slam singles titles include three Wimbledons. From the 1992 book, *The Last Word: A Treasury of Women's Quotes*

"I can never remember her cuddling me in her arms or saying, 'I love you, Ivan.' I wanted her to be softer to me. Once I saved up to buy her flowers and a box of sweets. But it made no difference."

> —Ivan Lendl, 1980s superstar from Czechoslovakia, on his hard-hearted mother, Olga Lendlova, who was obsessed with making him the champion she never was. From an unauthorized biography by Lendl's former friend, George Mendoza (1987)

"My mother was always snapping at me to eat my peas and carrots. But the more she yelled, the more I resisted her. Then she would start hitting me across the face. It hurt but I forced myself not to cry. If I had, she would have known that she had got to me—and I couldn't let that happen."

> —Ivan Lendl, on being tormented as a child. From an unauthorized biography by Lendl's former friend, George Mendoza (1987)

"I was pushed by my mother very, very hard. This is, of course, why I became a good player, why I was in the top ten, and why I won so many tournaments. But it was tough to have a mother who didn't give me any choice other than tennis in my life."

—Bulgaria's Magdalena Maleeva, who along with her older sisters Manuela and Katarina, comprise the only trio of siblings to achieve world top ten rankings (2002)

"Kill the bitch, Mary!"

—Jim Pierce's infamous outburst during an under-thirteens match between his daughter and junior rival Magdalena Maleeva

"I built the Ferrari and now I want the keys back."

—Notorious tennis father Jim Pierce, angry at being banned from women's tournaments at the request of his daughter Mary, who also took out a restraining order against him, citing years of abuse and threats against her life (1994)

"People say I put pressure on Mary. Do you think pressure is coming out here in the sunshine with a little yellow ball going back and forth over the net and running and hitting it and getting paid tens of thousands and millions of dollars a year to hit that ball? Do you think that's pressure?"

—Jim Pierce, interviewed by *USA Network* (1998)

"Parents aren't the story. People shouldn't talk to them, they shouldn't be interviewed. Alexandra [Stevenson] is a qualifier who has reached the semifinals at Wimbledon. That's the story, and what are we talking about? Her mother. Every time they talk about Jelena Dokic, they talk about her father. Same thing with Lucic."

—Martina Navratilova, infuriated with bad-behaving tennis parents who steal the limelight from their talented children (1999)

"Look at almost any of the great players. Would they have succeeded anyway if they hadn't been pushed? Would Agassi have been a great champion of he hadn't been pushed by his father? Would Monica Seles, if her father hadn't quit his job and pushed her? It's difficult to say. . . . I seriously doubt I would've been the player I became if I hadn't been forced into it in some way."

—John McEnroe, whose ambitious father pushed him and enthusiastically watched his weekend practice sessions. From McEnroe's 2002 autobiography, *You Cannot Be Serious*

"If he hadn't pushed me, I'd probably be putting food on supermarket shelves now. So I'm pretty grateful for him."

—Mark Philippoussis, on his father, Nick, who emigrated from Greece in the mid-1970s, after Philippoussis clinched the Davis Cup final for Australia over Spain (2003)

"She always wins. The problem is I can't always keep my eyes on the ball."

—Andre Agassi, on playing with wife and former world-ranked No. 1 Steffi Graf (2002)

"What do you want me to do, Mother, smile or win?"

—Intense teenager Steffi Graf, in response to her mother's comment, "Steffi, I would love to see one picture of you in the papers in which you are smiling."

"I think Lindsay Davenport's parents are terrific. You know why? I've never met them. Of all the teenage wonders I've known, she's the first one whose parents weren't hanging around all the time. I'm crazy about the Davenports."

—Veteran Pam Shriver, after being clobbered by eighteen-year-old Lindsay Davenport at the 1994 U.S. Open

"Some [tennis] parents feel they are the child. They get emotional. It's like you see in Little League baseball. I always walk away. I don't bother my kids."

—Soterios (Sam) Sampras, father of superstar Pete Sampras, in the *Los Angeles Times* (2002)

"Life is not perfect and neither is sports. But with a little bit of parental patience, guidance and common sense, every child should be able to play without fear, guilt, or pressure. They are entitled to nothing less."

—From Billie Jean King's 1978 instruction book, *Tennis Love: A Parents' Guide to the Sport*

"In which other sport would a twenty-two-year-old No. 1 have his parents traveling with him?"

> —Boris Becker, on Lleyton Hewitt, after the Aussie, as defending champion, was shockingly upset in the Wimbledon first round by Ivo Karlovic, a qualifier ranked No. 203 (2003)

"Why it becomes an issue now is beyond me. It says a lot about the fickle nature and jealousy of some people. It's at times like these when you find out who your true friends are."

> —Glynn Hewitt, father of deposed Wimbledon champion Lleyton, saying he and his wife found it strange there was no criticism of their presence when their son won Wimbledon the previous year (2003)

"My sisters have been spoiling me to death, and my brothers have been beating the crap out of me."

> —Patrick Rafter, 1997–98 U.S. Open champion, on his eight siblings

"Every emotion you can imagine was there—from worrying about how he's doing to worrying that he might beat me."

> —John McEnroe, after defeating younger brother Patrick in the final of a tournament in Chicago (1991)

"To play tennis you need the killer instinct. It's hard to have the killer instinct with your sister."

> —Magdalena Maleeva, who lost to one of her two older sisters at four separate Grand Slam tournaments (2001)

"It takes a Sutton to beat a Sutton."

> —Oft-used phrase describing the great success of the four Sutton sisters—May, Ethel, Florence, and Violet—in the early twentieth century. They combined to win the southern California championship eighteen times. May captured it nine times, the first title coming in 1900 and the last, amazingly, in 1928 after she had four children.

"You beat my sister. I owed you."

> —How Venus Williams greeted a stunned Anne Miller after easily beating her in a first-round match at Indian Wells (1997)

"For two women to compete, it can be awkward. For two friends, it can be difficult. For two from the same country, very difficult. For sisters, impossible."

—1960s Italian star Lea Pericoli, now a TV analyst, on the disappointing 2002 French Open final between Venus and Serena Williams

"It's not easy for me to play someone I care so much about."

—Serena Williams, before beating her sister, Venus, in the 2003 Wimbledon final, their fifth Grand Slam final in thirteen months

"To play your sibling is the toughest thing. You cannot play good tennis. It's hard to fight to win. You cannot pump your fist. You just hit the ball, and that's it."

—Olivier Rochus, world-class player from Belgium, after beating older brother Christophe at Wimbledon (2002)

"It was uncomfortable, unsettling. I hated every minute of it. I didn't want to lose to her, but then after I beat her, I felt terrible."

—All-time great Chris Evert, on her three professional matches against younger sister Jeannie, in the *Washington Post* (2002)

"I'm sitting over there and I'm thinking, 'Does Serena have enough sports drink?' I've always taken care of Serena. That's the way it's always been. I'm the one doing the driving late at night when we came home from school. I was always driving with her asleep. I'm the big sister and that's the way it will always be."

—Venus Williams, saying that she found herself thinking about her sister during the changeovers of her Wimbledon semifinal victory (2000)

"Tennis is just a game. Family is forever."

—Serena Williams, before losing to her sister Venus in the Wimbledon semifinals (2000)

ATHLETES ONLY NEED APPLY

"I wanted to do well because some people still think tennis players aren't good athletes."

>—Bjorn Borg, after winning six of eight events at the European Superstars competition in France, beating an Olympic medal-winning hurdler, among others (1979)

"This white boy can jump."

>—Pete Sampras, on his trademark slam-dunk overhead (1999)

"In tennis, you need everything. You need durability, hand-eye coordination, and mental endurance because it's a one-on-one sport. There's no help from your coach or manager or anyone out there. Tennis players are tremendous athletes, some of the best in the world. In some ways it's even more difficult to play tennis than to play in the NBA. There are no substitutions, no halftimes to recover. You definitely see someone's true character on the tennis court."

>—Pete Sampras (2000)

"I can tell you the incredible athleticism that it takes to play it well. In tennis, the greater the athlete you are, the greater your ability becomes to win and the more you separate yourself [from the field]. From that standpoint, it requires strength, it requires fitness, it requires eye-hand [coordination], it requires every component."

>—Andre Agassi (2000)

"Tennis requires a lot because you have to have an all-around athleticism."—Andy Roddick (*Susan Mullane/Camerawork USA, Inc.*)

"Tennis requires a lot because you have to have an all-around athleticism. You need speed, endurance, agility, hand-eye coordination and all that good stuff rolled into one. Whereas in some other sports, you can specialize in one or two particular aspects of athleticism."

　　—Andy Roddick (2001)

"A tennis player is the complete athlete. He has to have the speed of a sprinter, the endurance of a marathon runner, the agility of a boxer or fencer, and the gray matter of a good football quarterback. Baseball, football, basketball players are good athletes, but they don't need all those attributes to perform well."

　　—Bobby Riggs, triple Wimbledon champion in 1939 and pro champion in 1946–47. From his 1973 autobiography, *Court Hustler*

"Tennis is one of the most complete sports because you need to be strong in the upper body and lower body, you need to be quick, you need endurance and good reflexes. I chose tennis when I was younger because it was very complete. You need to have a little bit of everything to excel at it."

　　—Carlos Moya, 1998 French Open champion (2001)

"Tennis takes a lot of talent because you need to combine so many physical and mental skills, such as hand-eye coordination, speed, strength, endurance and flexibility. Even if all these physical skills are perfected, if the mental part is not as strong, it is difficult to succeed as a tennis player."

　　—Meaghann Shaughnessy (2001)

"Binocularity—the ability of both eyes to converge and focus on an approaching object and to fix by triangulation that object's exact position in space—may be the single most important ability in tennis, and very few players have it to any degree."

　　—From Dr. Robert Arnot and Charles Gaines's 1984 book, *SportSelection*

"The first two steps taken toward a tennis ball usually determine whether or not the ball will be reached, and therefore instantaneous speed, or *explosiveness*, is much more important in tennis than either aerobic or anaerobic power."

    —From Dr. Robert Arnot and Charles Gaines's 1984 book, *SportSelection*

"Tennis is a unique sport. In terms of sheer athletic ability, one has to be very powerful, strong, and explosive, as well as agile. Very much like basketball, movement is in all eight different directions, as well as jumping up and down. All that demands a lot from the body. Tennis is even tougher athletically than basketball because it's really the only sport that doesn't have an off-season."

    —Leander Paes, doubles star (2001)

"Some people talk about Tiger Woods being the greatest athlete in the world. That is absolutely laughable. If you talk about cardio-vascular fitness, he wouldn't last five minutes on a tennis court. And look at these guys—Montgomerie, Mickelson—they haven't seen their knees in years."

    —John Lloyd, former British Davis Cupper (2003)

"Golf is not a sport—it's an artistic exercise like ballet. You can be a fat slob and still play golf."

    —John McEnroe

"Golf is a game. Anything where you can drink and do better is not a sport."

    —Andre Agassi (1999)

"Agassi's ability to maintain his speed, reflexes and stamina at his age is nothing short of remarkable. We marvel at [baseball superstar] Barry Bonds' amazing play at the age of thirty-nine, but Bonds 'only' has to retain his talent as a hitter. He doesn't have to be as fast on the bases or as nimble in the field as he once was. For a tennis player, it's a different story. If any part of Agassi's game fails, he's gone."

    —*Sports Illustrated* writer Phil Taylor, in praise of thirty-three-year-old Andre Agassi who entered the U.S. Open ranked No. 1 (2003)

"Ten years ago you didn't have to be a great athlete—you just had to be a great tennis player. Then along came Martina [Navratilova], and the way she worked with weights, the way she was watching everything she was eating—she was giving 100 percent of herself to tennis, and that inspired women players."

—Chris Evert (1985)

"This is the toughest sport of all. Even in pro basketball, they don't play every night. Besides, when they're tired, they get a substitute. We don't. We play even when we're hurt. I've played with a sprained ankle. Lew [Hoad] finished a match one night after colliding with a wall and being knocked unconscious."

—Pancho Gonzalez, 1954–61 pro champion, in *SPORT* magazine (1958)

PASSION PLAY

"This was no passing dislike, but a blazing, virulent, powerful and consuming hate. I believed I could not win without hatred. And win I must because I was afraid to lose."

— Maureen Connolly, the first woman Grand Slammer in 1953

"She's out to kill them. You have to be mean to be a champion. How can you lick someone if you feel friendly toward them?"

— Eleanor "Teach" Tennant, who coached teen queen Maureen Connolly, on her protegee's fiercely determined demeanor. From the 1979 book, *Famous Women Tennis Players*

"I like to have the fans against me. I want to do everything I can to get them against me more. When they're yelling at me, I really get into the match."

— Anti-hero Jimmy Connors (1976)

"If I'm playing a foreign player and the crowd isn't for me, I feel like screaming at the people, 'Hey, I'm an American! Why don't you cheer for me?' Ninety-five percent of the time when the crowd's against me, it makes me tougher. I don't want to give them the satisfaction of seeing me lose."

— Chris Evert, renowned for her on-court stoicism, revealing the depth of her emotion. From the 1979 book, *Famous Women Tennis Players*

"After all, tennis is my life, my art. I love to play the game. Staying on top is tough, but there's nothing else in the world like it. That's why we all keep coming back for more."

> —Legendary Billie Jean King, on returning to competition after knee surgery at age thirty-three (1977)

"They don't like me because I win too much. That's a no-no here. It tells you something about why the English haven't had a really great player since Fred Perry. I'm sure it would be different if I were English. But I'm American. I'm competitive and hungry and intense."

> —Billie Jean King, winner of a record twenty Wimbledon titles

"Getting into those kinds of battles, I live for that. That's what I love about tennis."

> —Jennifer Capriati, after escaping two match points to beat Monica Seles in the Nasdaq-100 Open in Miami (2002)

"When I came off the court I just felt like the whole world was coming down on me. My heart was being ripped out."

> —Jennifer Capriati, after losing a heartbreaking 4–6, 7–5, 7–6 semifinal to eventual U.S. Open champion Justine Henin-Hardenne, having been two points away from victory on eleven occasions (2003)

"When I see him holding the Open trophy, it pisses me off. I feel like that should be mine."

> —Pete Sampras, after Patrick Rafter won the 1997 U.S. Open

"It is schizophrenic, and is the tour's biggest problem, that they want characters but forbid any passion. I would promote, and not ban, passion."

> —Marcelo Rios, railing against ATP attempts to curb the kind of behavior that earned him a reputation as the sport's bad boy (1999)

"Mr. Average American cannot sit in a stand and watch a game in a quiet detached way. Not only does he feel out of it but he is too emotional for dispassionate impartiality; he must voice his feelings, booing, cheering, shouting remarks at players and officials alike, and overall create an uninhibited hubbub. Thus he participates in the game, and that is important. Every sports fan is a frustrated player. Baseball and football have won him—tennis has not."

> —Gardnar Mulloy, a 1940s and '50s American star. From his 1959 autobiography, *Advantage Striker*

"I enjoy playing in New York City. The people here are crazy. They enjoy seeing two guys going at each other, spilling blood. That's the kind of guy I am."

> —Jimmy Connors, en route to his fifth U.S. Open title (1983)

"Why are you doing this to yourself? Why are you suffering for an event you've won five times already?"

> —Ilie Nastase, after seeing old sidekick Jimmy Connors, at thirty-nine, prostrate on the massage table during his amazing run to the U.S. Open semifinals (1991)

"You wouldn't understand. You're European."

> —Jimbo's retort to Nastase

"I am not the typical European clay player. You see, I like people who live life with a passion. And in tennis, as in life, I think everyone should go to the net. You can make mistakes but you have to attack. Take risks. Like 'The Three Musketeers,' attack and live dangerously!"

> —Yannick Noah, who lived dangerously by serving and volleying to the 1983 French Open title, in *Sports Illustrated* (1983)

"Tennis is like a woman I once loved, and I'm not in love with her anymore. I can't get rid of her. But I will. Definitely this year."

> —Yannick Noah, at the end of his pro career (1991)

"I like everything about tennis; the game, the courts, the competition, and doing everything you can to win. It's such a beautiful sport."

> —Martina Hingis, the ever-smiling Swiss champion. From the 1998 book, *The Best of the Best in Tennis*

"There is no sensation in the sporting world so thoroughly enjoyable to me as that when I meet a tennis ball just right in the very middle of my racquet and smack it, just right, where my opponent should be but is not."

—Bill Tilden. From his 1925 book, *Match Play and the Spin of the Ball*

"To hit a ball right, when you're on the balls of your feet, your body's working the way you want. . . . It's the greatest thing in the whole wide world."

—Billie Jean King, talking to journalist Grace Lichtenstein (1974)

"What's tough is knowing I'm not a professional tennis player anymore. I've wanted to be No. 1 in the world since I was eight years old. To say it's all over makes my stomach hurt."

—Jimmy Arias, after losing in the first round of the 1994 U.S. Open qualifying event in the final match of his career

"You reach these highs at a young age, then part of you keeps searching forever to re-create them. . . . That's why bad things happen with athletes more often than with other people. They can't get that high anymore, so they have to get it artificially, or, if they don't succeed, feel empty."

—John McEnroe. From his 2002 autobiography, *You Cannot Be Serious*

"I am a romantic. I believe in love. I believe in happily ever after. I'm not downhearted or bitter or disappointed. It's all part of this game called life."

—Boris Becker, known as much for his tumultuous love life as his legendary tennis career, in the *Daily Telegraph* (UK) (2001)

"Tennis is more than just a sport. It's an art, like the ballet. Or like a performance in the theater. When I step on the court I feel like Anna Pavlova. Or like Adelina Patti. Or even like Sarah Bernhardt. I see the footlights in front of me. I hear the whisperings of the audience. I feel an icy shudder. Win or die! Now or never! It's the crisis of my life."

—What Bill Tilden said to Frederic Prokosch. From the 1983 book, *Voices: A Memoir*

"The one thing I've always known is that people had better walk out of the stadium feeling that there's no way they'd rather spend their money."

—Andre Agassi, on the importance of being entertaining

"There are a couple of connections between art and tennis. People in the art business have a tendency to one day tell you you're the greatest artist that ever lived and the next second make you wonder if you'll ever sell a piece of art again. So I think I have a knowledge of that, because you have a fear when you go on the court: fear of failure. . . . I understand [artists] are needy and insecure."

—John McEnroe, talking to the *Independent* (UK) in 1994. He opened the John McEnroe Gallery in SoHo the following year.

"I feel that tennis is an art form that is capable of moving the players and the audience—at least a knowledgeable audience—in almost sensual ways. . . . When I'm performing at my absolute best, I think that some of the euphoria I feel must be transmitted to the audience."

—Billie Jean King

"The chemistry of a tennis player is different from that of a painter. The artist is not judged as harshly. The artist does not win or lose every day in black and white terms as we do. Picasso did not have a 5–3 won-lost record with Van Gogh. But I have to live with my 5–3 record against McEnroe and try to see that the balance doesn't change."

—Bjorn Borg

"It's hard everywhere as an artist. Why should tennis be different?"

—French racket artist Fabrice Santoro, who amassed a mere $6.3 million prize money during his career (2003)

"Excitable heart patients should be kept well away from TV sets when events like the Wimbledon final are shown. The risk of a fatal heart attack is much too great."

—Heart specialist Dr. Jan Soloski, in *Panorama* magazine. Dr. Soloski and his colleagues at the General Hospital in Malmo, Sweden, studied the link between heart attacks and sports events after fifty Swedes died of heart failure in their hospital rooms watching their hero, Bjorn Borg, win his excruciatingly tense Wimbledon final against John McEnroe (1980)

"Money doesn't matter when you have the gold medal."

> —Steffi Graf, crying with joy after adding Olympic gold to the Grand Slam she had consummated at the U.S. Open three weeks earlier (1988)

"I enjoy tennis when I'm intense about it. I enjoy my life when it's intense. And you can't have both."

> —Andre Agassi (1997)

"I feel my tennis reflects who I am. You don't have to know me to have a sense for me. And that's important to me."

> —Andre Agassi, confiding that his public persona doesn't differ much from his private one, after he won the French Open to ignite a dramatic career comeback (1999)

"I'd rather feel I missed out on some good tennis than some good living."

> —Andre Agassi (2000)

"I hate to lose more than I like to win. I hate to see the happiness on their faces when they beat me."

> —Jimmy Connors, after losing to archrival Bjorn Borg (1977)

"I'll follow that son-of-a-bitch to the ends of the earth. Every tournament he plays, I'll be waiting. Everywhere he turns, he'll see my shadow."

> —Jimmy Connors, vowing revenge after Bjorn Borg humiliated him in the Wimbledon final (1978)

"My basic problem was that I would get all tripped out by the negatives—bad calls, bad days, bad feelings—and anger got to be a habit. I was like a compulsive gambler or an alcoholic. Anger became a powerful habit."

> —John McEnroe, in a late-career interview in *Tennis* magazine (1992)

"Even when we get together now in Aspen [Colorado] for practice, the juices are flowing and we're out for blood."

> —Chris Evert, on her enduring friendship and competitiveness with archrival Martina Navratilova (1995)

"Italians are always wanting to murder somebody in the back. It was the same from the time of Caesar."

> —Cino Marchese, Italian client manager and tournament promoter for IMG, on how popular Nicola Pietrangeli, the Italian Davis Cup captain, was replaced because the players resented the attention he got. From the 1983 book, *Short Circuit*

"We should urge fans to scream and boo if they like, just like in baseball or football. The sport has too much stuffiness and protocol. It needs more pizzazz."

> —Billie Jean King, who created World Team Tennis in the 1970s to stimulate fan participation

"There are not too many places where you step on the court and people are telling you to go get a job, you bum."

> —Andre Agassi, on raucous U.S. Open crowds (1998)

"Serve the ball, ya sissy. Whaddaya think dis is, a library?"

> —A boisterous U.S. Open spectator, shouting at Stefan Edberg, after the Swede ducked mid-serve at the sound of a jet overhead

"Colorful European players are as plentiful as empty ashtrays in Paris."

> —*TIME* magazine (2002)

"How can you not love Hewitt? He's incredible for all of us that aren't 6'2". . . . He's giving everybody hope again to play this sport. This guy loves it so much he just loves every ball, he's just like . . . give me the ball. God, I love him. How can you not love this guy?"

> —Tennis legend Billie Jean King, on controversial No. 1 Lleyton Hewitt (2002)

DID THEY REALLY SAY THAT?

"I am a big fan of hers. She deserves some attention, doesn't she?"

—Unidentified twenty-year-old hacker from Holland, who claimed responsibility for a worldwide computer virus that used a photo of tennis vixen Anna Kournikova (2001)

"Tracy, I want you to know that I'm going to be much more famous than you."

—Pete Sampras, age ten, to Tracy Austin at their club in Los Angeles, after she won her second U.S. Open title (1981)

"I always talk like I'm stupid. I prefer people to think I'm stupid."

—Richard Williams, bizarre father/coach of Venus and Serena Williams (1999)

"People believe because I'm blonde, I must be stupid. But the blondes are the smart ones."

—Anna Kournikova, in the *New York Times*

"A haircut and a forehand."

—Ivan Lendl's scouting report on seventeen-year-old heartthrob Andre Agassi (1987)

"Why did you lose the fourth set?"

—What Wendi Stewart, then Andre Agassi's girlfriend, said was the first thing Mike Agassi said to his son on the phone after Agassi won Wimbledon (1992)

"I brought two hundred [headbands] with me, and I've already given away about hundred. I have no idea how many I have left."

—High school dropout Pat Cash, after taking inventory at Wimbledon (1988)

"Don't have one, I never read books."

—Andre Agassi, when asked to list his favorite author (1993)

"Half come to see him win. Half come to see him lose. Half come to see what happens."

—Ion Tiriac, world-class tour player and instigator in the 1970s and later a coach/manager and tournament promoter, on John McEnroe (1990)

"By the time I'm twenty-five, I'll become an actress. I'll be another Grace Kelly or Marlene Dietrich, or perhaps Julia Roberts or Michelle Pfeiffer—anything but a stick figure in a cartoon [a reference to her father, Karolj, who liked to portray her that way]."

—Monica Seles, age eighteen

"It's not really a shorter skirt, I just have longer legs."

—Anna Kournikova

"Nasty's done a lot of terrible things—there's no denying that. But he's done more for the game than any single player who has ever lived. . . . You wouldn't believe how many people come to see him."

—John McEnroe, on Ilie Nastase's court conduct (1979)

"Whoever stole it is spending less than my wife."

—Ilie Nastase, on why he didn't report the loss of his American Express card

"Winning the election, food, and sex. So what is your room number?"

—Former tennis star Ilie Nastase, who ran for mayor of Bucharest, Romania, when asked by a woman journalist what was on his mind (1996)

"I don't think he has to learn anything. . . . I mean, an actor was president of the United States."

—Ion Tiriac, on former sidekick and political neophyte Ilie Nastase, who ran for mayor of Bucharest and lost in a landslide (1996)

"It's not really a shorter skirt, I just have longer legs."—Anna Kournikova (*Susan Mullane/ Camerawork USA, Inc.*)

"McEnroe has got to sit down and work out where he stands."

—BBC broadcaster Fred Perry

"Chip Hooper is such a big man that it is sometimes difficult to see where he is on the court."

—BBC broadcaster Mark Cox, on the 6'6" American power server

"We haven't had any more rain since it stopped raining."

—BBC broadcaster Harry Carpenter

"Virginia Wade is thriving on the pressure, now that the pressure on her to do well is off."

—Harry Carpenter

"She puts her head down and bangs it straight across the line."

—Ann Haydon Jones, BBC broadcaster and 1969 Wimbledon champion. From www.tennisontheline.org

"And when Chrissie is playing well, I always feel that she is playing well."

—Ann Haydon Jones. From www.tennisontheline.org

"Agassi plays very quickly between points."

—Allan Stone, Fox Sports commentator, during the 2003 U.S. Open

"I had a feeling today that Venus Williams would either win or lose."

—Martina Navratilova. From www.tennisontheline.org

"It's cool, overcast, and cloudy here—but in a few moments two great players will take the long walk down the tunnel and emerge into the Melbourne sunshine."

—Australian tennis standout turned TV commentator John Alexander, before the 2004 Australian Open men's final

"When I first saw Andre at age two or three, I didn't think he was going to be any good."

—All-time great Pancho Gonzalez, probably figuring Andre Agassi lacked the size (1988)

"I'm going to retire when this kid grows up and beats me."

> —Jimmy Connors's somewhat prophetic statement after hitting with Andre Agassi, then four years old, at the Alan King tournament in Las Vegas. Agassi won both professional matches against Connors, in the 1988 and '89 U.S. Open quarterfinals. Connors retired from the ATP Tour in 1992.

"I enjoy playing guys who could be my children. Maybe he's one of them. I spent a lot of time in Vegas."

> —An annoyed Jimmy Connors, on teenage star Andre Agassi, after Agassi disrespectfully announced he had told his longtime friend, Perry Rogers, that he expected to beat Connors "three, three, and three" in their U.S. Open quarterfinal (1988)

"Why did you take your shirt off? You only got the girls more excited."

> —Question from a woman journalist to heartthrob Andre Agassi at Wimbledon (1992)

"If Pete's child is a girl, my son will like her; if he's a boy, my son will defeat him."

> —Andre Agassi. From www.tennisontheline.org (2002)

"How does it feel to be the most unpopular man at Wimbledon?"

> —British reporter to Pete Sampras, after he beat crowd-pleasing defending champion Andre Agassi in the Wimbledon quarterfinals (1993)

"Maybe she has a crush on me."

> —Pete Sampras, asked at Wimbledon if he noticed Princess Diana cheering for him (1993)

"He didn't set the world on fire."

> —Anna Kournikova, on Britain's Prince Andrew, whom she met in the summer of 2000

"This is the first . . . well anything I have ever won!"

> —Venus Williams, after teaming with Justin Gimelstob to win the mixed doubles at the 1998 Australian Open

"How odd Germany should have such personal interest in a court on which in 1940 they dropped a bomb."

—In *The Times* (UK) during Wimbledon 1985, when all regularly scheduled television programs in Germany were canceled for coverage of matches involving Boris Becker, the seventeen-year-old *wunderkind* champion

"It was fitting to my life but it was not my goal to marry an African American. I just fell in love with a person and much later I found out she was black. In the winter, she gets a bit pale. I didn't know she was black. We were already together three or four months and she was lying on white sheets in my bedroom. I woke up and there was a full moon outside and I nudged her and said 'Barbara, you're black!' You can ask her. I swear to God."

—Boris Becker, with a hard-to-believe claim, in the *Telegraph* (UK) 2001

"My best surface is my bed."

—Jim Courier, winner of two Australian and two French Open titles (1993)

"It's hard to find a horse."

—Martina Hingis, commenting on the down side of indoor tournaments

"I'm not sure exactly what his points are, but without even knowing what his points are, I'd say he has some good points."

—John McEnroe, on Wayne Ferreira, the leader of the new International Players Association, which sought more accountability from the Association of Tennis Professionals (ATP) for its policies (2003)

"I don't think I could see myself going fishing, period. I don't believe in messing with something that's not messing with me."

—Andre Agassi, when asked if he could see himself going fishing with Michael Chang

"At Wimbledon, the ladies are simply the candles on the cake."

—John Newcombe. From www.tennisontheline.org

"Why don't you go join the men's circuit and leave us alone?"

—Chris Evert, after being crushed by archrival Martina Navratilova

"If muscles are all that matter, how come John McEnroe is No. 1 in the world? He's a wimp."

—Muscular Martina Navratilova

"No, I prefer the Haagen-Dazs diet."

—John McEnroe, asked whether he used the Haas diet that was a key part of fitness fanatic Martina Navratilova's program in the 1980s

"I'd want someone a little younger than that. She's what I'd call a pitching wedge. She looks good from about fifty yards away."

—Pete Sampras, asked about Barbra Streisand's brief relationship with Andre Agassi (1999)

"It's just like you all expected: Edberg, Lendl, McEnroe, and Becker."

—Patrick McEnroe's quip to the media after he became the first player with a 100-plus ranking (No. 114) to reach a Grand Slam semifinal since 1978, at the Australian Open (1991)

"Last year, I lost to his brother [John], this year I lose to him, next year, maybe I can win against his sister."

—Goran Ivanisevic, after losing to Patrick McEnroe at the Lipton Championships (1993)

"My fines? I pay more fines than some guys' career prize money on the tour."

—Goran Ivanisevic (2001)

"Everybody thinks my name is Jerry Laitis and they all call me Mr. Laitis."

—Vitas Gerulaitis

"Was I then a man dreaming I was a butterfly, or am I now a butterfly dreaming I am a man?"

—Danish eccentric Torben Ulrich, asked if the butterfly that flew into his face when he was playing John Newcombe at the 1968 U.S. Open bothered him, replied with a saying of the ancient Taoist, Chuang-Tzu. From the 1975 book, *Carnival at Forest Hills: The Anatomy of a Tennis Tournament*

"Ladies, here's a hint. If you're playing against a friend who has big boobs, bring her to the net and make her hit backhand volleys. That's the hardest shot for the well-endowed."

—Billie Jean King

"That's the way the strap snaps."

—How shapely Pat Stewart, a former top twenty U.S. player and lingerie model, used to laugh off losses. From Bud Collins's 1989 book, *My Life with the Pros*

"There goes 1987."

—John McEnroe's response when his wife, Tatum O'Neal, informed him that she was pregnant with their second child

"Do you have any problems other than that you're unemployed and a moron and a dork?"

—John McEnroe, firing back at a heckler at the Lipton International Players Championships (1992)

"I still break rackets, but now I do it in a positive way."

—Volatile Goran Ivanisevic, on his changed ways (1992)

"Sorry I haven't updated my site for a while. I'll start again when Goran does something useful."

—Message on Jukka's Goran Ivanisevic Web site during the 2001 Wimbledon Championships, which Ivanisevic won

"I've attained my dream. I've become No. 2."

—Arantxa Sanchez Vicario, who went on to exceed her expectations and reign as No. 1 in both singles and doubles

"OK, do you want to get broken first, or do you want to let me hold?"

—What cheeky world No. 1 Martina Hingis quipped at the coin toss before her match against Lindsay Davenport (1997)

"I'm older than I used to be."

—Weary Venus Williams, just turned twenty-three, at Wimbledon (2003)

"Australia was started as a penal colony in the beginning. They went on to become patriotic Australians, got their own accent, moved away from the British, and here we are."

—Venus Williams, on the short history of Australia, when a reporter asked what she knew about the host country of the Australian Open (2001)

"I'm an actress, I'm a model and an athlete. I put athlete third on my list."

—Serena Williams, reigning French, Wimbledon, and U.S. champion and ranked No. 1 in the world, who played a jailed track and field star in the Showtime series *Street Time* (2003)

"I have a lot of boyfriends, I want you to write that. Every country I visit, I have a different boyfriend. And I kiss them all."

—Anna Kournikova

"I've only scratched the iceberg."

—Andre Agassi, mixing his metaphors (1990)

"I don't know why everyone puts so much emphasis on Wimbledon. It's just another tournament like all the rest."

—Bill Shelton, Andre Agassi's agent, trying to justify his client skipping Wimbledon (1988)

"I'm going to go fill this bowl up and get drunk."

—John Newcombe, 1971 Wimbledon champion, after Princess Marina had presented him with the silver bowl and asked him, "Now what are you going to do?"

"I've been through two wars and I've seen what they're like."

—Famed couturier Ted Tinling, on why he refused to design dresses for German and Russian players (1973)

"I'm blacker than Arthur."

—Billie Jean King, meaning she showed more fervor for feminist causes than Arthur Ashe did for racial causes

"She's Doris Day. My God, she's a normal person, the first one we've had in years. We've had the awkwardness of [Margaret] Court; the bitchiness of Billie Jean; the brown sugar of Chrissie; the butchness of Martina and the manic shyness of Graf. Now we shall have Seles and she will be wonderful. Completely wonderful."

—Ted Tinling, in a fax to journalist John Feinstein three days before his death (1990)

"If I had been Steffi, I would not have played in any tournament for a year. I would not have wanted to be a 'Knife No. 1.'"

> —Karolj Seles, unfairly blasting Steffi Graf for continuing to compete after his daughter Monica was stabbed in 1993 at a German tournament (1995)

"It would be a nice place if you took all the people out of the city."

> —Ugly American and eighteen-year-old tour rookie John McEnroe, on his first trip to Paris (1977)

"I'd go sight-seeing, but I don't think there's much to see in this place."

> —John McEnroe, continuing the ugly-American routine in London, after becoming the youngest men's semifinalist at Wimbledon (1977)

"I wanted to be like Jimmy Connors or Ilie Nastase. You don't idolize someone who is like yourself. You idolize somebody you'd like to be like."

> —Mild-mannered Mats Wilander (1988)

"If I'm a kid today, I'd choose basketball over tennis because it's more fun to be in a team sport."

> —Billie Jean King (2000)

"Are you glad you won, Martina?"

> —Question asked of Martina Navratilova (1978)

"It's Venus' Party and You're Not Invited."

> —Dopey message held up at courtside by Richard Williams during the 2000 Wimbledon final, won by his daughter Venus

"There is no one dumber than a tennis player."

> —Richard Williams's oft-repeated opinion

"Hi, I'm Richard Williams. There are those who want to ask me what I think of inter-marriage. Anyone that's marrying outside of this race that's black should be hung by their necks until sundown. Please leave a message after the tone."

> —Answering machine message on Richard Williams's phone during the late 1990s

"We couldn't care less what people think of us."

—Richard Williams, in *Sports Illustrated*

"Pete beat Andre four of five times in [Grand] Slam finals, but Andre's clearly the better player. . . . Andre has a way better game, but Pete had the ability to raise his game against Andre."

—Brad Gilbert, Agassi's coach from 1994 to 2002, in *Inside Tennis* magazine (2003)

"This is really strange, but I have this feeling that Michael is going to win the French Open."

—What Michael Chang's mother, Betty, said to her husband, Joe, right before the 1989 French Open started. Seventeen-year-old Michael shocked everyone by winning Roland Garros to become the youngest Grand Slam men's champion in history.

"My body hair is now secondary to tennis."

—Young Andre Agassi, on his changing priorities

"I don't know who is tall. Postman, maybe."

—A mischievous Ivo Karlovic, after upsetting Lleyton Hewitt in the Wimbledon first round, on how he turned out 6'10" tall when his parents are both average height

"So that I can finally find a companion."

—Why glamorous retired star Gabriela Sabatini said she developed another fragrance, called "Devotion" (2001)

"My breasts are really good because they don't sag. They are firm and perfect."

—Anna Kournikova, who clearly loves yet another part of herself. From the 2001 book, *Venus Envy*

"Having an orgasm—it's exactly like that."

—Billie Jean King, on the feeling of hitting the perfect shot. From her 1982 autobiography, *Billie Jean*

"Who is this Gullikson guy? Two weeks ago, he beat me playing with his right hand. Now he beat me with his left."

—German Karl Meiler, on losing to left-handed Tim Gullikson, two weeks after losing to his identical twin brother, right-handed Tom

TENNIS FOREVER

"The game is well enough for lazy and weak men, but men who have rowed or taken part in nobler sport should blush to be seen playing lawn tennis."

> —The Harvard *Crimson*, expressing alarm at the growth of tennis clubs on campus (1878)

"Tennis, anyone?"

> —Humphrey Bogart's sole line in his first play in the 1920s. Although Bogart jokingly took credit for the most famous tennis quote of all, its origins are lost in the mist of time.

"No. This is a man's war and tennis is a woman's game."

> —Memo from Gen. Dwight D. Eisenhower, after Ted Tinling, then a lieutenant colonel in the Royal Army Intelligence Corps, asked permission to stage an exhibition match for the Red Cross in Algiers (1943)

"Tennis in America is a socially conscious game, played mainly by the sons of wealthy parents. In Australia, any working-man's son can join a club, be coached and enter competitions, but in America his counterpart plays baseball."

> —Australian great Lew Hoad. From his 1958 book, *My Game*

"Tennis was seen as American imperialism, an influence of Western cultural invasion, so it was banned."

> —Iranian expatriate and 1989 French Open doubles finalist Mansour Bahrami, on why the 1979 revolution resulted in the closing of tennis clubs

"There are really two camps in tennis, the Anglo-Saxons who invented the sport as we know it and the Latins . . . who are playing it brilliantly and little by little taking over its leadership."

> —Philippe Chatrier, president of the International Tennis Federation (1985)

"If I ever become a great champion, I'll change tennis."

> —What twelve-year-old Billie Jean King, the daughter of a fireman, vowed because she disliked the stuffy, country club mores she found in tennis

"The other kids had nice tennis clothes, nice rackets, nice white shoes, and came in Cadillacs. I felt stigmatized because we were poor."

> —Rosie Casals, a twelve-time Grand Slam doubles champion whose parents immigrated to the U.S. from El Salvador. In *People* magazine

"This is the culmination of a lifetime in the sport. Tennis has always been reserved for the rich, the white, the males—and I've always pledged to change all that."

> —Twenty-nine-year-old champion Billie Jean King, after trouncing Bobby Riggs in the celebrated "Battle of the Sexes" (1973)

"There's a different breed of cats coming out here. Instead of hoi polloi, we're now getting Johnny Six-Pack."

> —U.S. Open referee Mike Blanchard, on the boisterous fans at Forest Hills the year before the tournament moved to the National Tennis Center in Flushing Meadows (1977)

"Boxing and tennis are rare, me-against-you games involving physical and mental skills, endurance, and a willingness to continue even though hurt. No bench. No substitutes. . . . Tennis is boxing without bloodshed."

> —Bud Collins. From his 1989 book, *My Life with the Pros*

"There's not a day that goes by that I don't run into someone who says, 'I never watched tennis until you guys came, and if you guys aren't playing, I still don't watch.' It doesn't necessarily have to be African American. I get that from everyone."

> —Serena Williams, countering critics who say the Williamses' dominance is dull by arguing that they have attracted a whole new set of fans to tennis (2003)

"Tennis's extraordinary mystique has been its capacity to survive, and that is due to its capacity to revitalize and present an image of totally contemporary people in every era."

> —Ted Tinling, Hall of Famer, tennis historian, and then chief of protocol for women's tennis (1985)

"To me, tennis is the most impressive sport. In golf, you hit your best shot and you can brag about it. In tennis, you hit your best shot and some little [expletive deleted] is on the other side hitting it back to you."

> —Fuzzy Zoeller, former U.S. Open and Masters golf champion (1986)

"Here's what's great about tennis. You learn self-discipline, self-worth and how to compete. You've always got that pressure, you've always got to take the shot. You have to be your own coach. Tennis helped me learn how to call plays in basketball. It's much more mental. In team sports, you can count on others."

> —John Lucas, All-American in tennis and basketball at the University of Maryland, NBA player and coach, and coach of former top tenner Lori McNeil

"Tennis should be played only in the long grass in the meadows— and in the nude."

> —George Bernard Shaw

"Those who cheated on the tennis court could almost always be counted on to cheat in the United Nations."

> —Andrew Young, former U.S. Ambassador to the United Nations, on what he learned from playing tennis against international leaders

"My biggest heroes are tennis players, film directors, and rock stars."

> —Salman Rushdie, acclaimed and controversial author

"Tennis fits my independent nature. It gives me an empowering feeling I haven't found in other sports."

> —Movie star Shannon Elizabeth (2000)

"Tennis is a lot like basketball in physical terms, and Chris Evert did everything with class."

> —Michael Jordan, when asked which female athlete he most admired

"You're [*sic*] a fat football player, a fat baseball player, even a fat basketball player, a fat prizefighter, a fat golfer, lots of fat golfers, but never a fat tennis player."

—Jim Murray, distinguished *Los Angeles Times* columnist

"Smashing a racket is no big deal. Hey, it's my racket. I broke it, picked it up, then bent it in half and the fans seemed to like that. I liked breaking it in half. Are we that wussy a sport that we can't break a racket?"

—Muscular macho man Jan-Michael Gambill

"The sport is best marketed as tough, athletic, and macho. The Williams sisters have done as much as anyone to market the sport as macho. Tennis players are up there with basketball players as the finest athletes in the world. They've got agility, power, and mental toughness."

—Arlen Kantarian, chief executive of the United States Tennis Association

"I like tennis because it's based on intimidation and the knockout punch—the big serve. Tennis is a blood sport, a very violent sport."

—Leroy Neiman, famous sports artist, on why he migrated to tennis after ten years in boxing and horse racing (1988)

"Writing free verse is like playing tennis with the net down."

—Poet Robert Frost. From the 1935 book, *Oxford Dictionary of Humorous Quotations*

"Acting isn't a very high-class way to make a living, is it? Shirley Temple could do it at the age of four. All you need is a saleable whatever-the-hell-it-is that people like to see. I think I could have been a great tennis star instead."

—Legendary actress Katharine Hepburn (1979)

"I wish I'd been a really great tennis player."

—Famed opera singer Marilyn Horne, when asked by *60 Minutes* if she had any regrets in life (1993)

"You know, Don, I always envied you. As a kid, I dreamed of being a tennis champion."

— Baseball immortal Joe DiMaggio, on meeting all-time great Don Budge at a New York restaurant

"If you can keep playing tennis when somebody is shooting a gun down the street, that's concentration. I didn't grow up playing tennis at the country club."

— Reigning queen Serena Williams, who grew up in violent, gang-ridden Compton, California (2003)

INDEX

ABOUT THE AUTHOR

Paul Fein is an award-winning tennis journalist and the author of *Tennis Confidential: Today's Greatest Players, Matches, and Controversies* (Brassey's, Inc., 2002). His articles have appeared in tennis, sports, and general interest publications in the United States and twenty-five foreign countries.

Fein's diverse tennis background also includes being a high-ranking sectional tournament player, a satellite tournament founder and director, a certified teaching pro, a New England tournament consultant, a cable television commentator, and a local tennis club and council president. He lives in Agawam, Massachusetts.